ASTROLOGY & COMPASSION

From early reviews......

"Roy presents new proposals that demand to be tested...a man of the 21st century; he is Utopian, idealistic, an Aquarius' Aquarian. He thinks so far outside the box that you are in a new country....Buy this book and read it. It will open your mind. **The book gives astrologers pride in our craft and introduces non-astrologers to a new way of thinking. It is a valuable addition to any library.**" **Arlan Wise** – Past President – *Organisation for Professional Astrology*

".. a personal manifesto by an astrologer with thirty-five years experience. Read it, agree with, disagree with it, challenge it or be persuaded. **But read it and listen to what astrologers in the twenty-first century really think.**" **Dr. Nicholas Campion PhD** – author - *The Dawn of Astrology: A Cultural History of Western Astrology*

"I look forward to the day when this valuable and truly comprehensive book will be used as a standard text book ..." **Ruth Rose**

Other books by Roy Gillett

Astrological Diaries 1978 to 1990
A Model of Health
Zen for Today's Living
The Essence of Buddhism

Astrology & Compassion

the Convenient Truth

by

Roy Gillett

Kings Hart Books

First published in 2007 by
Kings Hart Books
an imprint of Publishers UK Ltd
26 Beaumont Street
Oxford, England OX1 2NP
01243 576016
www.kingshartbooks.co.uk

First Printing 2007
Second printing 2008

Cover design Gerasime Patilas © 2007

A catalogue record for this book is available from the British Library.

ISBN 978-1-906154-07-3

Printed and bound by Lightning Source

The paper used in this book is from sustainable sources, certified by the
Forest Stewardship Council

Dedicated to universal understanding,

with compassion toward all creatures and phenomena;

however close or distant, familiar or unfamiliar.

Acknowledgements

The invaluable assistance of many people is gratefully acknowledged. Thanks for the following permissions to:

Astrolabe Inc [http:www.alabe.com] for use of *Solar Fire V6 deluxe* software to generate astrological charts; Astro Computing Services Inc [http://www.astrocom.com] for reproduction of the images from their *Astrological Mandalas* software used in Chapter 3; *The Astrological Journal* of The Astrological Association of Great Britain for the opportunity to explore and explain major astrological transits since 2002; Robin Heath [http://www.skyandlandscape.com/] for use of the Stonehenge diagram (figure 21 in Chapter 11); Dr Pat Harris for permission to give an extensive mention of her ground-breaking research into the relationship between astronomical factors and successful fertility treatment; Foundation for the Mahayana Tradition [http://www.fpmt.org] and the Foundation for Developing Wisdom and Compassion [http://www.essential-education.org] for permission to quote the outline of their *16 Guidelines to a Happy Life* in chapter 18.

The work, wisdom and achievement of numerous devoted astrologers, dharma students and people of good will in all walks of life have been the inspiration that has driven this work. I hope that everyone who knows me will recognise the part they have played. Special thanks to Alice Ekrek, whose early feedback ensured at least *some* scholarship was included; Rachael and Andrew Gillett for their helpful early comments; Jane Struthers for her invaluable proof-reading (any errors that remain are entirely mine); Gerasime Patilas for the unbelievably fine way his cover artwork responds to the book's vision; and Colin Shearing and Elizabeth Plant of Kings Hart Books for their generous and wise guidance through the publishing.

Most important, I thank Lama Thubten Zopa Rinpoche. Without Rinpoche's example and my wife Carolyn's untiring support my ability to offer these ideas would not have been possible and, in many other respects, the value of my life's endeavours would have been far less.

CONTENTS

We have bigger houses, but smaller families:
more conveniences, but less time.
We have more degrees, but less sense;
more knowledge, but less judgements;
more experts, but more problems;
more medicines, but less healthiness.
We've been all the way to the moon and back,
but have trouble crossing the street
to meet the new neighbour.

The Paradox of our Age
His Holiness the XIV Dalai Lama

Preface

In explaining and justifying astrology, this book both challenges and answers many of the problems, with which the world entered the 21st century. At first sight most people may find its title and claims ludicrously at odds with what seems likely and possible in our advanced 'modern' world. Before tossing it away unread however; consider two factors I suspect most people living today can agree on.

* Firstly, what is assumed to be true changes from one culture and time to another. As a view of reality becomes dominant and commonly accepted, it is institutionalised into a protected bureaucracy. This defends the now established order against alternative ways of seeing. Various inquisitions and racial persecutions throughout history bear brutal witness to this. Even in the development of our scientific society, some of the ideas we most prize today were mocked as impossible when first presented by brave pioneers.

* Secondly, conflict and consumption are the basic problems of the 21st century. They seem to be threatening the future of our planet and the freedom and privacy of our way of life. Yet dominant modern world opinion assumes that the competitive societies causing such problems are unavoidable facts of life.

Confronted with such an apparent impasse, we would be foolhardy indeed to dismiss radical alternatives without at least giving them a moment's consideration. This is particularly true of a system of understanding that has fascinated humanity for thousands of years, yet questions the *popular* view of linear cause and effect. We should remember that informed theories of physics moved on from such a simplistic Newtonian paradigm more than one hundred years ago. Truth can only benefit from giving astrology the floor to state its case.

It is an interesting paradox that to people with little or no knowledge of astrology, the very idea of there being any connection between planetary movements, behaviour and events is silly. Yet, to nearly everyone who has studied one or more of the many methods of astrology thoroughly, its validity and importance is self-evident and beyond argument. To date, discussion about astrology has been demarcated along these two distinct lines.

* ❄ *Those against* condemn it out of hand. Using oft-repeated *non-sequiturs*, they misrepresent what astrology is and claims to do. Answers to such criticisms that have been repeated many times are never properly considered and taken on board.
* ❄ *Those who support* speak in a complex symbolic language that seeks to express the intricate matrix of the working of the universe. Listening to them is rather like it would be to hear about mathematics, chemistry, or physics for the first time, without ever having studied it at school.
* ❄ *Never the twain shall meet!*

Even the satirical intelligentsia, who are usually ready to question establishment propaganda, ignore this cause. The public is left confused, with no way to be certain about the rather passionate, fascinating, but often unfathomable group of individuals who insist that astrology works.

The aim of this book is to ease and clear this logjam that keeps most people in ignorance. It starts with a plea for an open mind, and then confronts the rather mischievous misinformation about astrology that special–interest groups spread through their media networks from time to time. We then explore ways that astrology may work and offer a shortcut entry into its main concepts. Anyone willing to explore this far along the path will then be ready to ask what some may feel to be unthinkable questions about the role of astrology in various areas of academia. Then in Part Four, we take some audacious first steps to consider how our 21st century world might be improved if astrology was used with compassion, as an acceptable diagnostic tool in mainstream social institutions.

The intention is to give information and food for thought to anyone who has previously rejected astrology without really knowing it. I hope colleagues, whose expertise has convinced them already, will find some of the book's ideas complement their own, and so help them position and argue for astrology in contemporary society

Experienced astrologers may already have suspected that I have Mars in Aries and strong Aquarian/Gemini planets. What else could explain such an extremely impulsive and pioneering realignment of our contemporarily assumed world picture? However, I think the time is right to consider this. For three hundred years the spirit has been wrenched from our everyday lives because key methods to maintain heart and principle in material decisions have been marginalised. Astrology has been denied a voice in mainstream academia. Instead, we are being oppressed by the nannying of experts, who could help us so much better if only they would unburden themselves of the responsibility to organise the world in a way that makes them appear to be always right. Batteries of computerised statistical studies show us to be selfish, greedy individuals, who for our own good need to be contained and directed! Whether they intend to or not, such so-called expert studies encourage a life experience dominated by conflict and anxiety. Individual people become impotent, dependent upon following rules and regulations and having access to powerful medical techniques. Underlying it all is the economic need to be obsessed with consumption. We live to consume – what other purpose is there left to live for?

Is it satisfactory to live for no more than this? Something is wrong. We have to ask fundamental questions. This book seeks to make a start on doing just that. Its preliminary and incomplete answers will leave many gaps for the more rigorous scholarship of my colleagues to fill. Small selections of just a few of the best of their books are listed at the end of some following chapters. Together they develop and enhance the edifice of a more enlightened view of the world. I hope you will find moments of elegance in this book's rather rough-and-ready attempts to get things underway on a deliberately broad front. To start the ball rolling and lay out the territory, it is necessary to make and explore big claims.

Using astrology in the modern world will not solve our problems on its own. However, it will make available to humanity an intelligent conceptual language with which to address them. It will reveal what lies behind what we think we are talking about. Understanding the deep issues makes it easier to feel compassion. So, we are no longer obsessed with fear and the need to protect ourselves against the unknown. Instead, we support and enable each other's success.

To the scientist, astrology describes the relationship between the integrated effect of astronomical cycles and the earthly disposition of humanity and other phenomena. To the religious, it explores the structure of that area between heaven and earth, where God speaks to man. Used with compassion, it can relax and educate our spirit and so sets us truly free in a welcoming world!

PART 1

Identifying the Barriers to Understanding

How I Became Involved with Astrology

'What do you want to be when you grow up?' As a young boy there was only one answer to this question 'An astronomer.'

Of course, I did not really know what it involved – just that looking at a heliocentric diagram of the Sun, the planets and their satellites was incredibly interesting, but there was a problem. It was also incomplete. From where exactly was I looking? Clearly not where I was, because there was the circle of the Earth around the Sun and I was on it, yet looking at it from a long way away. I could only screw up my brow with puzzlement and leave the paradox unresolved. Then I learnt about what went on inside atoms. Of course the universe out there and in here worked the same way, was my simplistic conclusion.

About where that left me I was still uncertain. Then, at around ten years old, I had my first experience of being gripped by the fear of death. We were on holiday and that evening I had dropped the most delicious fish and chips I had ever tasted on the ground in a filthy alley way and, not being able to bear the thought of losing them, had picked up and eaten them, dirt and all.

That night I lay sweating and terrified in that Great Yarmouth holiday boarding house bedroom that I was sharing with my parents. I could not take my mind away from my realisation for the first time that the black void of death was my inevitable and unavoidable fate. Petrified at what my mother (I was to learn later the implications of her having four planets in Virgo in the 1st house!) would say and do, if I told her of my stupidity, I realised for the first time the totality of being alone.

Then I was sick. The next day was bright on the sand, with the distractions of penny amusement arcades. Even though the food poisoning had cleared, that night and many nights for years later it was difficult not to think about death without the sweat returning.

At that stage, such adolescent morbidity did not seem to have anything to do with theories of the universe, nor really with belief. I was a choirboy at an Anglican church and soon became caught up with preparations for Confirmation. Yet the routine of attending church two or even three times on a Sunday, occasionally for paid Saturday weddings and weekly choir practice, especially sitting through a half-hour sermon made religion a chore rather than an answer to my inner fears. Then there was rugby, athletics, swimming, the school choir, plays and operas and friends and games. Life was full, busy and creative. There was too much to do now to think beyond the next game, or event, or the irritating intervention of homework and lines for misdemeanours – just do not let your mind go there, when you close your eyes at night.

Then the obsessive immediacy of adolescent sex and romance gripped the focus of my life by the throat. How on earth does one pass examinations and make decisions about work and careers when confronted with such passion and the spectre of National Service and still always that morning paper round?

As adolescence grew into early manhood, the questions returned armed with an enthusiasm to use the libraries to find out for myself. I had always read the standard children's range. Now I started on the complete plays of George Bernard Shaw, with their incisive prefaces, and H G Wells and Jules Verne. Then over the two years in the Royal Air Force and immediately after, I discovered Oscar Wilde, Dostoevsky, Tolstoy, T S Eliot, Sartre, Camus, Aldous Huxley, Kafka, Auden, Isherwood, William Golding, read history, the Penguin philosophy range, the 'angry young men' of the late 1950s, then developments in film and drama in the 1960s. Having left grammar school prematurely at 16, at 23 I finally turned back to formal higher education as a trainee teacher specialising in English. There my reading broadened really to appreciate Shakespeare, Milton and much more. I was to discover, even act in, the drama of the Greek, English and continental classics. Along with this came a taste for voluntary public service.

What I felt at the time to be the end of my interest in religion and anything spiritual had occurred around the age of 17, when I noticed how sexually aroused I became when travelling to and from evangelical meetings. The feelings did not seem to match what I took then to be the Christian teachings. So I kept the sex and left Billy Graham to enjoy the devotion of 'purer-minded souls than mine'! To express an almost desperate need for meaning and to serve the community, I turned to social democracy, the struggle for fair societies in a world of equal opportunity for all classes and races. Secondary school teaching was a wonderful way of earning a living, while idealistically serving the community to create 'a better world'.

So, it was rather a shock when, after ten years of training and being a school teacher, a strange series of coincidences led to my astrological birth chart being drawn up and interpreted.

Full up with the secular, liberal and satirical arrogance that characterises a political revolutionary struggling for the moment of power to arise, I was patronisingly sceptical. I had never been told it was possible that understanding the cycles of those far-away planets could explain people's personalities, behaviour and experiences. Now here was a man who I had met only minutes ago not only describing my nature, but showing me how he did it from the book he was using! In the weeks that followed, I bought that book and several others and found they enabled me to do the same. My chart was ideal for a consultant astrologer. The more charts I studied, the more certain the validity of astrology became.

So at ten years old I had been right, almost! I had been born to be, and all my life had been trying to be, an astrologer and had said 'astronomer', because young boys in our society (especially in the late 1940s) did not know about astrology. Furthermore, as will be made clear in this book, astrology and compassionate insight always did have the wisdom to answer my simple boyhood questions. Together, they could explain the relationship between the inner and outer universe and how to approach and go through the experience of death.

Four years after that chart reading, I left school teaching to embark on a two-year world journey, studying and testing my own use of astrology and learning from colleagues in many places and cultures. I kept a detailed diary, in which were written planetary positions, with narratives of what was done on that day. Sometimes it was an account of contrived trials and the results. More often, it was just a description of spontaneous day-to-day occurrences. Reading the charts of people I met and listening carefully, I learned from the feedback clients gave me. All this continually confirmed and deepened my understanding. I have worked with, supported and taught the knowledge ever since.

It was and continues to be an unbelievable relief to be able to explain, understand, and put behaviour and events in perspective. At the same time, it is a tragedy of Greek proportions to watch people and societies deluding themselves and others into unnecessary suffering and hardship, when knowledge of astrology could guide them to easier and happier ways through life. Perhaps the saddest thing of all is the dismissive ignorance about astrology – especially from many well-known people, whose intelligence, general kindness and good intentions we have come to admire in their other activities.

In his *A New Model of the Universe,* P D Ouspensky describes the majority of humanity as living life asleep. There is sufficient wisdom for all. A group of awakened individuals are ever ready to teach this wisdom. Yet it is a quirk of human nature to dismiss, even attack, the very thing that would benefit it most - especially when it is so close and easy to grasp.

So, why not check out for yourself the possibility I am suggesting? Decide to read and consider this book to the end. You never know, it might turn out to be that very convenient truth that puts all your experiences in perspective and answers many questions of your life.

Chapter 1

A Lethal Void in 21st Century Judgement

> The unleashed power of the atom has changed everything but our modes of thinking and we thus drift toward unparalleled catastrophe.
>
> **Albert Einstein**

In 1941, the discoverer of the Theory of Relativity, Albert Einstein, famously wrote to President Roosevelt of the USA warning of the dangerous power of nuclear fission and the consequences of Adolf Hitler developing and using the technology first.

Taking the warning very seriously, the President arranged for more funding than that given to any scientific project before that time. In real terms, more was to be spent on what came to be called the Manhattan Project than was later spent on landing a man on the Moon. Vast teams of the best scientists gathered and worked exhaustively, until they finally harnessed the power of splitting the atom and produced nuclear weapons.

As well as the hubris of having at our fingertips a new, very practical power to change lives for good or ill, the coming of nuclear power to human consciousness atomised assumptions about what we could do in just about everything. If we could destroy the world, then maybe, like Doctor Frankenstein, we could forget previously accepted moral barriers and act exactly as we liked. We had unlimited power if we mastered technology and were deeply helpless if we did not.

Realising the horrific consequences, Einstein lived to regret the results of his letter and spent much of the rest of his life urging governments and the scientists to restrict and control further development. However, the genie was out of the bottle. Einstein did not find governments and the military so responsive anymore!

There are two very good reasons to remind ourselves of all this at the beginning of a book that seeks to establish the importance of astrological understanding in the modern world.

Firstly, the development of nuclear power in the early 1940s shows just what can be achieved when the best minds and resources are poured into a particular activity. It would be a mistake to assume that the outcome demonstrates the ultimate true nature of things. Nuclear power is just one of the many latent possibilities, picked out by an important man and given such resources that it has dominated and traumatised the contemporary mind ever since.

If the circumstances of 1941 had not been a general outbreak of madness, and it had been possible to put the same resources into developing an ecologically balanced planet, we may well have achieved it and be living in harmony with nature and each other today. If the investment in cars and roads had been put into railways, our contemporary quality of life would be very different. The priorities we choose focus outcomes. We believe them to be absolute at our peril. The world these priorities create is not the only, true world, or even necessarily the best possible one.

More recently, billions of pounds have been allocated to a mass-computer study of DNA variables in an attempt to map the genome. The ultimate aim is to treat each genetic factor in a uniquely appropriate way. Pharmaceutical and horticultural industries will create new medicines, even 'food medicines'. Fertility experts will develop ways of identifying and correcting pre-natal defects and abilities – even the sex of the child and cosmetic factors, such as eye and hair colouring.

With the lesson of nuclear power in our minds, perhaps we should not become excessively confident, or despondent about all this. We have still only discovered a fragment of what there is to know. What is academically in vogue may change. Certainly, we should never forget that, if the funds had been devoted elsewhere, our present and future world could be very different. If the billions of pounds in research had been devoted to studying naturopathic, or other holistic and traditional methods of understanding and healing the body, our view of reality, what help we need and where we go to find it would be radically different.

In 2005, the vast computer processing power to drive the *Millennium Run* project – a simulation of the alleged birth and development of the universe – was proudly announced. Some of the most inventive young minds are being guided into programming all that has been observed by optical and radio telescopes into models that it is hoped will answer our questions about creation. It would be interesting to see what would be discovered if all the astrological knowledge of all time were programmed in and run for a year or so!

Potential knowledge is limitless. We only get to know what we choose to know. So, if we choose to know about astrology and to put the same resources into this discovery, would we find a valid and better way of looking at the world we live in? Would a world grounded by knowledge of the cycles of the heavens give us clearer, more compassionate and healthier lives? At least, would it help us become more realistic about our choices?

Secondly, especially because what we choose to study determines what we come to believe, it is an act of lethal irresponsibility for scientists to bring material knowledge and power to humanity, when humanity is clearly not ethically and spiritually prepared to use the knowledge responsibly. Poor Einstein was reduced to fruitless campaigning against the nuclear weapons that were the unwanted children of his vision. Of course, it was too late to 'un-discover' them. Even the most repressive regimes find such backward writing of history at best temporary and in the end impossible.

We need to have inner knowledge and values that are as powerful as the outer devices and processes we seek to contain and channel. Yet we don't. Instead, our world belief systems conflict and we see our main purpose as a struggle for material success. This and the very academic process itself tend to institutionalise division and dispute. The question of who has nuclear devices, or any other great source of power becomes intrinsically problematic. We seek systems of assessment that show a fixed and mechanical relationship between phenomena. Yet, conflicting notions of absolute reality/truth frustrate decisions and lead instead to opinionated confrontation.

In such circumstances, are our assessments safe, self-critical and genuinely objective? The very systems that make us so clever or identify our culture confirm our prejudices and so drive cultures apart. Our educational systems, which should initiate *our* children into *our* world, are faced with two unsatisfactory options. Either they allow for different social and religious groups by omitting the teaching of most values, except., permissive secular materialism, or children are taught in separate faith-based schools and risk divisive misunderstandings.

Clearly there are gaps in our methods of social understanding and processes of conciliation that we vitally need to fill today, but mechanical science has not the capacity, or even the wish, to be more than an instrument in the hands of the highest bidder. We have turned away from the kindness of our parish priest to the advice of highly paid accountants and lawyers. Psychological solutions range widely from self-indulgent over-examination of who was to blame for early life trauma to behavioural mechanisms, or drugs that 'correct malfunction'.

It is remarkable that while material science has precise techniques to the level of nanotechnology, its studies of the emotional and mental causes of the human decision-making process are extremely rough and ready and based on a number of contradictory theses. Furthermore, be they the mechanics of behaviourism, brain structure and drug therapy, or Freudian early life explanations, most psychological studies focus on the 'abnormal' and treatments that will create 'normality'.

Those not diagnosed with 'mental health problems' are left in a state of mental and emotional anarchy, as the expertise that seeks to categorise and explain behaviour patterns and attitudes becomes increasingly contradictory, academic and hence distant. As ordinary people, we feel disempowered, with no right to have authority over our own lives. All we have to guide us may be impressions picked up from contradictory social, religious or peer group pressures. Our main motivation may be 'what Dad or Mum expect of me', the fact that I was rejected in bed last night. Such factors in the minds of those that lead us can trigger decisions that have a dramatic effect on the lives of millions, even billions, of ordinary people. To what extent are leading politicians or revolutionary activists still trying to prove something to their parents, wives, mistresses or children? The bigger and more powerful we are, the more we are free to exploit the system and make larger and larger errors. Dangerous drugs and machines may be carefully controlled. Dangerous politicians and administrators are free to let their minds and feelings run riot and produce the terrorised, consumption-obsessed chaos that is our 21st century world.

The answer of modern science as to the best way to organise the chaotic and amoral world it has created is that we should accept it as *reality*. It tells us we are mechanical beings driven by a natural need for genetic survival. To think anything more is possible has always made matters worse. To act as if playing poker or engaging in nuclear war, and so to believe everyone will cheat, lie and betray us, is the most mathematically sensible and beneficial way to behave.[1] To behave like this and take medicines and life decisions to gratify and ease any pain or dis-ease is the happiest course for everyone!

If we are to see beyond such an empty philosophy of despair, we need a systematic and consistent way of looking at behaviour and phenomena. It needs to describe in depth, but be capable of being learned and accessible to most people at varying levels of understanding. It needs to map emotional and mental pressures, the potential and the timing of their release, and how they may intensify and give opportunities for growth throughout life. Such a language should deepen understanding of what lies behind the expression of opinions and making of decisions. Being able to describe, explain and project human behaviour will help us appreciate other people and their situations. Knowing where we stand, there will be no need to protect ourselves against them constantly, as if they all were enemies.

This book aims to show that, properly understood and used, astrology is such a system. Astrology monitors the mechanics of cause and effect not only on the physical plane, as does conventional modern science, but on the emotional, mental and spiritual planes of experience as well. Because it is based on cycles of the heavens to which everything on earth is subject, it allows for the relative perspective of every element in the whole Earth system. So it can cut through many religious and cultural perspectives that tend to over-generalise, ignore individuality and alienate people into narrow and rigid cultural assumptions. While most branches of psychology may attempt to do this, few if any are free from contemporary Western assumptions and none based on a template of human behaviour that has stood the test of time. In Chapter 12, we shall see the importance of astrology in understanding Jung's theory of archetypes and as an important complement to recognising individual reactions to drug therapy and the importance of cyclical timing in mental heath. Most important, we will see that astrology is a tool specifically focused to describe mind and enrich behaviour, not a drug to reduce us to lowest common denominator indifference.

Aside from giving us tools to understand and help us address what we consider to be mental *illness*, astrology offers a language that can be learned and made more accessible to ordinary people. Vitally, it can be used without judgements of normality and abnormality that come from discussing ordinary human beings in psychological terms. A person with the Sun in Pisces, a Cancer Moon and the ascendant in Leo will be 'an extremely generous person, but need to avoid worrying about being responsible for other people'. It may not be necessary to diagnose, explain and treat 'self-obsessed paranoia, fuelled by an over-zealous guilt-ridden maternal responsibility for the suffering of others'!

While Astrology will not answer our problems, it does help us understand them better and hence decide an *appropriate* solution for ourselves, as healthy and properly recognised individuals, whatever value and belief system we live in. Vitally, it shows clearly what anyone with a problem wants to know – how other people are likely to feel about or react to what is planned.

Unfortunately, to make such claims for the social, political and psychological value of astrology (aside from the many other claims for astrology we will consider later) is likely to be considered ludicrous and to invoke derision. As at one time was the idea that splitting a tiny atom could actually destroy the world as we know it. In the 18th century, the trick of making fluff stick to amber when rubbing it with a cloth would not have been accepted as demonstrating the energy that would enable communication via the worldwide web.

Today, only the values of disputed religious convictions (if we have any) and the hard lessons of the ups and downs caused by the greed and struggle of the free market are there to discipline our crazed modern minds. Astrology suggests that everything we believe and the 'realities' of modern technology are contained and channelled by the cycles of the universe. We suffer, because of our own ignorance of the process. If there is anything in it, astrology could be vitally important. So, it is worth giving the matter serious consideration before we reject it.

To do so, we have to overcome a vital hurdle – that of misrepresentation. Chapter 2 shows how difficult it is for people today to find out about the real nature of astrology. Also that argument against it has degenerated into a mass of misunderstanding, disinformation and misrepresentation. In spite of what some scientists and some members of their press would have you believe, astrologers are not flat-earth-believing dinosaurs, with simple and gullible brains and very limited intelligence, who know little about the true workings of the universe. On the contrary, because astrologers understand and see the intrinsic limitations of material science's explanations and the dire consequences we face because of this, they have applied themselves with courageous original thought.

Read on and see if you agree with them.

Chapter 2
A Conspiracy of Disinformation

A cynic is person who knows the price of
everything and the value of nothing.
Oscar Wilde

A Western academic visited a Zen Master to discover his philosophy of
life and was offered a cup of tea. When the cup was full, the Master
continued to pour and spill, until the Westerner intervened to say the cup
was full. The Master replied. 'Like this cup, you are full of your opinions
and theories. How can I show you Zen unless you first empty your cup?'

Before we describe how it works and argue the case to claim a
positive role for astrology in modern and future worlds, it is important to
explain why it is on the margins of society. Why there is little or no
serious information about it in contemporary educational systems and the
media?   To understand, we must 'clear the decks' of the
misunderstanding, disinformation and misrepresentation that do exist and
masquerade as 'the facts'. When we do, the view commonly held by
'respected opinion-leaders', that 'no intelligent person can take it
seriously', is turned upside down.

How astrology was cast to the sidelines of our society.
As Christianity became the established religion of the Roman Empire,
the founding fathers narrowed contemporary esoteric wisdom, so what
was left would establish the absolute divinity of their view of the
Christian message for all time. Reincarnation and a range of subtle, yet
powerful, skills became denigrated as 'occult'. These, together with
many aspects of Christianity that did not suit those in power, were
outlawed to the 'dark' sidelines. It is often claimed that an important way
of preserving the cabalistic understanding of the structure of our spiritual
being was through the invention of Tarot cards. Herbal cures were
frequently looked on as satanic – the work of witches. The use and
acceptance of astrology and other esoteric skills was to vary considerably
during the centuries between then and now. The arrogant religious
divisiveness that haunts our societies to this day is a consequence of the
intolerance of Constantine's early Christian doctrinal decisions.

So, astrology's relationship with established Christian cultures was ambivalent. Much that survives today is as a result of early Arabic scholarship. It became more prominent during the second millennium and was taught in universities until the late 17th century. Astrological references abound in Shakespeare's plays. Milton's *Paradise Lost* draws on its imagery to describe the structure of the Lord God's created universe and Satan's descent from heaven. Systematic descriptions of human behaviour, health and personality, based on the apparent workings of the heavens, were commonplace. Astrology was too useful for the Church to reject outright, provided that astrologers did not seek to usurp the position of God. In the introduction to his *Christian Astrology,* William Lilly, the eminent 17th century astrologer, made this distinction clear with some elegance:

> 'To The Student In ASTROLOGY
> My friend, whoever thou art, that with so much ease shalt receive the benefit of my hard studies, and doth intend to proceed in this heavenly knowledge of the stars, wherein the great and admirable works of the invisible and alglorious God are so manifestly apparent. In the first place, consider and admire thy Creator, and be thankful unto him, be thou humble, and let no natural knowledge, how profound and transcendent soever it be, elate thy minde to neglect that divine Providence, by whose all-seeing order and appointment, all things heavenly and earthly, have their constant motion, but the more thy knowledge is enlarged, the more do thou magnifie the power and wisdom of Almighty God, and strive to preseve thy self in his favour; being confident, the more holy thou art; and more neer to God, the purer Judgment thou shalt give. Beware of pride and self-conceit, and remember how that long ago, no irrational Creature obey him, so long as he was Master of his own Reason and Passions, or until he subjected his Will to the unreasonable part.'

Clearly Lilly, his devotees in the 21st century and indeed most astrologers, whether they follow Lilly or not, did and do not see astrology to be in conflict with Christianity or any religion. Indeed they do not see astrology as a belief system, but rather a way of understanding the 'dictates of the heavens'. Indeed, Lilly goes to great pains to insist his students 'admire thy Creator, and be thankful unto him'.

From the global explorations of the Renaissance, Galileo's observations and what followed, the heliocentric nature of the Solar System was discovered. After several centuries of brutal religious conflict and persecution, in the late 17th to 18th centuries a new approach to knowledge emerged. It was called the Enlightenment. Towards the end of the 17th century, academia separated astronomy from astrology and ejected the latter from the 'academy'. It is an extreme irony that astrology, which had been reluctantly tolerated by Christian churches for more than 1300 years, was now rejected, because those Churches' world picture appeared to be discredited by modern science!

Yet the experience of living on the earth had not changed. We still struggled to survive on the same planet and were subjected to the same geocentric forces as our forefathers. The heavens still looked the same however deeply our observations penetrated what lay behind the appearances. It was the Christian claim that behind this observed universe was an all-powerful divine force that had created it in 4004 BC and guided it ever since that had been called into question. There was no reason to suppose that the astrological system developed by thousands of years of observation, before and after Christ, did not relate the cycles of the universe to human behaviour and natural phenomena correctly. Maybe a more sophisticated root cause and fine tuning of structures was needed, but the intrinsically observed relationships remained as valid as always. Indeed, relating these *inner* understandings to the new possibility of *outer* empirical observation was the great new hope for a fully comprehensive understanding of the universe.

Tragically, in one of the most infamous examples of throwing out the baby with the bathwater in the history of ideas, astrology was thrown out of the academy as a 'failed science'. That this happened is possibly explained by a fatal intrinsic limitation at the heart of material science from the very beginning – that it separated itself from art and the spirit, arguing they were illogical and so inferior facets of human nature. Even today, many material scientists see religion almost as an enemy. Such thinkers believe that, in time, statistical observation will build up sufficient bricks of 'irrefutable truth' to replace the soul with an entirely mechanical explanation of existence. To achieve this, it is necessary to deny any possible logical link between the spirit, mind and emotions of humanity and its material existence. Isolated beyond reason, the religious beliefs that humanity hold on to so desperately are merely childlike, primitive superstitions, left over from less enlightened times. In time they will wither away, leaving only the 'truly grown up' view of 'pure sequential reason' in a world of existential emptiness.

So, with adolescent arrogance, reminiscent of the perverse phraseology of Orwell's *Nineteen Eighty-four*, the 'Enlightenment', as it came to be known, rejected the wisdom of the ages, but left the ecclesiastical establishment to rant and rave about sacrilege, hoping it would wither on the vine. This left the new mechanistic approach to become the 'only true science'. Like a new fundamentalist religion, it went righteously on its own way, sweeping away the old and re-discovering the universe from scratch. The work was sub-divided into increasingly fragmented academic departmental bureaucracies. The result is not the hoped for ideal society of Rousseau's 'noble savage', or the genuine democracy visualised in Tom Paine's *Rights of Man* and William Morris' *News from Nowhere*, but the confused and amoral materialistic world we live in today. The fruits of three hundred years of *mechanical scientism*, as many see what we call science today, are pollution, global warming, and shortsighted exploitation of resources, lowest-common-denominator marketing media, confused and over-indulged adolescents, and focus-group-driven politicians. Today, even the great 20th century liberal hope of pure science fades in importance. Modern material scientistic statistical research is more like an industry that with sufficient funding can prove both sides of anything. Then ingenious technology can find ever more ways of imposing these newly discovered 'realities' on our increasingly exhausted natural environment.

Without advocators and defenders on any side of the Arts versus Science versus religion academic divides, astrology survived unexplained in the intuitive hearts of ordinary people, who continued to purchase almanacs through the 18th and 19th centuries. Then, in the late 19th century, interest developed in Eastern wisdom, where astrology had always known its place and been respected. This encouraged a deep re-examination of what was left of the Western esoteric traditions and the rediscovery of astrology. Since then, the voluntary dedication of small groups of intelligent and highly motivated experts has made a start on regenerating and developing the knowledge for the modern world.

Their task has been and is immensely difficult – rather like trying to teach the art of reading and writing to a society where its citizens for twelve generations over three hundred years have 'never needed to know how'. Imagine also that those citizens have been taught to consider writing as too primitive to have any use in satisfying the 'needs of the modern world'. For three hundred years no proper education or research in astrology has been allowed in our universities and schools. Astrological schools that developed in the 20th century were private and difficult to find.

With the development of the mass media, and especially radio and television, serious attempts to explain and show the workings of astrology have been banned, or severely curtailed, by regulators. Such official repression emanates from attitudes to be found in a long tradition Witchcraft Acts that date back to the Middle Ages. In 1604, activities considered connected with witchcraft became felonies under common law. No longer could offenders be burnt under church law. Instead they could be hanged under civil law and their properties forfeited to the State – a lively living for a new breed of Witchfinders General. In 1735, a gentler and more dismissive act was content to imprison, or fine, offenders as vagrants, or con artists. The last prosecution was in 1944 and the Act was finally repealed in 1951.

However, the spirit of Witchcraft Act prejudice continues in public institutions to this day. In Britain until 2004, astrology was specifically named as liable to give 'harm' and 'offence' to the general public – on a par with extreme violence, sexual abuse and demonstrations of suicide. The new Ofcom code continues to restrict a group of 'occult' and 'paranormal practices' as likely to be harmful and offensive and certainly not to be shown 'before the watershed, or when large numbers of children are likely to be watching'. If they claim the right to be listened to seriously in the media, regulation has demanded that astrologers are accompanied by one of astrology's detractors. Furthermore, unlike astrologers, such detractors do find funding in the psychology and scientific departments of state universities. So more money is spent preventing the serious study of astrology than in undertaking it!

Astrological activity as 'entertainment' is more tolerated. When written or spoken in Sun Sign columns it is seen as 'harmless fun', even though such generalisations are meant to be just that, yet prone to be acted upon by vulnerable people. Serious astrology can only be presented in the media as on trial. Nearly all this coverage aims to cast doubt, or even show astrology as 'clearly not true'. In a democratic society that rightly honours its legislation against racial, religious and cultural prejudice, it is difficult to understand how government-appointed institutions can believe it right to regulate against astrology in such a way.

All these circumstances combine to make genuine knowledge about astrology difficult to find. Yet its method and scholarship is vast, varied and profound, still in print and taught. The purpose of this book is to make such knowledge available. Then we will stress how vital it is to do so, if we are to fill gaps of crucial understanding in many areas of our modern world. We will embark on this task in Chapter Three. Before we do, it is important to dispel generally accepted myths and disinformation about the knowledge.

Dispelling the Myths and Disinformation
In spite of the standing of astrology's opponents, much of the task of defending it is much easier than might be expected. Astrology's debunkers have such contempt for its practitioners that few of them take the argument seriously. Often they rely on a series of assumptions and 'announcements' they repeat in the media at regular intervals. Although astrologers have fully and frequently answered most criticisms, similar or sometimes identical ones reappear; each time ignoring the answers that have been given many times already. This chapter aims to give definitive answers to the main criticisms once and once for all. So, listen carefully. I shall give these answers just one more time!

Assertion 1: Astrologers claim that you can predict events in a person's life by knowing the zodiac position of the Sun at their time of birth.
Soon after the birth of HRH Princess Margaret on 21st August 1930 the astrologer, R D Naylor, published a full chart horoscope and written interpretation of the royal arrival in the *Daily Express* newspaper. Like a long-awaited opportunity, it received immense interest. It was too time-consuming to answer readers' requests for similar information about themselves. So a grossly simplified version only considering the position of the Sun at birth was devised. Since the Sun passes through every sign for approximately 30 days during a year, it was easy to write twelve paragraphs – one for each of one twelfth of the world population.

Unfortunately, as can so easily happen with the popular media, the public took such gross over-simplifications to be specific advice to act upon. Others insisted that this was all there was to astrology and so condemned everything an astrologer does as generalised nonsense. Such columns might contain generalised grains of helpful advice, if written by an expert astrologer, but should never be taken as specific advice. The public hunger for astrology was and is so great that it has been impossible for most newspapers to exclude such columns ever since.

So, Sun Sign astrology is a mass popularised development well under one hundred years old. To see the paragraphs, however well written, as predictions or even individual descriptions may be an error in the minds of some readers, but never was nor is the intention of a genuine astrologer. While this Sun position is central to a person's nature, it is interdependent with many other lunar, planetary and earthly facts about a person's horoscope (birth chart) and its development and interaction with the heavenly cycles. To expect the Sun to describe every aspect of a person's nature and life is as daft as expecting an individual's physical heart to act for his whole body and run a mile, or eat his lunch, without legs, hands, stomach and all!

Of course the nature and condition of the Sun (heart) can tell us a lot about the life of the individual and how it would be best to approach what lies ahead.

'Eat less fat, more vitamins and iron, go for more exercise, or you will get sick' can be decided just by examining the heart.

Similarly 'Try to see yourself as more than a sensitive and vulnerable person, whose emotions can easily be manipulated by others' can easily be said about any Pisces Sun Sign.

Even 'Nothing will seem good enough today. Do your duty. Tomorrow you will feel less to blame' could be helpful advice for most Pisceans, when the Moon is in Virgo.

Just as the healthy heart advice would be helpful for most people with too much cholesterol in the blood, so would the Sun in Pisces comment be helpful in releasing most Pisceans from taking on too much responsibility.

Proper study of anatomy needs to be considered before treatment of the heart, circulation and body, as a whole, should be attempted. In the same way, informed courses of action and likely outcomes require careful testing and studying of the full chart. Even then, as we shall see, astrological insight is less specific than allopathic medicine. Astrology identifies pressures and possibilities. Rather like gathering and learning about the nature of food ingredients, before cooking a meal. The Appendix at the end of this book gives a brief outline of the main factors an astrologer would consider before giving a proper description of an individual and his potential. Many thousands of books have been written over several thousand years. At the end of Appendix is a bibliography indicating some accessible introductory books that describe meanings, associations and how to link and interpret them. At the end of some specialist chapters books that advance areas of study are listed.

To attack astrology as if it is just a series of Sun Sign columns is rather like condemning classical music, because someone wrote *Chopsticks* for all to play on the piano. 'How can you take nonsense like that seriously in the 21st century?' How indeed? But then, who limited astrology to just that? Is physics just about apples falling on people's heads?

Assertion 2: Astrology is based on the twelve constellations connected to the Sun's ecliptic. These are of unequal size. Also the stars that make up the constellations can be light years away from each other. Also, there are thirteen such constellations; hence there should be thirteen signs. Even if astrology had any validity, many people have the wrong signs.

The twelve zodiac signs used by astrologers are not the constellations, but the names given to exact 30-degree divisions of the 360-degree celestial sphere. Whether your Sun, Moon, planets etc are in a particular sign depends on the division, not the constellation. It is the same as Greenwich Mean Time referring to the zero hour first 30-degree time zone of the Earth's latitude and not to the area of London called Greenwich. No one suggests you have to live in that East London suburb to be in the GMT zone! Yes, these three criticisms of astrology are as silly as this!

Assertion 3: Because of the Earth's tilt on its axis, it appears to make a long wobble over approximately 26,000 years. As a result, when looking from the Earth, the position of the stars on the same day each year moves slowly backward. The position of the stars at the time of Ptolemy has changed by between 25 and 30 degrees. Most people should have their sun placed a whole sign earlier. Astrologers do not know about or understand this 'New Zodiac'.

Quite the opposite! Indian Vedic astrology has always allowed for this 'precession of the equinoxes' and used *the sidereal zodiac* as it is known. All astrologers use the precession to study a cycle of twelve ages that are each around 2,160 years in length. The present Age of Pisces is symbolised by the fishes, which was the early sign of the Christians. It has been a most Piscean period. The previous two ages were those of Aries and Taurus – again the sign qualities are typical of what archaeologists know about these periods in history.

The *tropical zodiac* (unchanged by precession) would be the only one, if the Earth were not tilted on its axis. It is measured from the first point of Aries (the Sun's position on the first day of Spring), which is used as the key reference point by astronomers. That the Western mind prefers to see signs cusps as constant over time and not submit to precession may say a lot about the hubris of imposing its 'truth' (including the scientistic mechanistic one!) upon nature. This could help explain the Western character. That the Eastern mind yields to take on board the reality of the Earth's tilt may explain its more accepting, mystical and holistic traditions.

It is my personal view that both perspectives of life on earth are valid in their own terms, and by combining them, we integrate heavenly and earthly understanding and so come closer to ultimate truth.

As we shall see later, astrology works mainly because of the relative position of the planets. We use the signs of the zodiac and their degrees to measure these planetary relationships, which are the same whatever name or even concept we give to the measuring framework. If we called an 'inch', an 'ipso', and changed nothing else, an ipso would give you the same information as an inch.

Assertion 4: There is more gravitational force in the midwife, who delivers the baby than the dwarf planet Pluto. How can bodies millions of miles away have any effect upon us?

Suffice it for the moment to point out that few astrologers are suggesting that Pluto, Venus, Mars or any other planets are having a direct effect on individuals in that they directly send rays of trauma, love and assertiveness respectively. How the planets combine as a complete system and how astrology might work is explained and illustrated in Chapter Three.

Assertion 5: In spite of numerous attempts by statisticians working with astrologers, it has been impossible to find any consistent cause and effect relationship between astrological cycles and the interpretations and predictions they suggest.
AND
Assertion 6: Astrology claims to predict. Yet, its predictions are unreliable and patchy, or so generalised that they seem to be applicable to anything that happens.

To start to answer these two points properly you need to read this book up to Chapter 6, as well its Appendix. Full answers would require a separate book that looks in depth at a very mixed range of studies and strategies from people who seem more intent on politicising their opinions than objectively defining and studying the science of astrology. The book list at the end of this chapter gives an idea of where to start. The rightness of the brief response below will become clearer as you study more.

Astrology's debunkers, even those most learned and respected in other academic fields[2], often refuse to study the subject. Others *appear* to have undertaken detailed study, but do not understand the intrinsic nature of astrology. Geoffrey Dean's ironically entitled *Recent Advances in Natal Astrology*[3] is a classic example. Dean lists a mass of experiments. Most, he claims, show inconsistent results, or replication failures. However in this book and all his future studies, he fails to develop and define a proper model of astrology. So how can he test it? At other times, he has offered a £1,000 reward to anyone who can prove Sun Sign astrology works[4] – as we have seen, a notion hardly anyone holds to be true! If Dean is not clear about what astrology is, how can he study what it can and cannot do? What Dean is testing is what *he thinks* astrology ought to and fails to do. His opinion is based upon a very basic understanding of early Newtonian mechanics, weights and measures, where only one rigid answer is valid. As we shall see shortly, astrology describes a much deeper and broader combination of consistencies.

Yet, even where the results of research are so strong that they appear to meet Dean's demands for mechanical rigidity, as in Gauquelin's *Mars Effect* studies[5], he cites implausible reasons to discredit the source data. On one occasion he even suggested that 19th century and early 20th century parents gave false data with regard to the births of their children.[6] For, Michel Gauquelin's 'Mars effect' findings from the study of the horoscopes of 5,000 athletes seemed so powerful that controversy concerning it continues decades later. At first, these findings and studies of other planets' positions near the angles of birth horoscopes seemed to establish astrology. In the event, Gauquelin's work may have set back, rather than advanced astrological research. For it created an impression that astrology could be what it could not be and could do what it would not be appropriate for it to do. Success in correlating the Mars and Jupiter positions to the achievements and professions of his 5,000+ sample created the hope in some astrologers and the fear in some opponents that astrological proof could be constructed in a kind of 'bricks and mortar' manner. Individuals, institutions and events could be created and predicted – built from their constituent 'astrological' parts like houses and motorcars. Such a simplistic view exposed astrology to a dangerous counter-argument. 'Because it cannot be shown to work mechanically, astrology has been "disproved". It is a "failed science". Hence astrologers practicing are deluded or "dangerous charlatans"'.

In his findings for Mars and other planets it could be argued that Gauquelin had fallen victim to a phenomenon most serious practitioners of astrology often come across – the highly significant and powerful pattern that 'cannot be denied' and seems to 'prove astrology without a doubt'.

There are patterns of planetary cycles and associations so similar to last time that they can be forecast with impeccable accuracy, but these are rare. Every time a planet enters a sign, makes an aspect, is exalted, in detriment, out of bounds, or whatever the astrological factor is, you can rarely be certain that what happened last time will repeat itself. There are at least three obvious reasons.

> ❋ While planetary patterns repeat themselves in predictable ways, every moment is a unique combination of these cycles. If the repetition is sufficiently strong (e.g. Mars on MC, stellium in earth signs), then outcomes may well be uncannily similar. However, no two moments are exactly the same. There will always be differences, leaving room for judgement and

guesswork. The more experienced the astrologer, the more likely is he able to synthesise the cycles into an exact projection.

❋ Even then, the individual planetary pressures can manifest at one or more levels. Transiting Mars conjunct natal Uranus in Leo in the 1st house expressed materially leads to (I kick down a barrier), emotionally (an outburst of anger), mentally (I plan to change my circumstances) and spiritually (I reflect upon my need to free myself from other people's labels). Furthermore within levels of expression there are many specific empirical outcomes. On the physical level one person may break down a barrier, another start a revolutionary movement and so on. In his *Cosmos and Psyche*[7] Richard Tarnas links this multi-level astrological expression with Jung's theory of archetypes.

❋ Because of the variables, we have the free will to make choices, <u>provided</u> that we are ready to face the consequences indicated by the underlying planetary patterns.

Because astrology manifests such a wide range of varieties, detractors dismiss it as generalised and unspecific 'Barnhamism',[8] capable of any interpretation that fits. Many interpretations perhaps, but that certainly does not mean ANY interpretation and never outside the range. Here comes the crucial – defining the range of variables, then testing for the range. Also, seeking to identify what other astro factors might make an exception to an expected outcome.

Such work being undertaken would be of immeasurable benefit to our modern world, where a narrow view of precisely measured mechanical materialism dominates societies in a state of chaotic emotional and intellectual anarchy. For by discerning, anticipating and explaining patterns in emotions, thoughts and beliefs, astrology offers an understanding that the purely physical sciences never can achieve and without which current social and psychological theories are incomplete.

Tragically, little or no public or business funding has been given to genuine attempts to do such research. Non-debunking research is nearly always the volunteer work of individual astrologers, working with meagre software and facilities. In contrast, considerable resources were put into disproving Gauquelin findings – even one replication study going to the extent of misrepresenting its own findings.

As already mentioned, some funding has been given to psychologists and sceptics, who seek to decide for themselves what would prove, or disprove, astrology and then publicise the disproving claims in high-profile media networks. These studies either ignore astrologers, or seduce well-intentioned, but unwary and inexperienced, astrologers into traps that are contrived to appear to fail. It would be unworthy of consideration to research physics, biology, and chemistry without involving experts in these fields in the main experimental and reporting design. Indeed, the usual approach is for experts to decide their own research and to be given funding, not to be put 'on trial' by outsiders, who know and respect nothing about the area of expertise under study. Why should astrology be treated so differently?

A good astrologer will describe the archetypal environment within which a person will have to work out his destiny during the period under consideration. A good astrology consultant will then discuss likely consequences of using the potential at varying levels, to help the client decide which level he is ready for and so will find most beneficial.

To seek to assess such activity by counting how many people had children, romantic affairs, developed their artistic achievements and so on is to fail to understand what the client and consultant seek and are trying to offer. Would we say a medicine failed if it built up the red cell blood count, but the patient was already too anaemic to survive? Or would a meteorologist's prediction of a 'wet time for everyone tomorrow' fail because the majority of the population saw the skies that morning and stayed indoors? Unless researchers listen to astrologers, identify and know what they are looking for and when they have found it, any experimental conclusions by statisticians for or against astrology are meaningless.

Assertion 7: The Holy Bible clearly states that, in seeking to predict the future, humanity usurps the omnipotence of God.
There is nothing in the Old, or New Testament that specifically says this. Certainly, the failure of Babylon's astrologers to affect the destiny of the Lord's chosen people is clearly shown. Generally, this criticism and other often quoted sections from The Bible concern human attempts to predict and change God's purpose. Such actions would be criticised just

as strongly by most astrologers. If astrology is used to understand, describe and celebrate God's creation, it no more contravenes divine law than does mathematics or gardening.

It is this very wish to understand and enhance this highest purpose of life that brings most people to astrology in the first place, as the quotation near the beginning of this chapter from Britain's renowned astrologer, the 17th century's William Lilly, shows. He was a highly regarded churchwarden and is buried under the Choir floor close to the altar of his church in Walton on Thames, Surrey.

Astrological symbolism lies at the heart of the essential messages of The Holy Bible. Its contributions to Christian and other religious traditions are studied in Part Three of this book.

Assertion 8: Media revelations 'disprove' astrology.
Often repeated news announcements about research disproving astrology appear in the media at regular intervals and, when they do, seem to spread surprisingly quickly to other media outlets all over the world.[9] It would be worth checking the source of such stories (usually the science editors of newspapers, radio and television). If you see such an article, check particularly the date of any research referred to, by whom it was undertaken and for what purpose. Often work done long ago and since discredited is re-reported in a summary of old work in an academic journal that has an anti-astrology editorial policy. Because this article has *just appeared*, interested parties report it as a 'sensational new finding'. In fact, the research will almost certainly have the shortcomings outlined above. It was never undertaken to test astrology, or was not designed and controlled by astrologers, or 'failed to prove' factors that astrologers would not seek to prove in any case – rather like relying on a Turner Prize artist to decide the validity of a recent theory in nuclear physics!

In conclusion, let us put these old, jaundiced, oft-repeated and special-interest accusations and arguments to one side.

There may be a whole range of intelligent and entirely justified reasons for rejecting the validity and usefulness of astrology to the 21st century and beyond. If there are, then we must come to this conclusion after extensive study of the facts. We must understand what astrologers are claiming and the deepest meanings of the language they are using.

We must identify how astrology might fit with, temper and improve modern understanding.

Our motivations and actions must be those of genuine scientists throughout all time. We must study without fear or favour for the outcome, always willing to let go of all assumptions and be pleased to be proved wrong – whatever the cost to ourselves in money and standing.

The truly great scientific mind allows no frontiers to block the pursuit of truth. It melts away bureaucratic barriers of self-interest. The genuine scientist has never been frightened to think the unthinkable. Perhaps a great misunderstanding did lead to a mistaken decision in the development of ideas in the $17^{th}/18^{th}$ century and that error does lie at the root of our 21st century angst, unhappiness and confusion. Perhaps astrology is a tool that would be invaluable in putting all this right.

This book claims such a possibility is sufficiently likely that you should study, consider and, if you agree, act on the following information. Be ready for surprises. What follows will be new to most people.

Further Reading
The following list is far from complete. It is selected to give you a beginner's introduction to the history, current level of debate and (mis)understanding about astrology. The books raise a range of contemporary criticisms and responses from astrologers, which the chapters that follow will address, answer and move on from.

Edited by Annabella Kitson *History and Astrology*
John Anthony West *The Case for Astrology*
H J Eysenck and D K B Nias *Astrology: Science, Superstition*
Geoffrey Dean *Recent Advances in Natal Astrology*
Michel Gauquelin *The Truth about Astrology*
Suitbert Ertel & Kenneth Irving *The Tenacious Mars Effect*
Neil Spencer *True as the Stars Above*
Garry Phillipson *Astrology in the Year Zero*
Correlation - published by Astrological Association; a bi-annual peer-reviewed astrological research Journal.

For more information about astrology, the media and Ofcom, visit the News area of: http://www.astrologicalassociation.com

PART 2

How Astrology Works

Chapter 3
Could this be How Astrology Works?

To see a World in a Grain of Sand
And a Heaven in a Wild Flower,
Hold Infinity in the palm of your hand
And Eternity in an hour.
William Blake

An explanation of the way astrology works needs to be fully heard before a proper assessment is possible. Yet from the beginning readers may wish to interrupt, challenge and argue. It is essential to refrain from this, if we are to give understanding a chance. Instead, suspend disbelief and be open to discovering new and unexpected knowledge. No progress is made when we dispute before we really understand what the dispute is about. The suggestion is only to *suspend* disbelief. Once you have the full thesis and facts to consider only then will informed study, experimentation and discussion be possible.

The aim is grand: no less than to describe the inter-relatedness of the patterns of our lives with our solar system's planetary and the Earth's daily cycles. Then we will show how knowing this does not restrict us, but liberates our minds and makes it easier to choose. Indeed, we can see astrological structure as the vital glue of appropriateness that puts all areas of knowledge and action in perspective.

Let us start from the material science's contemporary view of creation. Around fourteen billion years ago[10] a 'big bang' spontaneously caused an exchange of energy into the key elements of hydrogen and helium, which by nuclear processes developed into denser elements, then ever-expanding modules of matter and an ongoing coagulation/eruption process, which created the stars, clusters, planets and other cosmic debris of the universe that our telescopes observe today.

Without such instruments, meditators thousands of years ago went one step further to talk of an expanding *and* contracting universe. They built up a series of ever greater cycles within a period of 311,040,000,000,000 of our Earth Years, which we are only halfway through. We are said to be at the bottom of this great cosmic cycle they called the Life of Brahma. Others have referred to it as the 'breathing in and breathing out of Brahma'. We are near the maximum point of breathing out – hence material science's obsession with the 'big bang' and an expanding universe. Within this Life of Brahma are cycles from such immense to lesser and lesser lengths, until we finally reach periods of time comprehensible and relevant to a human lifespan. These are the cycles of the planets in our solar system.

For thousands of years, astrologers/astronomers have watched the Sun, Moon and planets move in front of the reference points of the star patterns, while at the same time observing behaviour on the Earth beneath. From this vast experience, observers have matched the poetry of words and images to planetary movement. We have developed a system of interpretative language, which is continually refined by further observation. This lies at the heart of the descriptions and projections astrologers use today. Is this the outdated fancy of gullible people? How and why can there be a causal and predictable relationship between the cycles of the planets, Sun, Moon and Earth and these words we use to describe them?

The mechanics of modern astronomy and space travel are founded on very specific observations of the interrelatedness of the bodies and clusters in the universe. We measure changes in the colour of light to determine the age and condition of stars millions of light years away. NASA calculates the gravitational pull of each planet precisely and uses this knowledge to catapult a probe to one of the moons of Saturn and beyond.

Astrology goes further. Its study of the same mechanics of the movements of the various objects in the universe is subtler than this. It is not like studying the behaviour of hard and solid snooker balls for three reasons. Firstly, the connection between the stars, planets and other cosmic phenomena is inseparable – more like a motor engine, in that every element is vital to the performance all the time. It is not disputed that, if a single planet in the solar system were to atomise and disperse, the effect on Earth would be catastrophic. However, what is often forgotten is that, unlike both the snooker balls and the motor engine, many of the elements (including ourselves) in this universal 'engine' are soft, pliant, malleable and capable of changing actions and reactions. Thirdly, the experience of occupants is highly dependant on pressures expended upon the planet as a whole, or upon particular places within it. Much of this is obvious. Unprotected sunlight, strong winds, and vast unsheltered plains, dramatic changes in temperature and polluted environments all force us to dress and protect ourselves appropriately. The relationship of the more subtle 'vibrations' of particular places to planetary cycles are more difficult to measure, yet no less powerful for that. Let us consider the possibilities.

Polar regions on Earth are colder than equatorial ones, because of the relationship between the Sun and Earth. The gravitational pull of the Moon and Sun on the Earth affects the height of the tides. Because it is observable and measurable with conventional instruments, many aspects of the relationship between the Sun, Moon, the Earth and its occupants are generally accepted. So is it illogical to insist the planets cannot have their part to play as well?

Dr Percy Seymour has written a number of books[11] that summarise many astrophysical research studies into the relationship between many kinds of animal behaviour and Sun, Moon and planetary cycles. He has synthesised these into what he claims to be a testable scientific hypothesis suggesting how planets could influence human behaviour and especially the foetus at the moment of birth. By carefully distinguishing the nature of gravity, magnetic force and resonance, he traces a pattern of possible relationships between organic life and planetary cycles, Sun spot activity, solar winds and planetary magnetism. Built into his model is the fact that apparently small factors can have substantial effects. We all know this. Making a decision to move a few switches can illuminate a whole stadium and who knows how many other sporting and entertainment activities as a consequence. Not making the decision could leave the crowd in a world of uncertainty and danger.

Even without the advanced scholarship of Dr Seymour's model, it is possible for most of us to observe enough about life to feel the relationship between planetary cycles and life on Earth deserves careful study. Since most of life is water, it is reasonable to suppose creatures formed of it might react to the same pressures, as we know the tides do. Many gardeners plant and prepare by the Moon, because they observe sap rising during its waxing fifteen days and falling during the waning half-cycle. Anecdotal reports from police stations and hospital casualty wards suggest there is excessive and insane behaviour in the build up to full moons. On 22nd December 2000, the *New Scientist* reported three studies. One showed that animals tended to bite much more at full moons; a second finding by British Telecom that people were more likely to make phone calls in the days leading up to full moons; and a third by Richard Neal at the University of Leeds that the number of patients visiting their general practitioner 's surgery peaks soon after a new moon.

In the 21st January 2007 edition of the British newspaper *The Independent,* Roger Dobson[12] summarised a number of everyday considerations that seem to be based on the Moon. Doctors and police experience the lunar cycle as affecting their work rate; gout and asthma attacks peak during new and full moons; murders and aggravated attacks in Florida showed clusters around full moons – generally more crimes were committed around these times. A four-year study found that the lowest number of accidents occurred on a full moon day, while the highest was two days before the full moon. Medical studies have found higher urinary retention among affected patients admitted during the new moon compared with other phases. Links have also been found between the lunar cycle and the likelihood of people being hospitalised with heart, bladder, and diarrhoea problems. The lunar cycle can also affect the menstrual cycle, fertility, spontaneous abortions and thyroid disease. Dobson quotes Dr Michael Zimecki of the Polish Academy of Sciences: 'It is suggested that melatonin and endogenous steroids [which are naturally occurring in humans] may mediate the described cyclic alterations of physiological processes. Electromagnetic radiation and/or the gravitational pull of the Moon may trigger the release of hormones."

Dr Seymour summarises a range of research that showed organic life responding to lunar cycles and magnetic forces.[13] The effect is not just caused by the increase of night light at full moons. Shellfish kept in total darkness still opened and closed in accordance with the lunar cycle. Richard M Pasichnyk[14] summarises a vast number of examples of organic life's reaction to Sun and Moon cycles.

Our dispositions, actions and their consequences may cause the subtlest astronomical cycles to have very material effects. Some people suggest there may be a relationship between financial market prices and Sun spot cycles, lunar cycles and eclipses. Before we dismiss the idea as impossible, we should remember that the behaviour of financial markets is the product of expectation and the mass hopes and fears that drive them. If astrology is a system that describes the cycles of these hopes and fears, then it may well help in anticipating trading decisions and hence price levels. Yet, since it is the emotions that astrology is mapping and the price level that we are seeking to anticipate, the results of planetary cycle study although helpful are likely to be patchy in predicting the markets day-to-day. They will be more reliable at powerful and obvious points in the cycles.

To really understand what is happening, we need to make a major leap from these lunar and solar examples to include the cycles of the planets and rotation of the Earth on its axis. While many of you would call this a 'leap in the dark' and 'a leap too far', do give it a chance. This is one of those seminal moments, when suspending disbelief can open and illuminate doors of understanding and make a big and beneficial difference to our lives.

At first sight, it seems patent nonsense. How can the poisonous, entirely uninhabitable planet Venus direct our 'love' and attitude towards possessions; the frozen methane wastes of Jupiter make it the bringer of justice, jollity and opportunity; and the distant, hardly-a-planet Pluto guide our life and death experiences in this life and beyond?

Throughout the ages, astrologers have not helped. They have become so caught up with the rich potential imagery and meaning in their grand interpretive design that the experience of the astrological language working has been enough for them. It was so strong that it no longer seemed necessary to consider how this might relate to the physical realities. The concepts and crude schematics we see in medieval and renaissance astrological illustrations are no more than reminders and rough drawings of what most learned people of the time took for granted. The gap between what was represented and what could be seen and measured materially was so great that, as we saw in Part 1, by the second half of the 17th century the old knowledge was thrown out 'boots and all'.

That this rejection of astrology is accepted blindly and held to without question by most modern scientific and academic scholars today is an example of how the brightest minds are as open to irrational prejudice as any others. Once again, let us remind ourselves that *we continue, as we always have, to live on the Earth.* So, having a better understanding of the true nature of the cycle of the Earth around the Sun, and exactly why the planets appear to dance backwards and forward against the backcloth of stars, should have enhanced knowledge and use of astrology, not sidelined it.

Astrological interpretation comes from the wisest and most skilful people of their time observing how cycles in the heavens relate to behaviour on earth. Whatever the physical cause of these cycles, while they continue to occur, why should the associations of the cycles to words traditionally used to interpret them cease to be valid? We may need another explanation of this, but the experience remains the same. To dismiss the experience as fanciful and impossible is hardly scientific in any sense – ancient or modern.

In contrast to Dr Seymour, who started from the viewpoint of a modern material scientist and then hypothesised a mechanical relationship between what has been discovered experimentally by astrophysics and astrology, it may also be fruitful to look from the opposite perspective. Let us start from what astrologers have observed over thousands of years, and then ask the question: if there were to be any validity in this knowledge, what sort of mechanical explanation might there be?

Quite often, when we close our eyes, we get a feeling for how things might be, even without the language and concepts. Like an identity-kit artist, an expert scientist listening to our description may make the connections, adjust and fine-tune what we describe. Perhaps we could harness the power of analogy to illustrate how we sense astrology to be working. This is what is attempted below, hoping that both astrologer and astrophysicist will show sympathy and respect for each other and meet in a middle way of understanding.

So, from the perspective of an astrologer, how might astrology work? How can we apply the language of symbolism to the ordinary world that we claim our knowledge describes so well? Is there a non-superstitious explanation that might be acceptable to the modern scientific mind?

The answer becomes clear when we look again at the inter-relatedness of the universe and, in the case of the human lifespan, the solar system. The Earth moves as it does because of its relationship with the Sun, Moon and every one of the planets, satellites and comet visitors of our system. The paths of the planets are not exactly circular and, from our perspective, do not appear to move at a constant speed. When racing, we know the difference between going around a tight bend and along a straight. Imagine that instead of our movement being based on the driving of our legs, or an internal combustion engine, it is controlled by the *combined effect* of the gravities, magnetic fields and other cosmic pushes and pulls of at least ten major and many other minor objects, each of which is based on the cyclic motion of each object. Let your imagination drift to visualise the gravitational relationships between the Sun, its planets and their moons. It is not one, but the complete composite situation, that keeps our Earth moving in its path and spinning on its axis. Because our Earth is pliable the pressures are different in different part of its surface. Because we are on it and dependent on the bounty of where we are, each of us experiences life differently. Yet, the closer we are to each other or the more similar our environments, the more similar we are likely to be in attitude and reaction.

This analogy may help. If you go on a dramatic roller coaster, or other theme park ride, you may come to notice particular objects each time you get to a certain point of the ride. Maybe you always see a candyfloss stand just as the carriage drops dramatically and you feel sick. If you had just woken up in that situation and did not know anything about the construction of the ride and its environment, you might think the candyfloss stand caused you to be sick. While this might be nonsense, it does not invalidate the importance of the connection between the candyfloss stand and the condition of your stomach. A sceptic, or debunker, who sets up a study which looks at all stands and shows that a very low proportion of people get sick when they see them, would be missing the point – particularly if he used the research to justify blocking all funding of studies into candyfloss stands and human behaviour relationships.

On the other hand, a genuine, objective scientist would suspend disbelief and investigate further. If he made measurements of the difference between the altitude and angle between the carriage and candyfloss stand, at the time when the sickening feeling is at its most intense and the lack of movement of the candyfloss stand is noted, he might begin to understand. It is our movement in terms of the fixed undulating structure of the ride and its relation to the reference point of the candyfloss stand that creates a sense of vertigo, which is of course the cause of the experience. If we do not like the experience, then we will learn how to recognise and avoid such rides in future. While we can now see that the candyfloss stand has no direct causal relationship with our experience, it has been a very helpful reference point to explain and correct our experience for the future.

Maybe it is on this level that astrology works. We find ourselves in a confusing Earth environment that at first sight seems solid and systematic. In fact, the Earth's behaviour is far more frightening and dramatic than the most traumatic fairground ride. It is speeding through space at a cumulative speed of 2,500,000 miles per hour. This is made up of 860 mph on its axis, 66,661 mph around the Sun, 31,000 mph of the solar system around Vega, 700,000 mph of Sun/Vega in this part of our galaxy, 559,350mph the rotation of our galaxy, and more than another 1,000,000 mph in relation to other galaxies. It is small wonder that our lives are subject to constant pressures, tensions, uncertainties, relieving spells of confidence, and depressing times of helplessness on this planetary ride that we just cannot get off! How anxiously exciting it is to start the fairground ride! How pleasantly exhilarating slowly to go higher and higher, see the view expand the first time and how nail-bitingly frightening every time afterward! How both relieved and just that bit cocky we may appear as we leave the ride.

In relating verbal response and image to particular moments of our ride through our life, astrology is an invaluable notebook of how and why things happen as they do. As we shall see in Chapter 12, psychologists could find the knowledge invaluable for diagnosis and treatment.

With the development of computer technology for astrological calculation, as well as the many measurements we make of our material world, astro- and geophysicists and seismologists could consider studying clues of how the detailed pressures of the universe express themselves in different places on our planet. The earthquake that occurred just off the Western coast of Sumatra on 26th December 2004, which led to the terrible tsunami was predicted by N Venkatanathan and his team. On 22nd December 2004, they presented a report about a possible Indonesian earthquake to members of the Department of Science and Technology, New Delhi, that was within 157.11899 km and 28 minutes of the place and time of the actual event. They were using what they called 'planetary angular momentum theory.[15]' May this break down barriers caused by prejudice and inspire much helpful collaboration in research between astrologers and material scientists!

Astrology does not just give us the chance to check up the physical causes that lie behind anecdotes of events; it also describes the person who is experiencing them. This comes from the notion that the astro-indicated condition, atmosphere, pressures of the place and time in which we are born form an imprint. This indicates the way we are disposed to react to experiences throughout our whole life. How could this be so?

If each point of place and time on earth has a composite impact, made up from the sum total of unique pressures that can be described using the ancient language of astrological understanding, then something new and vulnerable like a new-born baby may be affected by these unique pressures most of all – much in the way that Dr Seymour describes experiments that suggest organic creatures respond to subtle resonances. Turning on the light to illuminate a darkened room shows how a very small act can change completely what we see and so what we may decide to do next. A first meeting with an important person in our lives, starting a new job, meeting our future partner's parents, are all vital new experiences. They can form impressions that stay with us and determine our judgement/behaviour for much, if not all of our lives. Our first moment of independent existence has to be the most formative of all. The place we have been cast out of is to us the absolute protection of our mother's womb. Now we face total uncertainty. What it feels like must leave a lasting and crucial impression.

Freud saw the birth experience as so traumatic that it was the origin of all anxieties. So he proceeded to study ways of identifying, admitting and correcting the consequent psychosis, especially of our early life experiences. Assisted by wise maps of astrology, Jung developed a more neutral, less accusational and guilt-ridden therapy. This strengthened the subject by encouraging the acceptance of individuality and personal responsibility, rather than seeing others to be the cause of our personal problems.

Clearly whether the place of birth is hot, cold, noisy, sensitive, mechanical, sterile, embracing or reassuring is likely to affect the baby, but astrology looks deeper. It asks 'what is the condition of this point on the Earth at this time?' If the road is smooth and straight, we hardly notice our journey and can communicate with fellow passengers in relaxed and philosophical way. When we speed around a corner, or go over a bumpy road in a car, we feel less secure. We may shout out, demand and argue. How much more sensitive is a newborn child likely to be? So much so that astrology goes further and looks at the days immediately after a child is born as formative in the corresponding years of its life. From this we get a disposition at birth that is unfolding through life.

Many careful observers, who compare human behaviour with planetary and other astronomical cycles, are convinced that we are experiencing and responding to the astro pressures of where we are on the earth. Also, we develop familiarity, hence mastery and expertise, in the way we respond to more and more of these cycles as we grow older.

In the chapters that follow, we will look more systematically at the cycles, astrology's way of understanding and explaining them, and how we can benefit from this knowledge. Before we do, here are more clues that give possible explanation of the mechanical connectedness between the motions of the heavens and people's feelings, attitudes and actions.

At school, I was fascinated to learn how astronomers use time-lapse cameras to trace planetary movement from a dot for each observation, to draw a curved line through the heavens over time. When the cycle is complete, the line will return to its original point. Alternatively, we can trace the movement of two bodies, or two bodies as observed from a third body, and make straight lines to join the two curved lines at selected intervals. Both methods are ways of representing the actual relative movements of one or two bodies from each other or a third one. Since they are calculated by precisely measured mathematical algorithms of physical movement, they indicate actual relationships, which must be dependent on actual physical factors. Rather than planet A or B having a direct effect upon a person or event, could it be that their pressure of relationship to us, as revealed by the visually observable pattern of their movements, is what we are responding to? Of course, rather like the roller-coaster ride, it may not be the planets, or even the observable pattern, that is causing our experience, but rather something we are yet to discover and understand that is related to the patterns.

Are there factors in these actual physical patterns that are similar to patterns our ancestors have found to be sacred? Do the physical patterns compliment the verbal explanation of planetary cycles handed down to us by our ancestors? Positive answers to these questions are the clues that help us link the metaphysical with the physical and learn how astrology works.

The *Astrological Mandalas* computer program[16] draws such lines for any period at user-defined intervals and start-and-end dates.

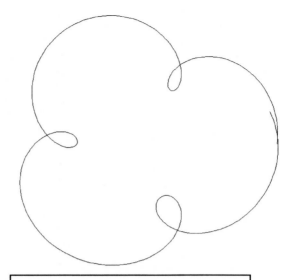

Figure 1 - Mercury to Earth over 1 year

Figure 1 draws Mercury's path (one dot for each day) in the course of one year, as it appears from the Earth. Imagine the Earth is in the centre of the diagram. Because Mercury and the Earth move at very different speeds, Mercury *appears* to move backwards and forwards (against the background of very slow-moving stars) toward and away from the Earth three times a year. Also, because Mercury is so close, it is often behind or too close to the Sun to be seen from the Earth. It is for this reason, rather than anything that the planet has on its surface, or does directly to us on Earth, that Mercury is associated with the quick, not always sustained, mental insights that come and go, change, disappear and re-appear.

Figure 2 above shows Venus' movement as viewed from the Earth over a ten-year period. Although Venus completes a cycle of the Sun in less than a year and its path around the zodiac in terms of the Earth is roughly one of our years, it takes about ten cycles to form the balanced mandala shown. It is its steady build up to completing the drawing of this symmetrical rose pattern in our minds that captivates and focuses our consciousness on the persistence and completeness of material beauty and devotion. Its archetype image is the inspiration of many stained glass church window designs. Yet, until the development of this technology, its relationship to the material world could not be seen – only *felt*. Felt so strongly and profoundly that Venus has been associated with the flower, the rose and hence love and beauty for thousands of years. This is why this inhospitable body was defined as a planet of beauty and love by our ancestors. Of course that was how they experienced it and, in spite of all the information master telescopes and probes tell us, it is how we continue to experience it today.

As all the planets move we feel their changing pressures, in the form of images that their paths wrest in our subconscious. We experience a build-up of the beautiful and ugly, balance and imbalance, relaxation into harmony, or the unsettling opposite.

Figure 2 – Venus to Earth over 10 years

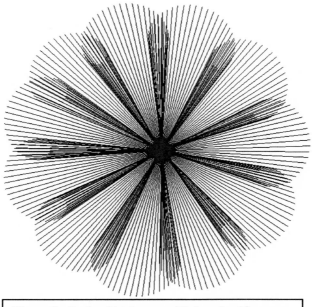

Figure 3 - Jupiter/Earth every 10 days for 12 years

What do you feel about and learn from these? Figure 3 is a line drawn between Jupiter and the Earth every ten days over twelve years. Figure 4 is the pattern of Saturn to the Earth over that same ten-year period.

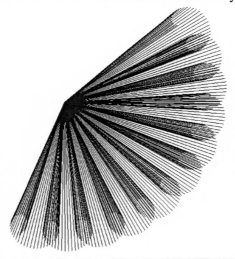

Figure 4 – Saturn/Earth every 10 days for 12 years

Figure 5 below shows the interactive dance between Jupiter and Saturn. The Earth is in the centre.

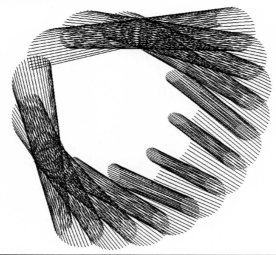

Figure 5 – Jupiter/Saturn every 10 days for 12 years from Earth

Note how similar, but subtly different, are the Jupiter/Mercury and Jupiter/Venus mandalas.

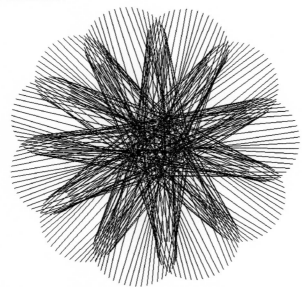

Figure 6 Jupiter and Mercury viewed from the Earth over ten years.

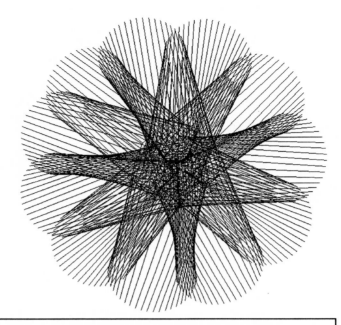

Figure 7 Jupiter and Venus viewed from the Earth over ten years.

To understand the mental patterns that drive whole generations, consider Figure 8, which depicts the dramatic relationship between Uranus and Pluto from Earth over one hundred years.

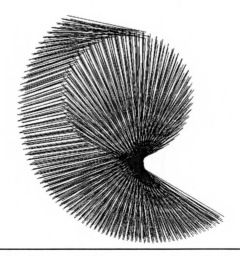

Figure 8 – Uranus and Pluto from the Earth for one hundred years

Then there is the massive culture-changing generational cycle of Neptune/Pluto. Figure 9 shows 100 years of this.

Figure 9 – Neptune and Pluto from the Earth for one hundred years

The *Astrological Mandalas* software that generated these images can draw thousands of astronomically exact representations of the patterns that show the cycles of our solar system, from many perspectives.

These cycles are the pressures that create the archetypes in our subconscious minds. For the subconscious does not see the ground as firm, solid and permanent, but knows the fragility of being attached to this body at this point of time. It experiences how secure, wonderful, frightening, seductive and much more is our present situation. Out of this subconscious matrix emerges our dispositions, potentials and resistances; not only at birth, but as they change and develop through life.

Of course, it is only in recent decades that astrologers have had access to the technology that can represent the relationships between the planets and ourselves in this way. For centuries, astrologers had to visualise from numbers in almanacs developed from on-the-ground observations, recorded over time. The three hundred year separation of astronomy from astrology has led to divergence in methods and terms of observation. These gaps of understanding are apparent, not substantive. Although astrologers use a geocentric language and references, they are perfectly aware of the most recent heliocentrically based discoveries and use them to fine-tune their interpretations. Yet it is valuable for astrology to continue to use a geocentric language, because it is inextricably linked to a vast tapestry of intrinsic understanding of human behaviour and events on Earth thousands of years old.

This ancient language of astrology shows the reflection of the extrinsic universe to this intrinsic understanding, like an intricately detailed and fine-tuned Platonic mirror. Having these invaluable linking resources makes astrology a truly remarkable combination of art and science. It is a science, because everything is based on the measurement of the cycles. It is an art, because the meanings of these measurements are expressed through words and images that are reflected upon, juxtaposed and integrated with the skill of a poet.

This language seems alien to most people in the modern world, because it introduces a concept that has been absent from most intellectual circles for more than three hundred years – that of a synchrony between astronomical movements and our behaviour. We are told the very notion of such a possibility seems at best quaintly anachronistic and irrelevant.

Yet, is it really good enough to consign this very complete system of explaining behaviour to the 'dustbin of history' without open-mindedly applying modern methods to delve deeply into it? Surely we should study this ancient astrological language, make allowances for the limited technical resources available at the time it was developed, and seek to discover whether our forefathers knew something that would benefit us today. To refuse to do so would be as unscholarly and unscientific as it would have been (before the Rosetta Stone was found) to cast aside Egyptian hieroglyphs as primitive scribbling.

If we open our minds to the language and structure of astrology, as it has come down to us, then we may just begin to see complementary links between the way we explain the universe today and the way our ancestors used astrology to explain the structure of their lives. We may even find answers to what modern science is yet to understand and explain.

If we give its ideas and theories a chance, allow in new information and let it settle, then who knows what we may see and understand in a radically different light?

Further Reading and Study

Dr Percy Seymour
     Astrology: The Evidence of Science
     The Scientific Basis of Astrology
     The Birth of Christ – Exploding the Myth
     Scientific Proof of Astrology
Nick Kollerstrom & Mike O'Neill *The Eureka Effect: Astrology of Scientific Discovery*
Rick Levine *Quantum Astrology* (DVD from http://www.sacredmysteries.com)
Rique Pottenger *Astrological Mandalas* (software published by ACS Publications http://www.astro.com)

Chapter 4
The Workings of Astrology

The whole is far greater than the sum of its parts.
Georg Wilhem Freidrich Hegel

To explain each moment of time, astrologers consider at least three combinations of planetary positions. These are known as the birth, progressed and transit charts. At least ten points (Sun, Moon and eight planets) can occupy any one of twelve zodiac signs (segments of the celestial sphere, named after one of the main star clusters on the ecliptic) in any one of twelve houses (calculated from the diurnal revolution of the Earth on its axis). The 1440 variables in each of the three charts combine to make nearly three billion variables in all.

Yet built into the structure of this immense range is a limited number of key concepts, which modify each other. Rather like children's bricks, or a Meccano set, the number of possible constructions is far, far greater than the limited range of basic materials. As we get to know the possibilities of each unit better, the range and complexity of what can be built increases. Yet, astrological key concepts are much more than solid, hard-edged construction units. They are more like colours and textures in painting that mutually inter-adapt and combine together to create uniquely different outcomes. In spite of immense variety, the cultured eye of the astrologer can still discern the primary ingredients.

དགེ་སློང་

At first sight, learning the language of astrology is more difficult than learning French, Greek or even Tibetan; for there are no immediately recognisable functional comparisons. To know that *moine* means 'monk' immediately makes us feel at home with French. To know the script above this paragraph means the same encourages us to continue learning this strange way of writing.

However, to be told that 'you have an Aries Sun, because you were born at that time of year' still seems to have little relevance to your life. You need an astrologer's insight.

'Aries is a positive, cardinal, fire sign ruled by Mars and so its key words are "assertive", "pioneering" and "courageous".'

'Well yes, I am inclined to take more risks than most people and am impatient to get on with things, but I would not act on it.'

'That's because your Aries Sun is in the 12th house and you have the ruling Mars conjuncted by the Moon in Cancer in the 4th house, squared to Saturn in Libra in the 7th house. Your relationship with your mother made you frightened and defensive about other people and left you bottled up inside.'

'How did you know that?'

Now we are cooking!!

To develop such proficiency, we need to build a considerable understanding of the language step by step. However if we try to learn it will not be long before flashes of insight encourage us on our way. There will also be crisis moments of intense disappointment – the feeling that astrology does not work and has 'betrayed us'. These come usually just before our minds open to enable great leaps forward in understanding. Astrology's most vehement detractors are people who, at such moments, lacked the humility to broaden their minds and achieve a major breakthrough. Be patient and persist. Bear in mind we are embarking on a study of an inclusive system that has a time and place for every conceivable concept and thesis in the universe. If it is any good, it is bound to force you to adapt your position in some pretty radical ways.

The Appendix at the end of this book is a carefully prepared introduction to the main concepts and workings of astrology. It gives the key images and associations and structures and describes how they can be combined to provide the kind of insight illustrated in the dialogue above. Those who know these basic concepts need do no more than give The Appendix a glance to check up and reflect again on the power and potential of the imagery.

However, if the concepts in the Appendix are new to you, then it is only possible to consider the rest of this book, and so do astrology justice, if you spend whatever time it takes to master them. You may also need to follow up by studying some of the books, or using the computer software, recommended in the Appendix's bibliography. To do otherwise would be as daft and impossible as to try to argue in French when you only know English!

SO, HERE COMES A PAUSE OF ANYTHING FROM A FEW MINUTES TO SEVERAL LIFETIMES, WHILE YOU ENSURE YOU UNDERSTAND THE KEY CONCEPTS OF ASTROLOGY. YOU DO NOT NEED TO ACCEPT OR BELIEVE IN THEM. ASSESSMENT COMES LATER. ALL WE ASK FOR NOW IS THAT YOU LEARN AND UNDERSTAND, BEFORE YOU PRESUME TO JUDGE.

To do this, please refer to the Appendix and return to this page once you feel you have mastered the key concepts and have an idea of how to synthesize them.

-oOo-

WELCOME BACK!

Now you have astrology's key concepts, we need to fine-tune your understanding of the cycles and how we use them to enhance insight into our lives. This chapter will look a little deeper into the nature of planetary movements and qualities and how this helps us understand individuals. Chapter 5 will explain astrology's key contribution to our understanding of social and historical change. Chapter 6 will show how astro-cycles can help us see the universe as logical and just. Then we will have all the elements to understand in Chapter 7 how to give astrological advice.

Let us start by asking a question. How could the very different way astrology looks at the world and phenomena be related to everyday experience? Is it really possible that by incorporating its methods we could understand the relationship between the universe and ourselves better – even enhance it? To answer these questions, let us take a little time considering the poetry of astrological interpretation alongside the mechanics of planetary movement.

Poetry and mechanical movement

Some people see astrology's key concepts as immeasurably valuable, even if no mechanical explanation can be found. They are satisfied to see the concepts as an inspired descriptive language. The colour red does not actually cause things to happen, but without it there is much we would not be able to describe or understand. Similarly, to know that the lunar side of a person's nature reflects other people's behaviour back upon them can be very helpful, even if saying so gives you no idea of when or how the effect will occur. So, even in this limited sense, astrological concepts are useful.

As can be deduced from Chapter 3, I would not so restrict astrology. There are causal relationships between the planetary cycles and what happens, but these are broader and operate within a spectrum of variables that can be considerably affected by the participants' choices. Astrological knowledge is not the same as modern mechanical knowledge, based on rigid and exact measurements of cause and effect that enable us to build vast conurbations, construct the most advanced systems of transport, and create other machines that ease the practical pressures and enhance the pleasures of our lives. At the same time, astrological knowledge is a far more suitable means of explaining and guiding the initial decisions to build and construct such conurbations and transport systems – instead our society does not use it and suffers.

The astrological chart gives a broad, yet incisive and remarkably pertinent, outline of contrasting attitudes and dispositions. Determining what will happen requires considerable skill of juxtaposition and deep past experience of similar cycles. Many astrologers see themselves as objective interpreters of the cosmos. They feel it more proper to help clients understand the issues, but leave decisions to them. The astrologer interprets the archetypal details in ordinary language that will help the client to fit the pieces together in a way that makes sense in terms of their experience. 'I saw a white shape on the distant hillside' might mean 'I saw a sheep, a rock, or a house'. 'It flashed past me at enormous speed' may mean a bicycle moving at no more than 10 ten miles an hour, if the witness were a tortoise! By describing something very real and logical in this broad, person-related way, astrology can bring both order and freedom to the chaotic emotional anarchy that often traumatises individual and group experience in the modern material world.

In Chapter 3, we made a start in explaining how these planetary cycles (and hence their words and symbols) work. The solar system exists in an integrated universe, in which each element is co-dependent. Gravitational pressures, the interrelationship of the planets' easing and/or disruptive magnetic fields, or maybe subtle individual experiences of centrifugal force, may dispose us far more than researchers can discern with the crude tools of contemporary observation and statistics. Causes may be indirect. What happens when Mars is in Aries may be as much to do with where Jupiter or Saturn are at that time; or where the Earth is in its path around the Sun. Indeed everything we say in astrology about the particular cycle of a particular planet may have little or no direct relationship with that planet at all. If physicists and astronomers are to discover the mechanics that lie behind the strange, but irresistible observations of astrologers, they need to find statistical tools and theories of movement and co-dependence.

In the meantime, astrologers have found it more useful to explore and systematise their direct experience of the language handed down to them. They take account of the precise mechanics of planetary movement and apply it to a profound body of poetic perception. They continue to record their observations, ever ready for a more enlightened time, when suitably sensitive, flexible and interactive research tools are available. When we reach such a time, astrology's key concepts and their underlying patterns may well be explained. When they are, our understanding of both science and astrology will be the better for it.

Archetypes that structure the poetry of the zodiac signs
Bear in mind by the zodiac we do not mean the star constellations, but a frame to observe the planets moving in front of them. We divide the celestial sphere into twelve equal segments. The movement of the planets we observe is determined partly by their movements and partly our own. So what are we saying physically about these cycles, and especially the measuring frame of the zodiac, when we say: every fourth sign of the zodiac has the same element and from Aries, the first, the order is earth, air, or water? Again is there a physical explanation for astrologers' suggestion that from Aries, every third sign is in order cardinal, fixed, or mutual; and every second sign is in order positive or negative? Should we consider the integrated effect of the shape of the paths of all solar system planets, or just the Earth's? What are other co-dependent planets doing when a particular planet is in cardinal, rather than fixed, or mutable signs?

The zodiac, the Sun and the seasons
In the northern hemisphere at least, the Sun's movement through the zodiac signs seems to mirror easy-to-observe seasonal factors. Aries is

the bursting of the seed in March/April (positive, cardinal, fire). Taurus in April and May sees plants working underground, building roots and strength (receptive, fixed, earth). Gemini is a time of branching, early flowering and dancing in the breeze (again positive, but now mutable and the air element). Cancer consolidates and protects the seeds that will perpetuate the plant (receptive, now cardinal with the nurturing of water). Leo symbolises the birth of the child, the great hope for the future, also the bud opening of the great and glorious flowers and plants in the garden (positive, fixed, fire). Next comes the Virgo time of anxious conscientious harvest and the careful storage in Libra. Scorpio represents the temptation to indulge that comes from having access to so much. Sagittarius represents the generosity and danger of over-optimism; Capricorn the hard reality of proper order and control as winter approaches. Aquarius points to a broader sense of organisation for the benefit of all and Pisces the capacity to feel for and sacrifice to the needs of others and so prepare for the redemption of a new beginning in Aries.

Of course in southern latitudes the process is reversed and in equatorial regions the entire year may be fertile. Yet this does not discredit the analogy of northern temperate zones. Conception, birth and life may be stimulated by fertile conditions and an energy source like the Sun is essential to the process. Yet our Sun and its seasons are but the triggers and sustainers, not the intrinsic nature of the process itself. The development of the twelve signs of the zodiac, similar to what Buddhists call the Twelve Dependent Links, are the essential steps of manifestation, be it in the darkest cave, the deepest ocean, the brightest and most open air, and by whatever life force it is triggered and sustained. Our familiar seasons may well be the manifestation of a deep twelve-point process that lies at the core of life itself and varies its expression in different environments. The same twelve-point process expresses itself through the periods of the planetary cycles explained below and also can be found in the diurnal movement of the Earth's angles as it revolves on its axis.

The planets and annual variations
Mercury and Venus keep close to the Sun, sometimes ahead, sometimes behind. Like it, they are seasonal. The three bodies' varying relationships to each other year on year go some way to explaining why each year is not exactly the same. More variety is explained by how all this connects

to Mars's two-year cycle, Jupiter's 12 years, Saturn's 29+ years, Uranus' 84 years, Neptune's 165 and Pluto's 244. In Chapter 5, we will study how the slower-moving planets from Jupiter outwards explain social development and history.

Retrogression

For some part of its cycle, every planet (but never the Sun or Moon) *appears* to move backwards (retrograde) against the backcloth of the stars. This is a product of the relative speeds of both the Earth, from which we are observing, and the planet being observed. Because it travels around the Sun in 88 Earth days, while we take 365-6, Mercury presents what appears to us to be a triple retrograde loop every year. Being closer to our length of orbit, Venus retrogrades once a year. Taking nearly twice as long to go around the Sun as the Earth, Mars retrogrades every two years. Being much further away, each year the outer planets tend to spend a few months in apparent retrograde and the rest of the year in forward motion. Retrograde motion indicates reflection and consolidation of the qualities associated with that planet. Mercury retrogrades are often times when errors in past decisions show themselves. Quick decisions made during a Mercury retrograde period tend to be inadequately considered. Saturn's apparent changes of direction are often associated with structural reassessment; often this shows itself in the financial markets.

The signs in which these retrogressions occur advance through the zodiac in regular patterns. So, as well as the cycle from one retrogression to another, there are much longer periods to consider from a retrogression period occurring again in exactly the same position of the 360-degree zodiac.

Aspect relationships between the planets

Aspect patterns are another example of how the statistical relationship between the times taken between certain astrological events contain hidden within them indications of other cycles. For example, Jupiter opposes Saturn every twenty years, but every sixty years this opposition occurs very close to the position of the 360-degree zodiac in which it occurred sixty years earlier. The intervening two oppositions occur approximately 120 degree apart. In 1989/91 the opposition was across Capricorn-Aquarius/Cancer-Leo, 2010/11 it will be in Aries/Libra;

2030/31 in Sagittarius/Gemini. These positions move 10 degrees every sixty years. So the sixty-year opposition after 1990, in 2049/50, will start at the very end of Capricorn/Cancer and complete in Aquarius / Leo. Sixty years later it will be full established in Aquarius/Leo.

We have identified three cycles between these two planets: that from opposition to opposition; from opposition to opposition in a section of the zodiac area about 10 degrees ahead; and when opposition returns to exactly the same place again. These cycles can be many hundreds or thousands of years in length. Similar levels and variations in timing can be discerned by the interaction of the Sun, Moon and the eight planets, in pairs, threes and more. Studied together, the cycles form a rich tapestry that reflects the shortest- and longest-term interactive patterns of history.

Interest in such dynamic structural relationships between outer planetary cycles and the history of group behaviour on Earth in the past, present and future has particularly increased in the 20th century and continues today. Some important examples of recent findings are outlined in the next chapter. Finding material explanations for the connections (provided that researchers are willing to synthesize and not fragment concepts) could fruitfully reintegrate our wisdom and repair many centuries of damaging misunderstandings.

The deeper conceptual wisdom of astrology's ancient traditions
Recent years have seen a remarkable renaissance of interest in what is known as traditional English/European, classical Greek, Chinese and Indian Vedic astrology. Although these systems are based on careful calculations of planetary positions and the orientation of the Earth on its axis, their interpretation methods are conceptual and incisively poetic in nature. At first sight, they may seem very different to the dynamic structural explanations of astrology earlier in this book. Yet these ancient methods still aim to describe precisely and predict specifically. They have been built up by thousands of years' of observations without modern astronomical technology. Careful research may show our forefathers came to a deep and very real understanding of the underlying structure of planetary relationships in a way that might seem unlikely today. Let us consider them at face value and see where that leads us. It may put what we now know in a very different perspective.

Rulerships

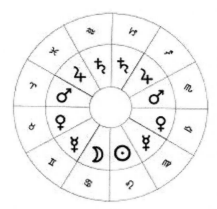

Figure 10 – Traditional Planetary Rulers of Zodiac Signs

Figure 10 is a good starting point. It shows the symmetrical and reflective pattern of the allocation of traditional rulerships of the signs. A planet is considered to rule the sign that is essentially of its nature. For example, the pure action of Mars ideally suits both Aries' fiery impulsiveness and Scorpio's watery needs for passion. Venus' attachment to beautiful earthly possessions and comfortable friendly understanding suits earthy Taurus and airy Libra precisely. Behind such eminent imagery, do the reflective pairs building from the Sun and Moon at the bottom to authoritarian Saturn at the highest and most public top area of the chart have a material explanation in terms of what we now know about the planets?

Rulerships and more

By including rulerships, with dignities, exaltation and fall of planets in signs, Figure 11 takes us one step further in working with these complex and unbelievably fascinating concepts of meaning[17]. The notion that a planet can be placed well (in rulership or exaltation) or badly (in detriment or fall) in a sign lies at the heart of astrological interpretation. Mars works well in Aries, because the sign concerns courageous quick action, but in the opposite sign (Libra) it is too quick and sudden and so leads to instability. The reverse is so with Venus, which gentles understanding in balancing Libra, but can lead to sudden, but poorly sustained infatuation in Aries. The Sun shines full of new-born hope in

Aries, but Saturn there can undermine whatever we try, before we even get started. When considering the effect of a planet in a sign, it helps to consider how such a planet would relate to the ruling or exalted planet for that sign. For example, Venus and the Moon are likely to be ravished by the intense passion of Mars in watery Scorpio. Saturn and Mars can be too harsh, restrictive and violent for the Moon-ruled gentle, maternal water of Cancer.

	RULER	Exaltation	DETRIMENT	Fall
♈	♂	☉	♀	♄
♉	♀	☽	♂	
♊	☿		♃	
♋	☽	♃	♄	♂
♌	☉		♄	
♍	☿	☿	♃	♀
♎	♀	♄	♂	☉
♏	♂		♀	☽
♐	♃		☿	
♑	♄	♂	☽	♃
♒	♄		☉	
♓	♃	♀	☿	☿

Figure 11 – The Planetary Qualities of Zodiac Signs

Now consider how we might seek a technical explanation for all this poetry. Refer again to Figure 11. Imagine placing the RULERS from the first column on the circular zodiac of the signs in Figure 10. Now consider the fourth column (DETRIMENT). Note that the planets in this column are on the opposite side of the zodiac wheel to the rulers. Do the same for the planets in the third (Exaltation) and fifth (Fall) columns. The same principle applies, except that Leo and Aquarius do not have an exaltation or fall, Taurus has no fall and Scorpio no exaltation. Is there a physical explanation for planets being 'well placed' in one sign and not in another? Are there clues in the way the structure is designed for the resources of modern astrophysics to explain why this is? Jupiter rules (is of the nature of) Sagittarius and Pisces, is exalted (works eminently well) in Cancer and strong in Aries, Taurus and Libra. Is there a physical reason for Jupiter to be in detriment (counter-productively excessive) in Gemini and Virgo and in fall (struggling with excessive didacticism) in Capricorn? Could structural factors in the orbits of Jupiter and co-dependent other planets confirm this ancient tradition?

Could modern science study and explain this structural logic? If so, it could reveal a science of poetic juxtaposition that could radically illuminate understanding.

Applying rulership and planet strength to specific charts
When we use this knowledge with other key astrological methods of interpretation to interpret the horoscope of Ludwig van Beethoven, his intransigent and expansive genius is clearly explained. The chart in Figure 12 on the next page is drawn for noon on the second of the two possible birth days. It explains his tempestuous, yet relentless, attitude to music and his personal life very well.

The 15th and 16th December both have Sun and Moon in Sagittarius, ruled by Jupiter. The Noon-time gives Pisces as ascendant, which is also ruled by Jupiter. However, Jupiter is in fall in Capricorn and totally unaspected. This means it has no major accepted angular relationships to other planets in his chart. Sagittarius is excessively expansive, Capricorn determined to structure and control. With no aspects, there is no easy channel to release the intransigent Jupiter energy. Just by combining these concepts we get the notion of someone with an intense need both to be free and to control at the same time. Yet the chart shows little or no outlet for this need. With the Sagittarian Sun and Mercury (in detriment), opposed to Mars in Gemini, the sign ruled by Mercury, outbursts of anger, disputes and argument are inevitable.

That the time of birth may well be right is suggested by the fact that Beethoven disputed with his father, but was obsessed with his family name and fought his sister-in-law for the custody of his nephew. All these things are 4th/10th house matters. Since houses are based on time of birth, the facts of his life may well confirm the time he was born. With both ends of this opposition in a T-square to Chiron[18], rising near the ascendant, it is possible that this is connected with health problems. This is strengthened by Saturn in Leo, the ruler of his Jupiter sign, being placed in detriment in the 6th house of health, squared to Uranus. This pattern could explain his deafness, as well as the revolutionary nature of his work. Work is a 6th house matter. Venus in Capricorn, ruled by

Saturn, sesqui-square to Neptune, suggests misunderstandings with women.

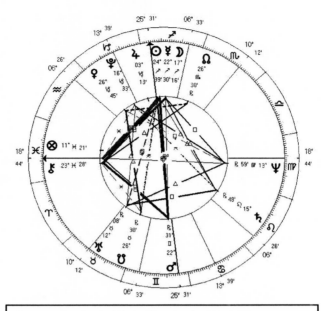

Beethoven
Natal Chart (3)
16 Dec 1770 NS
12:00 LMT -0:28:20
Bonn, Germany
50°N44' 007°E05'
Geocentric
Tropical
Placidus
True Node

Figure 12 – Ludwig van Beethoven Birth Horoscope

If he were born at noon, with Pisces on the ascendant, the intense frustration suggested by the planetary combinations could only be released to the world through another Jupiter sign. The intensely sensitive, expansive water of Pisces (also ruled by Jupiter) is often found in musicians' birth charts. Appropriately this would also place the Sun next to the Midheaven, with the unaspected Jupiter culminating. The astrological symbolism describes precisely this stormy, frustrated musical genius and his private life. Central to the planetary picture is the ruling Jupiter placed, unaspected in detriment, in Capricorn – representing heroic triumph over adversity. It led him to write in the remarkable last movement of his *Ninth Symphony* – the music to Goethe's *Ode to Joy,* which became the European anthem.

Understanding an ancient astrological tradition

What has been explained places us only at the edge of the 'outside door' of the highly detailed and systematic methods of modern, horary, traditional, classical, vedic and several other traditions of astrology. Working with concepts introduced so far is just a very early entry point to a vast field of techniques that were or have been explored by astrologers in China, India, the Middle East, Greece, Rome and Western societies for thousands of years. The more we open our minds to this knowledge and seek to find underlying explanations in terms of our contemporary scientific understanding, the more old and new will educate each other. Then, we will fill those gaps of understanding that so savage our lives. At the end of this chapter is a bibliography to help you do this.

If your head is buzzing, be reassured. Discovering more concepts and methods is not essential. We have touched on sufficient key concepts to consider how astrology could enhance our understanding of individuals, society and our place in the universe. Now it is possible to proceed to the rest of the book and assess what it suggests.

Remember astrological interpretation is multi-level.
It is important to reiterate this point made already in Chapter 2. Astrology's planetary pictures can manifest at a variety of levels. Remember the 5th house is where one looks for romance, children, generosity, creative expression and partying pleasure. Jupiter placed there can mean an expansion of one, more, or all of these things. The astrological suggestion is that art, offspring and giving yourself over to pleasure all come from the same driving force – the same archetype. In the same way, the essential archetype of the 4th house produces the mother, the home, the foundation of our lives and the values by which we live them.

Every concept in astrology – be it house divisions, zodiac or planetary positions and aspects – can manifest in this multi-level manner. It can also manifest in a *positive* and/or *negative* way. Pisces offers willingness to sacrifice, support and care for others. It also makes one vulnerable to drugs and alcohol, prone to self-pity and one's sympathetic nature being manipulated. Piscean men especially can become so scared that they deny anything symbolic and cling desperately to simplistic logic. Sagittarius makes us open, expansive and generous, but over-stretched – too willing to say 'yes' to everything. Scorpio explores the passionate, the dark and sexual, but also is incisively focused and so suited to research. Mature Scorpio can find the nub, the crucial turning point that brings healing.

Realising these last two paragraphs is an absolutely essential consideration for any researcher into astrology. Just like the motorcar or any other tool of our modern world, we are studying criteria that can manifest for good, ill or at a range of levels. This brings us to the very heart of what astrology is about and why we practise it. We do so to recognise our potential, be intelligent about our choices and know what action will make us more effective and happier. If Saturn is transiting the 7th house, we can expect structural changes in our relationships, but they can manifest on a range of levels – divorce, separation, illness or injury to a partner. It may also mean a relationship with someone of a different age, culture or country to ourselves. Maybe we are supporting a partner with a disability. We study and use astrology not to prophesy or gain advantage, but to understand the essential archetype behind what is happening, and then make the best use of its possibilities for everyone's benefit.

When we are ready to take this entire chapter on board, we will be ready to use and research astrology in appropriate ways that show exactly how it works.

Further Reading
In addition to the introductory books summarised at the end of The Appendix, the books below go deeper into the some of the main branches and more advanced techniques of astrology referred to in this chapter and will lead you to excellent additional books to broaden your understanding of astrology even further.

Classical and Traditional Astrology in chronological order
Claudius Ptolemy *Tetrabiblos*
Abu Ma'shar *The Abbreviation of the Introduction to Astrology* [Edited and Translated by Charles Burnett]
William Lilly *Christian Astrology* [Modern English edition David R Roell]

The modern revival in chronological order
Alan Leo
    Astrology for All
    How to Judge a Nativity
    The Key to Your Own Nativity

> *The Art of Synthesis, the Progressed Horoscope*
> *Horary Astrology*
> *A Thousand and One Notable Nativities*

Charles Carter
> *An Encyclopaedia of Psychological Astrology, Mundane Astrology*
> *The Astrological Aspects*
> *The Astrology of Accidents*
> *Symbolic Directions in Modern Astrology*
> *Essays on the Foundations of Astrology*

Alice A Bailey *Esoteric Astrology*
Reinhold Ebertin *Combination of Stella Influences*
Robert Hand
> *Planets in Transit*
> *Planets in Composite*
> *Planets in Youth*
> *Horoscope Symbols*
> *Essays on Astrology*

Alan Oken *Alan Oken's Complete Astrology*

Contrasting views from three esteemed contemporary astrologers

Geoffrey Cornelius *The Moment of Astrology*
Dennis Elwell *The Cosmic Loom*
Robert Zoller *Fate, Freewill & Astrology*

Eastern Astrology

Philippe Cornu - *Tibetan Astrology*
Ronnie Gale Dreyer *Vedic Astrology – A guide to the Fundamentals of Jyotish*
Dennis Harness *Nakshatras*
B V Raman
> *How to Judge a Horoscope Vols. 1 & 2*
> *Muhurtha – Electional Astrology*
> *Essentials of Vedic Astrology*

Komilla Sutton *Lunar Nodes – Crisis and Redemption*

Chapter 5

Astrology, History, Social Change & Politics

What does Joan say?
Ronald Reagan

Because they occupy signs of the zodiac for anything between one and twenty years, naturally the planets from Jupiter outward are in the same place for people of the same age. So, they are often referred to as generational or sub-generational planets. For this reason, they describe and so help us anticipate historical assumptions, fashion and changing social behaviour. Because they are convinced of a view of reality indicated by their generational planets, generations of people become convinced of the rightness of their time. Yet when future generations, convinced by a different set of generational planets, look back from the future they can see obvious flaws. Of course, the assumptions of this later generation will in turn be considered flawed in retrospect from further in the future, and so on.

Because this is so, astrological understanding can liberate us from destructive over-confidence in the present, constant condemnation of the past and exposure to condemnation in the future. It would also deny politicians and planners refuge in that tedious old cop out – 'of course, with the benefit of hindsight, it is always easy to see what we should have done'. As illustrated by the examples below; with astrology we have the benefit of all three kinds of sight: hind-, fore- and current. With the right motivation there is no reason why we cannot see things as they really are, avoid many errors and do the 'right thing' far more frequently, to the never-ending glory and gratitude of succeeding generations. Let us explore the concepts and see if this is so.

Pluto takes 244 years to return to the same point of the zodiac. On average, it changes its zodiac sign twenty years, but, because of its irregular obit, such changes can take longer than this, or as little as thirteen years. From its keyword, we can see that for the period of time in which Pluto occupies a particular zodiac sign, the *transformation* it indicates is of the nature of that sign.

With Pluto in Gemini, the 20th century opened with culture-changing ideas. They prophesied an explosion of change in humanity's power over nature and the values of society. From the time of the Pluto ingress in the mid 1880s, the science fiction of Jules Verne and H G Wells, and the revolutionary ideas of George Bernard Shaw and Oscar Wilde, had burst upon the literary scene. Van Gogh died penniless in 1890, but his painting and that of his Expressionist and Impressionist contemporaries, and those schools that that followed, radically changed what we consider to be great art. First presented in 1905, Einstein's Theory of Relativity was to become a seminal point, from which our understanding of the universe was transformed.

This explosive bubble of new ways of seeing the universe became more anxious, defensive and painful from 1913, when Pluto first entered Cancer – the sign of the home, the mother and the very mores of society. Its time there was associated with radical changes in the foundation of the family on many levels. European ruling royal families warred against each other and consequently saw their power diminish and decay. At the same time, a long struggle commenced to restore balance in the relationship between the sexes. The authority structure in individual families changed. Public moral values were revolutionised and the class struggle led to radical changes in political structures.

At the end of the 1930s, Pluto entered Leo – the sign of egocentricity and creative power. It remained there until the second half of the 1950s. This period saw megalomania in our leaders and their enterprises and tales of proud heroism. The subsequent Virgo period until 1972 was one of intense criticism that saw traditional values being questioned and swept away. The Libran period until 1984 brought radical tolerance that liberalised what was acceptable in relationships. At the other extreme of Libran possibility, it also saw the development of a frightening arms race. The ingress of Pluto into Scorpio saw the advent of AIDs and an intense expansion of knowledge of the whole gamut of sexual behaviour, which had been previously unknown to large sections of the population. Pluto's movement through Sagittarius since 1995 has seen such an expansion in cheap air and road travel that it threatens our environment. At the same time, we have the Internet that enables us to be in many places without moving.

Neptune's cycle is 165 years. It spends just over 13 years in a sign. Its keyword indicates that it *inspires* the way we see the unknown, the artistic and the fashionable – what we feel *inspired* to believe.

Being in Cancer at the beginning of the 20th century, belief in the family, welfare and the role of women dominated the first decade. Its movement into Leo in 1914 inspired the First World War and belief that each side was fighting for its own personal survival. After the war, it fuelled the fashion of individual pleasure and freedom. The Roaring Twenties, prohibition in USA that only encouraged the use of alcohol, and the booming Stock Market were all expressions of the cult of individual freedom and choice.

Just over one month after Neptune was fully established in Virgo in September 1929, the Stock Market crashed, poverty followed and simplistic gospels of fanatical 'purity' ensued – especially in Europe. The ingress into Libra in 1942 provided the romance and dreams for the future that maintained hope through dark war years. When in passionate Scorpio from 1956, it heralded rock 'n 'roll and free love.

From 1970, its Sagittarian period saw Western society radically changed by travel to and interest in foreign cultures and religions. From 1984, with Neptune in Capricorn, the rule of the financial markets, multinational capitalism and a questioning of the Welfare State dominated. Developments instigated when Neptune was in the opposite sign of Cancer were questioned and reversed. From the Aquarius ingress in 1998, belief in the Internet, mobile phone technology, genetics, and the patronising of ordinary people by scientists took hold. In 2003, ruling Saturn in Leo led the technology to start limiting individual freedom.

Uranus' keyword reveals the nature of *invention,* social upheaval and change, depending on the zodiac sign in which it spends each seven years.

The 1912/19 Aquarian period saw radical revolution throughout the world, followed by the painful post-war recovery of the 1919/20 Piscean transit. Its time in Aries during the late 1920s helps to explain the impulsiveness that led to the 1929 crash and rise of Fascism. Its time in Taurus from 1934 until 1942 symbolises the development of machines that could bomb civilian populations and explode the Earth. When in Gemini until 1949, it triggered a range of new inventions such as radar and the practical applications of atomic power. The Cancer period sired a sub-generation that would challenge the very basis of the family and social values. Ironically, in later life the same group would legislate to protect, even indulge, children and create a 'nanny state' obsessed with health expenditure and centralised restrictions, introduced for the individual's 'own good'.

Uranus in Leo from 1955 until 1962 sired the punk rock generation, who were to grow into the self-interested 'yuppies' of the late 1980s and early 1990s. The Virgo period until 1969 saw the beginning of development of home computer and games technology. Uranus in Libra from 1969 until 1975 combined with Pluto (and Libran John Lennon!) to suggest 'love and peace'. This changed marriage and how we view same-sex relationships. When in Scorpio until 1981, self-indulgent promiscuity became the norm. The subsequent Sagittarian period brought in computer trading technology to serve the worldwide financial community.

From 1988, the Capricorn ingress tested and brought down systems that were industrially and socially incompetent. From 1995, now in Aquarius, the sign it rules, inventive force activated the technological infrastructure of the 21st century. In Pisces, as I write, many people feel lost and ignored in the midst of the technology that has been introduced to protect and ease their lives, but leaves them impotent.

Pluto, Neptune and Uranus together

Of course these three generational planets, as they are known, work together, not in isolation. So, when we use astrology to understand what lies behind social and political change, it is the combination of the three planetary archetypes in their current signs we have to consider. Consider these examples:

* The First World War is explained by Neptune being in Cancer in the build-up period and retrograding back and forward across the cusp of Leo through 1914, while Saturn (the indicator of authority and limitation), entered Cancer to conjunct Pluto just as the war was starting in September that year.

* The combination of Uranus in Aries and Neptune in Leo encouraged the bravado of the pre-crash boom in the years immediately before 1929. When Neptune moved into Virgo at

the end of July 1929, a realistic accounting was essential – the crash happened just over a month later.

❋ The profound social changes in the second half of the 1950s were triggered by Pluto, Neptune, Uranus and Saturn all moving into new signs within a year of each other. The process was intensified as Uranus approached its conjunction to Pluto in 1966.

Generational planets make cycles with each other
We measure them from one conjunction's date to the next.

❋ The Neptune and Pluto cycle takes 494 years. The beginning of the cycle marks a seed regeneration of spiritual attitudes, throwing out the assumptions of the past cycle. As the cycle matures, so do the new attitudes. Study history, seeing the years of the conjunctions 411, 905, 1398 and 1892 AD as seed points.

❋ The Neptune/Uranus cycle takes 171 years. At the conjunction revolutionary beliefs undermine existing social values and control. In Britain, this conjunction has seen fundamental conflicts between male and female authority in the monarchy: 1136 saw the conflict between King Stephen and his cousin Matilda; 1378 was three years after the end of the Wars of the Roses and the establishment of the Tudor monarchy; 1650 was a year after the execution of Charles I; in 1821, George IV barred his Queen Caroline from his Coronation; in 1993, Prince Charles separated from his wife Diana.

❋ The Uranus/Pluto cycle is less regular. Because Pluto moves within, then outside of Neptune's orbit, the interval can be as little as 113 and as many as 140 years. The year 1597 was a time of uncertainty towards the end of Elizabeth 1's reign; 1710 marks the crisis of the succession, because Queen Anne's children did not survive into adulthood; 1850 saw considerable revolutionary instability in Europe; 1966 was a time when all values and social authority were questioned.

We shall see later, the 90-degree squares and 180-degree oppositions in the cycles between outer planets are also critical.

Uranus first observed 1781, Neptune 1846, Pluto 1930

Yet they have always been there, playing their part in the dynamics of the solar system and its effect on the underlying pressures of society, if not so consciously upon our individual selves. Since their discovery, these planets' characteristics have played a far greater part in our conscious knowledge. So, their qualities have become more noticeable. Uranus' discovery and association with invention and social change was appropriately reflected in the agricultural enclosure, movement of populations into towns and accelerated industrialisation from the second half of the 18th century. With all this came consequential demands for political change and 'the rights of man'. Soon after the discovery of Neptune, electricity, the telephone, film and petroleum became a dominant part of our culture. At the same time, a fascination with other religions and ancient wisdom experienced a renaissance. It was not long after the discovery of Pluto that atomic power became harnessed and humanity became able to atomise its environment.

Jupiter and Saturn

The cycles of Jupiter and Saturn are intermediaries between the three generational planets and the inner, personal ones. Respectively, they describe yearly and two-and-a-half yearly sub-generational developments. Jupiter's twelve-year cycle means that each year has a different zodiacal 'flavour' of expansive opportunity. When Jupiter is in Aries, a general atmosphere of impulsiveness is likely. The following year practicality and consolidation are more likely, and so on. Saturn takes more than 29 years to cycle the zodiac. The sign it occupies describes where problems, structure and order are likely to be focused. For example, in 1990, when Saturn was in Capricorn, governments were put to the test and found wanting in different ways in the USSR, Britain and the Middle East. Between 2003 and 2005, when it was in the opposite sign of Cancer, it was the people who had an increasing range of restrictions placed upon them by their governments.

Putting the outer planets together

Of course, moments of the conjunctions between outer planets are just one part of their interactions. The 90-degree multiple aspects (squares and oppositions, as well as conjunctions) indicate moments of stress and challenge that can be used to develop strength and genuine achievement.

When the planets are 120 degrees apart they tend to support each other, but may make it too easy for what is gained to last. The cycles from conjunction to conjunction of the same planet or different outer planets each have a waxing and waning phase. Growth is much easier in the former and more difficult to sustain during the latter.

When we consider a moment in history, the stages of each combination and cycle have to be born in mind. At the end of 2005, the world was experiencing growth, but we were deeply worried about its consequences, because:

* The Neptune/Pluto cycle approached its waxing square.
* The Uranus/Neptune cycle was at an uncertain early waxing stage.
* The Uranus/Pluto cycle was about to complete its waxing square.
* The interplay of opportunity and control that the Jupiter/Saturn cycle brings was at its waxing square.
* Jupiter, Saturn and Neptune were building to a tense T-square.

With Uranus and Neptune mutually receiving each other in revolutionary Aquarius and mutable Pisces, and Pluto in mutable Sagittarius, everything seemed possible, but the then social development seemed to be running out of control, with unclear purpose. Philosophies contradicted and confused each other.

Overall consolidation seemed vital, but the astro-cycles were pushing people into uncontrolled growth.

(Of course, all the planets move. Jupiter moves as much as 30 degrees a year. So, the composite pressures will be different when you read this. Readers are encouraged to consult an ephemeris and make the necessary adjustments. Then look at the history of social developments since 2005 and consider how this fitted the changing cycles.)

Astrological cycles explain historical and social change
The test of this thesis is that repeated patterns bring similar outcomes. As well as the general trends outlined above, it is even more fruitful to look at moments in history in more detail.

✻ In 1789, the year of the French Revolution, Pluto in Aquarius
   opposed Uranus in Leo. The very nature of kingship (Leo) was
   called into question and government by a people obsessed with
   executions (Pluto in Aquarius opposing the Leo) was
   proclaimed in France. The consequences are still being felt
   today.
✻ In 1917, at the time of the Russian Revolution, Uranus was in
   the opposing sign Aquarius, and opposed to Saturn and
   Neptune in Leo – the Tsar was deposed and executed and a
   'dictatorship of the proletariat' established.
✻ The build up to the Uranus/Pluto conjunction in critical Virgo
   1965/6 can explain the breakdown of social control in the mid
   1960s. It was time to find fault, but be less certain of answers.
   From then onwards, the notion of following leaders has been
   fundamentally questioned.
✻ The fall of the Berlin Wall and end of Soviet Communism in
   1989 was driven by Jupiter in Cancer, exactly opposing Saturn,
   Uranus and Neptune in conservative Capricorn – this 'counter-
   revolution' returned government to rule by money and
   personal gain.

The above examples, explanations and interpretations are only a taste of
a vast potential area of study. In his *Cycles of Becoming* Alexander
Ruperti gives a systematic description of the outer planetary cycles. A
study of this book alongside the events and developments of history
provides remarkable insights that transcend and put in perspective
conventional historical assessments. Further reading is given in the
bibliography at the end of this chapter. An especially thorough modern
contribution is Rick Tarnas' *Cosmos and Psyche.*

What makes using astrology to understand history so valuable is
that such understanding does not trap us in the 'lessons of the past'. By
offering profound, objective insights into the past and present and future,
it gives far broader and incisive guidance as to the best way to approach
what lies ahead.

Astrology study of a specific policy and those shaping it
Using the slower-moving outer planets to describe the broad sweep of
historical and social developments is just a part of this mundane

astrology – the name for the study of the astrology of everyday events. It is possible to combine the outer with faster inner-planetary cycles and individual charts of people, institutions, countries and events. This can reveal in great detail the links between the development of a political process and the individuals involved. The second half of this chapter will now use the astrology of the USA/British-led war in Iraq and associated Middle East problems to illustrate the possibilities in detail.

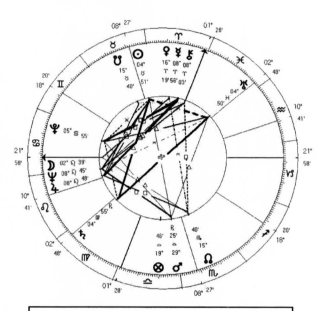

Figure 13 – Middle East Mandate Horoscope

Figure 13 is a chart drawn for the moment in 1920 when, at a conference in San Remo in Italy, the victorious powers finally decided the structure of the Middle East, following their victory over the Ottoman Empire in the First World War. The countries we know today as Lebanon, Syria, Iraq and Jordan were created and a Mandate was given to France and Britain to foster their establishment and development. Also, Britain was mandated to oversee Palestine and arrange for the return of some Jewish people; a decision that was to prepare the ground for the creation of the state of Israel in 1948. Kings were appointed and constitutions drawn up, not without considerable resistance from many sections of the peoples that were to live there. It is now well known that in the 1920s, Winston

Churchill as Colonial Secretary considered dropping gas from the air upon the Kurdish population of Iraq. T E Lawrence, whose relationship with Jordanian Arabs was crucial to the British victory over Turkey, became so disheartened by these decisions that he resigned his commission and sought to commence a new life under a new name.

The chart for this seminal moment in Middle Eastern and world history reveals in great detail both the inappropriateness of the time to make such a decision and exactly why victorious powers presumed they could act in such a cavalier manner.

For the purpose of this analysis, we will select the most crucial of the indicators. In the 1st house are Jupiter and Neptune conjunct at 8 degrees and 45/48 minutes of Leo, with the Moon (which moves roughly 12 degrees each day) applying to join the conjunction in 12 hours. From our appendix keywords, Jupiter in Leo means 'expand imperially'; Neptune there means 'inspire without responsibility' and the Moon 'react egocentrically'. It will also be noticed that Mercury is in Aries in an almost exact trine to the Leo conjunction. Mercury in Aries means 'communicate suddenly'. Also Venus is nearby in Aries; this means 'love impulsively'. If we combine these keywords, it is plain to see the impulsive lack of considered judgement and genuine understanding of the situation and the peoples for which the conference was making such earth changing decisions. Even though they had only recently presided over a war where millions had died, it is clear that the politicians of the time had not learned humility and were certainly not open to seeking insight from the astrology that lay behind their decisions!

It is important to make this point, because we continue to base notions of 'right', 'wrong', international 'legality' and national legitimacy on what was decided then. Yet, the predictable consequences of the San Remo agreement are well known. Of the countries concerned, only Jordan has maintained its established structure, mainly due to the inspired leadership of the late King Hussein. Instability, revolution, dictatorship and an ongoing state of war have intensified. Millions of people have been killed, injured or displaced. Today, the problems of the Middle East lie behind much suffering and conflict throughout the Islamic world and are now threatening stability and freedom in Britain, USA and France – the very countries that presided over the original decision.

The astrology behind the original 1920 decision continues to haunt us. The 1948 establishment of the State of Israel has a T-square in fixed signs close to the degree of the Leo conjunction in the 1920 chart (Moon, Pluto and Saturn between 4 and 16 degrees of Leo; nodal axis 14 degrees Taurus/Scorpio). In 1990, Saddam Hussein invaded Kuwait when there was a grand cross[19] to the 1920 Leo conjunction in the middle of fixed signs. Also, the nodal axis was at 7 degrees of Leo/Aquarius. If we focus on more recent events in Iraq, the astrological theme of the 1920 Leo conjunction comes into even sharper focus.

Figure 14 is a chart drawn for the first solar return of the 9/11 attack on the World Trade Center. (A solar return is for a birth anniversary, precisely calculated for when the Sun returns to the position it was at the original birth moment.) The first birthday of the 9/11 atrocity was at 1430 EDT on 11th September 2002.[20] At this time, President Bush gathered many world leaders together at Ground Zero. The following day, he addressed the United Nations, focusing particularly on the need to act on the problem of Iraq.

On this day there was an exact opposition between Jupiter and Neptune at 8 degrees 39 minutes of Leo/Aquarius – just 6 to 9 minutes of arc from an absolutely exact conjunction/opposition to the 1920 conjunction of the same two planets! From this moment, the build-up towards the 2003 invasion of Iraq seemed unstoppable, in spite of massive demonstrations against the planned invasion on 15th February 2003 – the day before retrogression had led to a second exact opposition between Jupiter and Neptune! Equally remarkable is that the meeting of world leaders to decide what was to happen after the war occurred around 3rd June 2003, when the third opposition of these two planets occurred and completed this series. Significantly, these last two oppositions were not so exact, being at about 11 and 13 degrees of Leo – so their effect on events was not so incisive. Studies of the moment the war was announced to the American people show similar connections. While a Jupiter/Neptune conjunction does have an opposition 82 years later in close degrees of the same sign axis, for it to be within exactly the same degree is very rare indeed.

Notably, the higher arguments for the benefits of the war were very similar to the original 1920 simplistic decision – that it would benefit and bring democracy and individual freedom to that country and make it a positive example for the rest of the area. To date, as in the 1920s and afterward terrorism and destruction, not peace and democracy, have ensued.

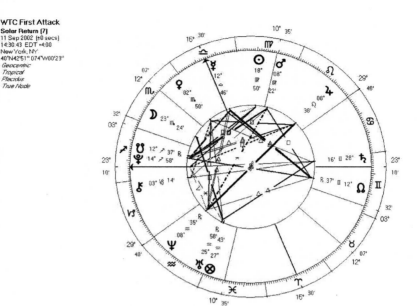

Figure 14 – 1st Solar Return (birthday) of 9/11 attack

As well as transits to the 1920 Mandate chart marking the development of its issues, connections to individual people's charts indicate the ones that will become crucially involved. With the Mandate Jupiter/Neptune point in a tight square to the midpoint[21] of Saddam Hussein's Sun/Uranus conjunction in Taurus and his Moon and Mars in Sagittarius trining the Mandate point, he was clearly destined to be the intransigent trigger to what was to happen. George Bush Senior's chart[22] has no close links. He sought to end the Gulf War and bring the troops home as soon as possible. Bill Clinton[23] had his Mercury within 1 degree of the Jupiter/Neptune conjunction point, but it was trining Mars, Neptune and Venus in Libra in his 1st house. So he contained Saddam and kept an uneasy peace.

When we consider the birth charts of the two leaders - George W Bush and Tony Blair - behind the coalition that invaded Iraq, the astrological explanation for their actions could not be clearer. President Bush has his Ascendant, Mercury and Pluto between 7 and 10 degrees of

Leo, exactly what is needed to push the world into this war. Tony Blair takes up the other end of the opposition. He has his Moon/North Node between 7 and 11 degrees of Aquarius in his 10th house. He was to exploit and so sacrifice his public standing and the esteem in which his countrymen held him, by joining the USA's disastrously managed war. Interestingly, both are traumatised men with their Suns and other planets in their 12th houses. This helps to explain the obsession with surveillance, security and the war on terror that has characterised the time of their working together.

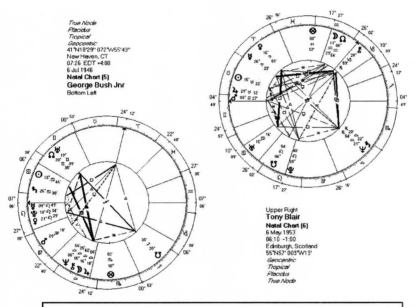

Figure 15 Birth Horoscopes of George W Bush & Tony Blair

This mundane branch of astrology is invaluable, because historical facts can be compared with its cycles and so research is confirmed. Even this limited analysis explains what is happening in the world – why people in the news behave as they do. It can also give us clues as to their thoughts and what they will do next.

Even more crucially, our understanding of these astro-cycle connections helps us put the times and our leaders in perspective. The public knowing the astrology that is driving decisions and actions could take obsession, delusion and simplistic propaganda out of the frame and temper our leaders' behaviour.

Could understanding the astrology of the Middle East and its protagonists have helped changed the course of history, as it did when Ronald Reagan was President and made peace with the USSR?[24] If the purpose of using astrology is to inform free will and put the actions and motivations in perspective, then it could.

What would have been the outcome if, instead of seeking to play down and hide Ronald Reagan's use of astrology, we had celebrated its role in ending the Cold War?[25] If we had continued to apply it to more and more world crises, could we have done better than move merely from one *contained* global Cold War conflict to an endless, *undefined* 'war on terror'? Could we have avoided our freedom being the price we pay for promised 'protection'? If we had used astrology to assess policy decisions and individual appointments, we may have avoided the massive corruption at the end of Soviet Communism and the 2003 Iraq War

One certain benefit of knowing the astrology that lies behind people and events is that we are less likely to believe and become whipped up by present spin and promises for the future. Indeed, by giving a far better understanding of events, astrology could enable us to become more patient and tolerant. Vitally we would have a way and so be willing to consider long-term factors. We would still enjoy the fashion and style of the times, but not be so extravagantly and self-destructively consumed by it.

When you understand astrology's relationship to life, even the most difficult political times become far more like a ship we sail, rather than a burden we carry.

Further Reading

Key books on planetary cycles and Mundane Astrology
Nicholas Campion
>   *The Book of World Horoscopes*
>   *The Great Year*
>   *Mundane Astrology* (with Michael Baigent & Charles Harvey)

Rick Levine *Quantum Astrology* (DVD see end Chapter 3)
Joan Quigley *What Does Joan Say? My Seven Years as White House Astrologer to Nancy and Ronald Reagan*
Alexander Ruperti *Cycles of Becoming*
Richard Tarnas *Cosmos and Psyche*
The Astrological Association publishes *The Astrological Journal* every two months. From 2002, it includes Roy Gillett's regular mundane astrology column *Working with the Planets*

Chapter 6

A Fair & Logical Universe

If you thought about cause and effect
You would stop being reckless.
Lama Tsong Khapa

Something feels wrong

The apparent irreconcilability between our contemporary physical descriptions of the universe and the fragmentary, apparently anachronistic explanations of traditional religions leave many people in a cultural vacuum. Alienated, desperately materialistic and deeply unsatisfied, they are exposed to religious fundamentalism as the only compensation.

Is this new? Throughout recorded history views of reality have been dramatically contested. Empires have risen and fallen for many reasons from the most materially self-indulgent to profound religious conviction. Yet, each culture focused upon a unified ideal vision – a view of 'ultimate reality' where the practical area of that society always served the spiritual. Persians, Greeks, Romans, Huns, Vikings and all based their lives on central convictions. Then they used their practical skills to expand the amount of territory where those convictions would be accepted. When new notions of 'truth' changed societies, they became the norm. The Roman Empire became Christian. Christendom split into the Roman and Orthodox branches. Cultures developed accordingly. Practicality was a lesser artisan activity, to be performed in the 'service of God', however a particular culture chose to define him. Even today, some Christian churches seek to move into new areas of the world to 'save the souls' of the people living there.

However, the 16th century saw the beginning of a very new centre of focus that was to change such processes radically over the coming centuries. From this time, human discovery started to become the central determinate of 'ultimate truth'. By the late 17th century and particularly as we reached the 19th, material scientific discovery seemed to suggest humanity was capable of explaining God's universe. So, from the crude visions of Frankenstein to the subtle genetic skills of today, man sees himself as the creator of life and its values. If life progresses through the survival of the fittest, what need do we have for God?

Modern mathematical games theory goes further. If God is a redundant figure of primitive imagination to advance beyond, our society does *not* require values and judgements – they are inefficient and counter-productive. Recent market economic theory claims to discredit even 19th century rational humanitarianism. It considers the notional of the human being as a naturally moral being, well intentioned toward others, to be a dangerous delusion. Rather, he is a mechanical creature with rudimentary drives based on the need to survive; capable of being assuaged and adjusted by appropriate chemicals. The freedom of the market is seen as the determiner of what is best and so the provider of all our needs. So, power to control and expand by developing industrial expertise gathers strength. Humanity has completed a 500-year journey from subservience to harsh regulations of the Church to serving another harsh 'realism' dictated by free-market capitalism. Is that all there is in the gospel and cultural heart of the 21st century? Have we made values so rudimentary and the provision of resources so efficient that we have created a unique culture that finally equates values exclusively with possessions?

If this is so, individuals and groups in society are left clutching at straws in the search for purpose in their lives. Can a sports team, hero, pop idol that we look up to and envy and condemn (if found wanting) fill the gap? With so many 'things' to 'have', it is difficult and economically inappropriate to be satisfied. For some purpose that is never really explained, to be happy we need to work harder, 'consume' and not question the need for a market economy. Then we may well live comfortable lives until we die. 'After that, be a big boy and accept that is all there is,' say some geneticists.

Of course, this book sees an essential error in such a view. By refusing to consider the emotional, mental and spiritual implications of humanity's life on this planet and dismissing its responsibility after death, the emerging scientific world rushes with hubris and arrogant pride into one material discovery after another. As a result, it has created a world of lost souls constantly needing to consume to keep going.

Yet, as we need to continue reminding ourselves, whatever has been discovered about astronomy and physics, we continue to live on the planet. In the deepest sense, it is its subtle effect on our dispositions, emotions, thoughts and beliefs that decides how we feel and how we act.

It is not too late to retrace our steps back to earlier times; not to reject anything that has been discovered and understood since, but to seek to move forward again 'holding on to the baby' this time! Is there a view of the universe that accepts all the findings of modern science, without invalidating or alienating us from our emotions, thoughts and beliefs? Here is a description of a philosophical/ religious model that seeks to do just this. It allows us to celebrate the discoveries of material science, while putting them in a disciplined perspective.

A super-modern model of the universe

What follows may seem to be drawn more from some cultures and belief systems than others. However, a deeper study of the mystical traditions of all religions will reveal considerable common ground. Language and assumptions about meaning may cause problems, for language is a tool of relative comparisons. It works less well at the margin; where the relative meets the absolute. At this level, concepts like an all-seeing, all-encompassing God; the one and only Great God; and dissolving of all phenomena into emptiness that is empty of its own emptiness; are really saying the same thing. Ultimate truth is beginningless and timeless. Things that *seem* to arise do so only because they are dependant on something else. Our essential nature is universal mind. Each religion has a way to realise it. Christ, Mohammed, Krishna, Buddha are true ways to find this experience, as are many other practices when followed purely. All bring us to the same place.

Blake told us we can see 'eternity in an hour', 'a world in a grain of sand'. The Buddha went further. He taught that each of us can be aware of all the time that has ever existed and will ever exist. We have lived every possible life and experienced every possible relationship. Knowledge of this has become clouded because we look at things from the perspective of the place and time we were born. We develop and become attached to particular relative views that are mere illusions. These illusions distort our essential inner universal understanding. The truth becomes clouded. As we shall see in a moment, karma from a previous lifetime attaches us to this time and place and its illusionary clouds of confusion.

Accept provisionally for a moment that each life starts at a particular time and place that has inbuilt and developing negative and positive patterns. Now go one step further. Consider the challenge of life as being to see beyond the partial truth of the relative focus that we become attached to at birth. How might we clear our vision? Firstly, we need to let go of the automatic reactions and feelings our circumstances activate in us. When caught up in, but not fatally injured by an explosion, the sooner we stop running around screaming 'Help!', start binding our own and others' wounds and seek medical expertise, the happier we and everyone will be. This is the way we should look at birth karma and cause and effect. The cause was being attracted to a place where there were bombs. The effect is broken bodies. All we can do is bind wounds, repair breakages and encourage healing.

To many materially minded people, karma seems no more than a 'wishy-washy' excuse, used to avoid reality and logical consequences. It is much more than this. It has an invaluable healing logic that moves us beyond mere physical cause and effect. Every action, word, thought has a reaction. The universe is certainly full of circling bodies, pulsars, quasars, black holes, chemical elements, raw materials and machines, and all have very logical actions and reactions. It is also full of ideas and feelings, which can lead to actions that can fundamentally harm others. As Dostoyevsky showed in *Crime and Punishment*, everything we do creates an imprint on our minds. If we kill, we attract a world of punishment, even death. If we cheat and steal, we fear being stolen from. If we hunt, we feel hunted. If we lie, manipulate and spin, we assume everyone will do the same to us and are unable to trust. So our negative actions create minds that draw us toward and reinforce ever more negative environments. In contrast, positive actions of patience and kindness bring clarity, free up and open our minds to truth.

The karmic consequences of negative actions can bring problems for ourselves and others right away; or they can be delayed until some time in the future – even a future lifetime. Karma broadens and deepens our understanding of actions and their consequences. It is not just 'John upsets Jill, so later on Jill gets her own back', but rather 'John upsets Jill and, in doing so, become attached to a negative pattern with inevitable negative consequences'. So, some result that is not quite so obvious occurs. This result may not just be a consequence for John, but also for Mary, who has created karma unconnected with John's action to Jill, but it is exactly appropriate for John and Mary to work it out on each other. Karma is not a 'cop out' by which we shrug off responsibility for our actions; quite the opposite. The law of Karma is based on the idea that each of us is fundamentally responsible for everything that happens to us. God is not cruel, or unjust. The universe is fair and logical; if we look at life beyond the lifetime we are living.

The nature of reincarnation is frequently misunderstood – especially in cultures that have a conventional Christian heritage of guilt. To correct this, we start by asking what is claimed to be left after death. The answer is emotional attachment. Without a physical body through which to express this attachment, the consciousness is left floundering for expression. Unlimited by physical considerations of time and space, the consciousness is drawn to an entirely appropriate new point of time and space that has the characteristics through which its residual aggregate of the previous life can express itself. So a new incarnation occurs. There are infinite possible incarnations. If we were fully awake, we would be aware that all time and space is within us and we have experienced all possibilities. The emotional attachments we cannot let go of urge us to see reality from just one perspective. The reincarnation view of the universe seeks a broad objective view of all realities, rather like a material scientist. The vital difference is that modern science is trapped in the material, constantly looking for that crucial missing elemental material glue that holds its *Theory of Everything* together. It cannot be found, because the essential element is beyond the material and requires a higher logic to understand thoughts and feelings.

Here comes astrology's role. The birth chart is the diagrammatic representation of birth karma. It tells us how we are likely to be disposed to react to circumstances. Because planets move on, so do our dispositions. Because we can compare birth planetary positions with current ones, we can get an idea of whether our experiences will be easy or difficult. When we have an understanding of the operation and nature of all this, we find it much easier to handle what happens to us. As a result, we understand and respect others. As consciousness expands, we start seeing from many more perspectives and realise we have a much broader and more meaningful destiny. Paradoxically, because we are less trapped in ourselves, we are more in control over our circumstances. Almost without trying, we have greater free will than a frantically self-seeking control freak. Far from enslaving us in a fixed fate, knowing our astrology chart sets us free to know better what is happening. So we can make more effective decisions – just as having a road map helps us reach our destination far more easily.

However, the purpose is to do more than make this life easier for ourselves. Just as an undisciplined dog will wreak dangerous havoc in a flock of sheep, our ignorant, spontaneous emotions wreak havoc on our societies and our world. By understanding others and ourselves better, we discipline what we think, feel, say and do. Vitally, the more we realise the higher logic of the universe and act with deeply objective compassion for everyone, the more we see the full nature of reality. We see all lifetimes, all perspectives and so cleanse ourselves of emotional attachment. This cleansing clears our minds, so we see the true nature of reality. We remain conscious and maintain control through the death process. The less we are able to do this, the more residues of emotional attachment remain to swoon us into unconsciousness. This draws us inevitably to the next point of time and place, appropriate for the working out of the karma of the next lifetime, with a new astrology chart to guide our way.

Various cultures use methods of prayer, meditation and yoga to cleanse the consciousness and so attain this ideal state of mind at death. The Roman Catholic priest offers absolution. While some describe the afterlife in terms of ideal states of bliss and suggest only their practice is the right one, all suggest that a clear and kindly state of mind is the way to liberation. At death, we face a key test to discern whether we have achieved it. Most spiritual paths that avoid attachment to personal benefit lead to what are in essence very similar experiences of liberation.

Being based on exactly measurable cycles that repeat regularly, but combine in the same way hardly if ever at all, astrology can give logic and system to any karmic pattern in any culture. By measuring cause and effect systematically on emotional, mental and spiritual levels of behaviour as well as the physical, it helps us see how to let go of attachment step-by-step.

Without a system like it, we are able to calculate the outcome of physical actions exactly, but have no method of controlling the outcome of emotional and mental actions. This is the very recipe for disaster that confronts us today. If you have the money and bluster you can have the most dangerous things at your disposal. The moral rules to contain and direct the use of such things are ineffective, because of indifference and dispute.

We are so caught up in the material today that it is difficult to explain and grasp the high logic of spiritual justice. Instead, we blame an 'unjust God' for our suffering. As a consequence, we deny his right to exist and in desperation turn entirely to the mechanical. Immersing ourselves in the struggle to possess and enjoy distracting pleasures as of right, we divert our minds from confronting what we 'know' will be the final end of everything at the time of our death.

In 500 years we have advanced from a time when human societies were unified in a general misunderstanding about the workings of the universe and the relationship between it and its citizens. Now we face a time of clear physical predictability, but problematic moral understanding. It is a bit like handing out hand grenades to each member of a kindergarten class! Yet, the very knowledge that helps us understand our feelings and thoughts is as available today as it has always been. With the development of even more exact astronomical observation and computer technology, astrology can now provide even greater precision. The knowledge of the cycles this offers does not determine our lives, but help us see far more clearly the implications of our actions, and understand the universe from every perspective.

Astrology, the knowledge that was 'cast out of the academy' in the late 17th century can work systematically with emotion and mind. As is so often the case, the solution that is staring us in the face is one that irritates us the most and we feel like dismissing first. When we embrace the 'enemy' of astrological understanding, we find ourselves at one with our dearest friend and, combining it with compassion, transform our delusions into clear light.

Chapter 7
Giving Astrological Advice

> If we can accept the propositions that there is a level of consciousness where past and future are one, it becomes a great deal easier to see why astrology can indicate the pattern of the future.
> **Ronald C Davison**

Enough of the theory! What exactly are we supposed to do with it? This chapter aims to answer this by giving you the experience of being in a modern astrologer's head and workspace. Illustrating the way a good practitioner might approach some common tasks will help you get to know his/her way of thinking. We will look at individual consultations, and then show astrology providing insights into social, economic and political events, as well as the personalities that drive them.

Accept that the technical concepts may seem a bit dense at times! Be happy to be treated as an informed equal. Also be reassured. This chapter concludes our introduction to the essential concepts and workings of astrology and our aim to inform you of its *basic* possibilities.

Armed with this understanding, in Parts 3 and 4 you can consider how the wisdom you now have might enhance academic and social institutions. What follow in this chapter are experiences to prepare your judgement for the rest of the book. It will enable you to decide what benefits, if any, astrology might bring to society at large.

Personal consultations

Good consultants relate the insights explained in Chapters 3 to 6 to their clients in ways appropriate to each person's circumstances. Consultants develop skills to explain the basic language and synthesise the concepts. Knowing the generational cycles enables the astrologer to speak appropriately to each particular age group, and then look at the inner planets, to relate each individual's unique nature to his group. Many, but not all astrologers, will have a way of taking account of karma.

Amazingly, clients are drawn towards a consultant they will feel comfortable with and who specialises in the very issues and astro events that dominate their present lives. This alone tends to confirm that astrology works. Astrologers can range from the practical, who respond to simple down-to-earth questions, to esoteric interpreters of 'spiritual paths'. Most are a mixture of the two.

There are many approaches. Some consultants will look carefully at a chart and, using no astrological terms, translate the meanings into everyday language. The listener immediately feels understood, without realising how vital was the insight given by astrology. Some years ago at a parents' evening for my then young son I wanted to help the teacher handle his Capricorn intransigence, but did not feel mentioning I was an astrologer would help his cause. So, with his birth chart clearly in my mind, I just translated the symbol meanings into ordinary language. 'Mr Gillett – you really understand him and have explained his behaviour very helpfully' was the teacher's response after a few minutes.

On the other hand, bringing in astrological terms *can* help, because it gives an objective explanation for behaviour and experience. Having my own chart read in the early 1970s was an incredible relief, because it gave me reasons and a right to be myself, yet helped me let go of trying to persuade everyone else to be the same. This blessing is something many religious, political and other opinion leaders sorely need to learn!

When the consultant moves on to life developments, the timing of the progressions and transits can give some hope of change and solutions in the future. Consultants will vary in their attitude toward causality and prediction of the future. Some draw on traditional techniques and seek to give very specific practical descriptions of a person's situation and what is to come. In the traditional 17th century work of William Lilly[26] and his colleagues and in Indian Vedic[27] astrology there are intricate techniques for doing this. Excellent scholarship is re-discovering and applying these techniques in the modern world.

In contrast, many other modern Western astrologers tend to see the consultation more as having an advisory function. As was explained in Chapters 2 and 4, and will be studied in more depth in Chapter 12, the chart is best seen as a map that sets the scope of a person's life. It uses understanding of archetypes to show the many possible paths that could be taken. Also we can use progressions and transits to track the possibilities and issues that have and are pushing and will push themselves to the fore at particular times. The chart is rather like an A-Z map of a town. We may not visit every street, but we could visit any street, if we set our mind to it. It is more likely we will concentrate upon particular places, once we have decided to journey from A to F. Furthermore, there are ways to approach a particular destination. We can get there quickly, or take the time to admire the scenery. We may organise ourselves to arrive at a particularly convenient time and do other things on the way. The kinds of consultations that my clients find most satisfying work very much like this.

Of course, the border of the particular town the A-Z map covers limits the options. A Southampton book will be of little use to find our way around London. So, each of us is limited by the scope of our chart in some way. Paradoxically, though, identifying other people's limitations can help us find more freedom for ourselves. We may buy a *London A-Z* and use our knowledge of the way the *Southampton A-Z* works to master the London one more quickly. We can get to know what it is like in London, without ever having been there. Similarly by understanding our own horoscope, we open doors of knowing and tolerance toward others. In our own astrological details, there is almost always some kindred experience that we can extrapolate into an understanding of what it must be like to be someone very different to us. This is the beauty of astrology and the sheer wonder of being a consultant astrologer. To be able to understand, respect and even love so many radically different people is an incredibly liberating experience. To help people use the knowledge to make decisions and master their lives, their feedback on how valuable this has been to them; all provides a great sense of purpose. This really confirms the value of astrology.

It is the process of such an approach and motivation that is described below. The aim is to explain the method and the thinking behind it, rather than become too technical.

An outline of an astrological consultation

Some astrologers start with a discussion of the client's reason for coming and what they seek from the consultation. In contrast, I would prefer to know as little as possible at this first stage – I want the chart to do the talking. Hence, I check the client's knowledge of astrology and any previous consultation experience, ensure the birth data is correct, and then interpret the birth chart in a way that I feel they will understand.

At this stage the consultant is more like a translator just speaking words in response to another language that the listener may hardly, if at all, understand. Yet this language is not one of sequential concepts, as it would be if one were translating French into English. Interpreting an astrological chart is more like describing a painting to someone at the other end of a telephone. You want them to see the whole picture all at once, not a series of isolated images. Every image needs every other image to express the full effect of the picture. We are everything we are.

This key point of synthesis in chart interpretation has already been touched on at the beginning of Chapter 4 and in a little more detail under *Interpreting Marilyn Monroe's Chart* in The Appendix. This art of poetic juxtaposition kindles joyous motivation in the heart of all consultant astrologers. Skilfully you synthesize details of Sun, Moon, ascendant and planetary relationships, house positions and aspect connections into an increasingly distinctive personal statement. Before you is someone who entered as a stranger, yet after about 20 minutes of explanation will say; 'You seem to understand me better than anyone in my life ever has before now.'

When a client gives the reasons for saying this, the situation becomes even more amazing. The actual experience of interpreting a chart for someone you know nothing about can be automatic, abstract and tiring. At this stage you are just translating symbols, listening to your words and trying to understand what they mean. You may be developing a good idea of the potential range of possible work, relationships and financial situations. You may feel you know their attitude towards creativity, children and so on, but uncertainty is there all the time. Amazingly, nearly every time you are given their actual circumstances, the information does not just confirm your expectations; it enlightens them! For what you now learn about their lives hardly ever contradicts and nearly always confirms the validity of their chart and, in doing so, enhances your ability to interpret for future clients. You have to understand the astrological conceptual building blocks to inform this experience. However, once you do, every chart you interpret confirms your conviction that astrology works.

The period of interacting to fine-tune understanding from both the consultant and client perspective will inevitably bring up issues. It will also reveal client's grasp of life and the situations they are in. How objective and compassionate is the client ready to be, or do they need to be? The consultant should not moralise; rather, he has to respond in ways that are relevant and helpful, explore options that the client is capable of benefiting from. The consultant may see the best course of action, but suspect the client is unready to follow it. So he will sow seeds for the future. Maybe he will say something on the recording of the interview that he hopes will be understood when the recording is listened to later. With or without a recording, a point can be made in such a way that it will stay at the back of the client's mind ready for later use. If this is not possible, it may be best to give advice until a particular time in the future, and then suggest a return appointment. The experience in the intervening period may well just be what is needed to help clients to be ready to understand better, when they return in the future.

However, we should not go into the future on the basis of the birth chart alone. At an early stage, as the client's current issues become clear, I like to return to objective analysis, using techniques that indicate likely experiences in the future. There are many methods, but here we will focus on the two main ones – secondary progressions and transits.

We have referred already to the unfolding of the chart being indicated by secondary progressions. By taking each day after birth as a year of life and studying the Sun one-degree-a-day (= one year) movement, we can see that, after the number of degrees left before its end the Sun will change sign. For example, someone born with Sun at 15 degrees of Leo will develop an overlay of Virgo at the age of 15 (30-15=15 years). Then the Sun will be progressing through Virgo for thirty years, and then Libra for the next thirty - perhaps entering Scorpio too if the client lives into old age. Other planets will move at their relative speeds and may change sign as well. Such changes give great hope for new experiences and opportunities at many different times in our lives, as what we are disposed to be and accept gradually changes.

In the case of Mercury, Venus and Mars the pace of movement can vary – even appear to retreat due to the apparent retrograde motion explained in Chapter 4. Retrogression can indicate periods of reversal or reconsideration in a person's life with regard to the quality of the planet: with Mercury it is their way of speaking and thinking, Venus their devotion and attachments and Mars the effectiveness of their actions. The outer planets do not cover much ground. Changes to direct or retrograde motion can indicate important moments in a person's life. Alongside all this is the Moon's movement. Taking a year as a day means it moves on average twelve degrees a year and makes a complete cycle in about 27.5 years. This cycle indicates important stages in emotional development. 7 years represents the end of complete dependence on the home/mother, and 14 years, heralds teenage rebellion. 21 was the traditional age of adulthood. I always feel that 28 has to be reached to achieve genuine maturity! When we consider the transiting Saturn return[28], we may wish to make this 29 years.

We study progressions to discern how we are likely to develop through life. They indicate an inner maturation that may predispose the client to look for different experiences and what when in their life this might occur. Our birth chart does not indicate a fixed unyielding nature, but an unfolding process of opportunities to develop and grow.

How the world 'out there' is ready for and will receive our dispositions and changes is another matter. This is indicated by the transits – the positions of the planets at any particular point in time and space. Our birth chart is the same as a transit chart for the time, date and place at which we were born. How each future transit chart relates to this birth chart indicates how we are likely to experience life at that moment and location.

The potential advantages and disadvantages of time-and-place transits in view of how a client's life is unfolding by progression now take up the heart of the consultation. Progressions and transits can both complement and conflict with each other. Often what the client is ready for meets what the world is likely to offer. The end of the progressed Moon cycle is just two years before the key transiting Saturn return cycle. Hence the last years of our twenties confront us with emotional uncertainty and social realities that can lead to much upheaval, especially if we have been overconfident and reckless during younger years in the first cycle. Many people find this is the first time they begin to *take on board* the realisation that they cannot live forever.

By skilful use of these and other associated techniques the consultant will be able to link events in the past to experiences in the present and likely outcomes and opportunities in the future. The second half of Chapter 5 showed how events and people link over history. A rigorously detailed study of what has happened in the Middle East since 1920 would show frequent and remarkable astrological links.

The same is true in every individual person's life. Perhaps a client suffered problems in her career when Saturn made the first of three transits to Venus in the 10th house. Due to retrogression, two more are to come during the next six months or so. The advice would be to take control and seek to implement firm, disciplined action to put matters right on the second (retrograde) connection. Then the client should continue to work at this, with the expectation that when the third and final completion event occurs, she will be more established in her success than she was when the first problem happened. Counsel, however, that because Saturn is involved, this will not be easy. She has to be serious, determined and persistent.

Astrology liberates us and provides regenerative power to work in this way, because it shows that events are not entirely determined and unyieldingly linear. Because life is cyclic, the one who has the determination and facilities to dominate will not always force his or her way to success. Adolf Hitler may have conquered much of Europe in a hurry with Jupiter fortunately placed on his chart, but it moved on. So, with Saturn and Uranus following, he was to shoot himself in a bombed-out bunker within five years. Most of our experiences of the cyclic nature of existence are far less extreme and melodramatic, but they are just as genuine. If a Jupiter transit seems to be influencing a person's life, the astrologer will look back to when the Jupiter transit was at the same degree twelve years earlier, or maybe at the squares and oppositions three, six, or nine years ago. What happened then? How similar and different were the other progressions and transits then? Often a missed opportunity or mistake that led to disappointment in the past can be redeemed many years later – if you know and use the cycles.

Studying retrogression in progressed planets can be profoundly beneficial. Perhaps a client was born with Mercury retrograde in Gemini the 12th house just behind the ascendant. His early life experience was one of being overlooked, not listened to, and considered to be inarticulate. This was made worse by Saturn being in Gemini in the 1st house, the other side of the ascendant. Thirteen days (years by progression) after birth, Mercury moved into direct motion and he was sent to a public school at the age of 13 years, where he was happier than expected. However, because of early life experiences confirmed by the Saturn in the 1st house, he kept himself to himself and never felt equal to others.

As Mercury moved forward and grew stronger (by progression) in succeeding years he was in fact becoming an expert in his own private world. So, he did qualify for university. As he visits for the consultation, he is about to leave university at the age of 23 with a good Master's degree. Progressed Mercury has finally returned to the point it occupied at the time of his birth, but in the coming year it will conjunct natal Saturn in the 1st house. Clearly he is due to be rewarded in the public arena for all his hard work. He may even gain a first-class degree. Yet he is unlikely to believe this and may well aspire far too low and allow himself to be undervalued. Realising and explaining all this, the consultant should be able to encourage ambition way beyond what the client felt was possible when arriving for his appointment. There may be factors in other parts of the chart that enhance such optimism and inform strategy but, in any event, knowing how long it will take for the progressed Mercury to reach and move on from the Saturn will indicate vital timing. For, once Mercury is upon and then past the Saturn, the client could well discover himself to be recognised as *the* authority in his area of expertise.

As explained in Chapter 6, the birth chart is a diagrammatic representation of birth karma and the progressions and transits, opportunities for karmic growth. By understanding our astrology, we can become conscious and in command of our situations and our lives. We work through, master and transcend the challenges we were born with.

So, the consultation proceeds at whatever level the client is ready to address issues. Perhaps the question relates to the making or ending of a marriage, work or a business decision. It may concern children, or other creative endeavours. The range is as broad as the list covered by the Houses in The Appendix. The discussion may help a person decide if they are ready to make or end a commitment. We study the birth chart and its development and connections through life to explore all sides and options of the issue. We do not seek to decide 'what will happen', or 'what should happen'. We can explore alternatives. 'If I go to a certain place, take a job, marry this person and so on, what is the experience likely to be?' Each alternative answer will bear in mind the astrological potential of the client – especially the transits and progressions that are due. Let him choose from several opposite alternatives and examine his feelings about each. Let all this rest in his mind; then he will know what he wants and decide with clear commitment.

Working with clients in this way can bring intimacies that require careful handling. The key consideration is that the client leaves the session more independent and aware than when he or she entered. The use of astrological techniques should not have confused, dominated and created false hopes or fears for the future. The consultant may have succeeded brilliantly in understanding and describing the client. Yet the consultant will have failed if that client now feels in a special relationship and dependent upon the consultant. It is my opinion that, should the consultation be entirely an astrological one, then there should be no dependence. If the astrologer is a qualified therapist, then temporary dependence in accordance with the principles of that therapy may be acceptable.

Usually, the client will leave refreshed, because what he already knew subconsciously has been drawn up to his conscious mind. He is on good terms with himself and his life. He knows what to do and is able to recognise, understand and know how to handle whatever happens next. Although such an ideal state of mind may not always be possible to achieve entirely in one session, the astrological consultant should never forget that this is the prize a good astrologer seeks.

It helps to do so, if the consultant cares for his or her position. The consultation can be intense and really personal. I find the easiest way is to give myself entirely to the client for the duration of the consultation, without attachment to personal needs. Paradoxically, this state of mind is easiest to achieve if one looks at the situation materialistically. The client has purchased 'x' number of hours of your life. You will let go of yourself and be guided by the astrological indications that give the best objective understanding of the client's needs. This creates the most beneficial neutral environment for the consultation and the client. The corollary of that is that once the session ends, so does your involvement with and responsibility towards the client. If this is so, then it is your responsibility before the session ends to ensure clients are ready to proceed with life on their own. Maybe another session is needed and arranged. Even in this case, the client should be left independent between times.

What is outlined in the previous paragraph is my ideal. While it may not always be possible to be sure it is achieved, it is important to try to do so. Just as important is to be able to know you have and tell yourself you have done your best to achieve it. Many clients have traumas they will have to face, however good the advice. The deep intention and motivation to leave our clients free and strong is the key to our doing the best we can.

Using mundane astrology to 'advise the world'!

As well as people, our lives are full of significant events that also have their astrological characteristics and can form part of an astrologer's advice.

Whatever their religious, non-religious or cultural assumptions, nearly every society, group and family feels it important to mark special occasions with some kind of ceremony. Be it a christening, marriage, the launching of a ship, new building, business enterprise, a country's independence or the end of a war, usually an important person will arrive, perform a special symbolic deed or say some special words. This will be seen as the real beginning. The exact time, date and place will be carefully recorded – often by a legal document, a metal plaque or even a stone.

Some special ceremonial moments can be grandiose in the extreme. The inauguration of the President of the United States of America takes place on an open-air, elevated platform in the company of the most important people in the land. It is followed by a day full of receptions and celebrations. The coronations, anniversaries and weddings of the British Royal Family bring the whole of London to a standstill. They are televised and watched all over the world by billions of people.

Clearly there is a reason for the most powerful organisers of our societies to go to so much trouble and expense to make such days special and honour their anniversaries ever afterward. Indeed, many ordinary people mark their lives and relationships by bringing to mind how they felt at those special times for the famous. Such days mould our identity and so have a profound influence upon what we do.

Religions use anniversaries and inaugurations to perpetuate traditions and instil qualities of spiritual excellence by performing particular ceremonies on particular days. Jewish, Muslim, Buddhist, Hindu and even most Christian religions decide most of these by astronomical calculations. These are often lunar-, sometimes solar-based – more often both.

Whether astrology is accepted, or even known about, implicit in this practice is the assumption that there is important solar and lunar energy in particular moments of time. Hence, it is certainly reasonable to ask if we can learn something about any moment from the symbolism of its astrology chart and the cycles that will develop from it. Perhaps we can even anticipate developments, when transiting planets relate to the planetary positions on a chart drawn for 'time of birth' of a particular institution, event or process of activities? We call this study mundane astrology.

Chapter 5 introduced this by considering the workings of historical cycles. It then offered a first taste of the way that natal and event charts can be combined with such cycles and used to explain events and the people that control and contain them.

Before we go further, however, it is important to keep in our minds what was said at the end of that chapter and also with regard to prediction in Chapter 2 and much of Chapter 4. What will happen is not inevitable. With foreknowledge, insight and compassion, it may be possible to turn the most difficult situation around. Astrology is not a precise predictive tool but a describer of the environment in which we have worked, are working and will work.

Mundane astrology may give precise predictions, but its main aim is social healing not prophecy. To be famous as the predictor of massive death and destruction is hardly a cause for celebration. It is far better to use astrology as a diagnostic tool that measures pressures, possibilities and social trends. Such understanding guides our lives skilfully and helps us to learn from dire dangers and have the insight to turn failure into success. The calmer and more aware we are when driving along the road, the less chance there is of an accident, however badly others are behaving.

Astrology's great value is that it can show very clearly *why* things happen and may even give clues as to exactly *what* might happen next if we do not change our course of action. One of the main reasons Western religious leaders have held it at arm's length is what they see as the danger of Man seeking to 'usurp the role of God'. They are right to warn of the dangers. Attempting to 'possess' a process/technique, to 'own' and take pride in a prediction, leads to ego-driven madness.

Mundane astrology is best used to serve the world. It is much better to be the person who helps to avert disaster by a timely and appropriate warning, than to become notorious and hounded by correctly predicting a sensational earthquake, assassination or political crisis. We have free will. We study astrology to know the circumstances we have to work with, so we can make the best use of their potential. The astrologer is a counsellor, not a seer. Maybe his or her uncanny knack of anticipating the future inspires awe, trepidation and a need to sit up and take action, but it should never make people feel powerless and impotent.

From March 2002, I wrote a column entitled Working with the Planets for astrologers who read the bi-monthly *Astrological Journal*. It involved picking out the key astro events in the coming two months and giving choices and advice on how to make the best use of the possibilities.

Due to copy deadlines, I was writing two to three months ahead of events. So, in March 2002 just as my first piece was published, I was preparing my May article. I noticed that on 26th May the last of three Saturn/Pluto oppositions (the negative driving force of the 9/11 World Trade Center atrocity) occurred conjunct the nodal axis, Mercury turned retrograde and there was a lunar eclipse. This day was just five days before the planned, very public, Golden Jubilee celebrations for HM Queen Elizabeth II over an extended holiday from 1st to 4th June. This was to be followed on 10th June by a solar eclipse with Pluto on the MC in London at that moment.

Clearly the Jubilee celebrations would bring immense crowds and much public exposure for the British Royal Family. At the time, just six months after 9/11, the world and Britain were anxiously anticipating the next attack. With trepidation, I studied the chart for the climax of the four-day celebrations, a lined procession to St Paul's Cathedral for a service of thanksgiving followed by a return procession and a parade in the Mall. The Pluto end of the opposition was retreating, but Saturn was applying to the nodal axis. The Moon was applying into Aries to square Mars throughout the afternoon. Yet there were good indications. The Moon and Mars, although uncomfortable or in fall, were mutually receiving each other and Venus was very close to a conjunction to Jupiter also in Cancer in the 11th house of the religious service chart. Danger could be turned into sensitivity and kindness, a respect for the homeland traditions. With Mercury culminating, followed by the Part of Fortune[29], Sun, Saturn and North Node and then Mars, Jupiter and Venus, the service and the hours that followed would see London at its most public, with just about every mixture of information, creativity, problem, danger, opportunity and love. It was easy to visualise the worst kind of disaster and danger to dignitaries and spectators, but how would it help to say so?

At times like this there is usually no alternative but to pray and be positive. Maybe there are words and images that can sow seeds of hope. Maybe the sheer fact of possible danger will turn people's minds away from it, distract anxiety and divert actions to more fruitful pursuits. So having outlined the transits above, I wrote the following:

So are we predicting disaster for London?

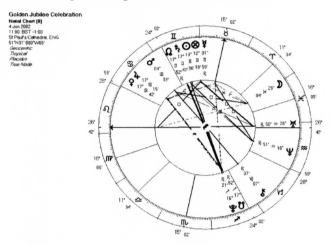

| Figure 16 – HM Queen Elizabeth II Golden Jubilee |

Not necessarily, in between 26th May and 10th June HM the Queen's fiftieth jubilee celebrations reach their climax. From Saturday 1st June until a special ceremony … on Tuesday June 4th 2002 there will be four days of holiday celebrations. Do you remember the chart for the wedding of Prince Charles and Princess Diana in 1981? Whatever their relationship's long-term outcome, when the wedding happened it deflected major social conflicts. Not only in Britain, but all over the world, attention was focused on this regal British ceremony. 1981 had started with desperate dissent; it could so easily have grown into a 'hot and bloody summer', but instead was transformed into innocent hope by a fairytale wedding that captured most people's hearts. A simple comparison of the Royal Wedding and Golden Jubilee charts show that same high-profile focus. Both have massive stellia being transited by the MC well into the afternoon. The Queen is due to enter the Cathedral just before 11 am, then lunch at the Guildhall afterward and is most likely to appear on the balcony of Buckingham Palace in the afternoon, just as the Venus-Jupiter conjunction is on the MC. Do you remember that shy, awkward balcony kiss of Charles and Di with Venus in Virgo on the MC?'[30]

Writing the July/August article in early June 2002, I was pleased to be able to comment:

'And in the end the love you take is equal to the
love you make' The Beatles - *Abbey Road*
The success of the Queen's Jubilee celebrations amidst difficult eclipses, the Saturn/Pluto opposition and other challenging astro events (outlined in the May's *Working with the Planets*), shows just how much can be achieved with negative astro energy – providing there is respect for and co-operation between people and their sub-cultures. The processions and concerts did this great work really well. As a result danger melted away. The 49 Hell's Angel motorcyclists screeched to stop their speedy path along the Mall to salute and honour, not harm the royal family, so vulnerably placed on a very low dais. The supersonic Concorde rose majestically up and away from the palace. The fire on Saturday night did not reach the masses of fireworks stored elsewhere in the building. What could have been disastrous was good, because our love and devotion made it so.[31]

Insight into economic and political developments – oil
As well as describing changes in fashion and socio/political developments and helping us behave positively through important moments in history, the charts for vital achievements are particularly significant. The astrological charts of a discovery can describe the nature of the moment and its context. Future connections to this chart can indicate important developments and consequences.

The following piece was written in May 2006. It shows just how important understanding the links between resources, business and politics can be. It is often claimed that oil is the reason for Western involvement in Middle Eastern affairs. What follows shows how astrology can help us see the extent to which this is so.

'What's oil got to do with it?

'With petroleum oil and conflict so dominating the news and very likely to do so even more in the future, it seemed a good idea to search out some data of key dates and compare them to the present time. So on the recommendation of a friend; I purchased *The Prize* by Daniel Yergin,[32] a 900-page Pulitzer Prize-winning account of this key ingredient that underlies so much of the fashion of contemporary life and its attitudes towards knowledge. Although there are accounts of the collection and use of naturally standing 'rock oil' and spontaneous fires since the dawn of written history, the first time that petroleum was successfully drilled for is given in the chart on the next page. Yergin's account records 'the drill dropped into a crevice, then slid another six inches', just before end of work on a Saturday afternoon. The following day plentiful quantities of oil were gathered in containers. Pumping started on the Monday. So the time of breakthrough could be between 1700 and 1800 hours on the Saturday.

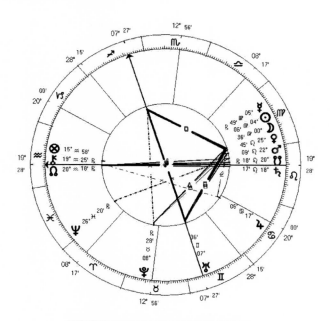

Oil First Drilled
Natal Chart (9)
27 Aug 1859 NS
18:00 LMT +5.18 42
Titusville, Pennsylvania
41°N37'37" 079°W40'26"
Geocentric
Tropical
Placidus
True Node

Figure 17 – Oil First Drilled

The chart clearly shows intense speculative endeavour. Indeed, the drilling project was severely out of resources and about to be closed down. Particularly interesting for our purposes is the position between 18/19 degrees Leo/Aquarius of the nodal axis, Saturn, Chiron and, if 1800 LMT is the time, the ascendant/descendant axis as well.

Yergin gives many other dates and accounts, but especially relevant for the importance of the Middle East in our destiny today are three of these.

* ✳ The *Red Line Agreement*[33] was signed in 1928 when the interested European parties agreed the proportion by which they would to divide the oil and to 'work jointly together' as a cartel to explore the entire Arabian Peninsula, including Palestine, Iraq, Saudi Arabia and Turkey. Although the agreement was set-aside at the end of 1948, it set a principle of Western involvement in Arabian oil that continues to this day.
* ✳ The *nationalisation of Iranian oil* in May 1951[34] led to the exile of the Shah, then his Western-backed return a few years later, and, in 1979, consequent revolution and
* ✳ The *return of Ayatollah Khomeini*[35], which haunts the West and our access to oil to this day.

The charts of these three key moments continue the middle degrees of Leo/Aquarius theme and extend it to the other two fixed signs. The *Red Line Agreement* chart has Venus in 16 degrees [36] Leo, having recently squared Jupiter and Chiron and applying to square Mars in Taurus. *The Nationalisation of Iranian Oil* chart has Pluto in 17 degrees of Leo, with Sun and Mars in Taurus applying to square it. At the *return of Ayatollah Khomeini,* Jupiter was in 21 degrees of Scorpio, with Mercury, Sun and Mars in Aquarius applying to cross the critical 8 to 18 degree area, and then square Jupiter during the 11-day period from his return until the army gave him full power.

Of course, as we have seen previously [in Chapter 5 of this book], the 1920 Middle East Mandate chart has Jupiter conjunct Neptune at 9 degrees Leo, the three Jupiter/Neptune oppositions in 2002/3 that seem to have driven the War in Iraq were at 9, 11 and 13 degrees of Leo/Aquarius. The Saturn/Neptune opposition on

31st August 2006 is at 18 degrees. Jupiter squares Neptune on 24th September 2006 at 17 degrees of Scorpio/Aquarius. Neptune is retrograding very close to the same degree in Aquarius, when Jupiter squares Saturn on 25th October [2006]. It would be fascinating to discover what a fuller study of oil's chequered history would yield?

The autumn of 2006 will see the coming together of fundamental karmic issues, as we reap what has been sown with regard to oil and the involvement of the West in Middle Eastern affairs. As we continue to see constantly, astrology works and would help us understand what we need to do to put our problems right, if only we would allow ourselves to learn from its wisdom. The speculative intensity of the great fire-producing liquid and the brilliant technological innovation needed to harvest, contain and exploit its potential is so clearly described by the interaction of Jupiter, Neptune and Saturn in Leo and Aquarius, plus the other fixed signs that square them. The great kingly generosity and humanitarianism that intermingle with and give moral justification to material and business considerations describe this Leo/Aquarius astrology on another level.

So we have a wealth of energy and bi-products that helps us move, be everywhere and provide everything – to set everyone on earth free and comfortable. Yet, we find ourselves diverting the wealth to conflict and constant destruction – little different to prospectors in the old 19th century Wild West going through all manner of privations, only to fight and destroy each other once the 'prize' (be it oil, or gold) is discovered. The source of the wealth that makes the West strong is the same one that makes our 'opponents' strong enough to oppose us. The oil, its silicon and plastic bi-products are crucial to the technology that creates the weapons that explode whole neighbourhoods and make the exploded wish to explode the exploders in turn. When explosions explode people, it is just a matter of personal perspective to decide which explosion is good and which bad.

We need a profound understanding of Aquarian humanitarianism if we are to contain and direct truly this ultimate fiery product of Leo for the benefit of all. Aquarius can be the wily whore-chancellor serving the destructive ego of the king, or the custodian of universal wisdom channelling his ruler's philanthropy so that everyone can be happy. When everything is measured and weighed on gross and material scales, only the lesser science, the illegitimately arrogant Aquarius can rule. Oil may well destroy us, if we cannot see and do any better than that![37]

Putting our leaders and their actions into perspective

If decisions are based as much on taste and emotion as reason, then choosing the right leaders can have a dramatic effect on our lives. Yet, our 21st century ways of selecting those we look up to is flawed. Desperate for a super-person to follow, we idolise too quickly, condemn too absolutely, then lose faith in leaders all together – 'they are all the same!' Who is in and out in celebrity culture becomes more a gladiatorial contest than genuine respect?

Having an accurate astrological chart for the leader in question can prevent false hopes. It can also provide some helpful pointers that will reveal how well they are really doing. Such insights are essential if informed democratic decisions are to be made by the people.

Of course, only for the past two and a half centuries have ordinary people's thoughts mattered. Uranus in Leo opposed to Pluto in Aquarius in the late 18th century kick-started a rebellious process that led to what is known as modern democracy. There was much injustice to address and many powerful vested interests to confront. The battle between classes, economic interests, colonialists and commercial pressure groups was bloody, destructive and frequently polarised. For most of the time, the process was so full of contradictory mixed messages that issues of ends and means blurred who was right and wrong and therefore, who we should follow.

As we approach the end of the first decade of the 21st century, the relationship between the people and their leaders seems to be breaking down into three broad structures.

✳ In many democratic parts of the world, millions of ordinary people are, or are moving towards, being richer and having more freedom of expression than ever before, providing they are willing to be supervised and guided by experts 'for their own good'.

* In other more traditional and 'undeveloped' parts of the world, millions of people are open to exploitation by their own leaders in collusion with foreign interests.
* Other millions feel morally outraged by what they see to be the 'godless degenerate nature of the privileged countries'.

If any ordinary people are to have control over their lives, those in the first group, so-called modern democracies, must have the means to assess and control their leaders' judgement and emotional stability.

This has been made all the more urgent by the recent transits of Uranus and Neptune through Aquarius, being opposed by Jupiter in 2002 to 2003 and by Saturn between 2004 and 2007, while Pluto was transiting Sagittarius. As well as conventional religious intolerance, these cyclic patterns have combined to expand potentially self-destructive scientific advances. We live under a kind of technological fundamentalism that assumes mechanistic and statistical experimentation should be the sole basis of truth. It seems statisticians are wiser about what is best for us than we are ourselves. Some doubt we are even capable of choosing our leaders.

Cyclic changes in outer planetary positions between 2008 and 2012 will bring the Earth to a number of nemesis points and difficult decisions. Many people will feel the need to look for more than mechanical statistics for answers. It would be lethal to turn instead to leaders who manipulate emotionally and deceive. Are there deeper ways to remove the clouds and clarify issues? Break down barriers and find them!

Public interest in the 'one person, one vote' electoral system has diminished dramatically in my lifetime. Many feel that, because politicians lie and obscure the main issues of what they plan to do, one occasional vote has little effect. Special interest groups, appointees and experts, who then patronise the public, make the real decisions behind closed doors. Multi-national business has the power to influence and even control national political decisions.

Even when there is a major election the battle of ideas is conducted like a perverse advertising campaign of promise, slur, spin, distortion and misleading image building. Buzz words such as 'education, health, crime, old people, children, protecting the public against terrorism' are thrown around; as if just uttering the words somehow sanctifies the speaker and obliges you to vote for him or her. Many of these problems have always been there in political debate, but recent decades have allowed little real choice. It seems we have replaced the class struggle with a middle-ground meritocracy, which has reduced political voting decisions to little more than choosing between rival washing powers on a supermarket shelf.

Clearly we need a better, objective way of cutting through the marketing and empty promises to the real people behind the contrived 'voter-friendly' image of our prospective leaders. If we knew what they were really like and allied this with the insights we have already seen astrology providing in world affairs, then to vote would be an intelligent and exciting prospect. Nor would it finish there. Knowing the birth chart, progression and transits of the successful candidates would enable us to assess how they may serve us in the future. Would the world have followed George W Bush and Tony Blair into Iraq, or even allowed the original 1920 agreement, if they had known the astrology of the time and the people involved?

Here is a study of contemporary British political leaders, written for the July 2007 *Astrological Journal*[38] that shows how astrology can be used to get behind the image to get into the heart of the people in whom we place our trust. For those of you not so experienced in astrology, immediately below is a *background paragraph* that explains the article's key astrological concepts.

Background If they know the time you were born, astrologers can allocate your planets to the twelve 'houses' (areas of your life) described in the Appendix. The most mysterious and threatening of these houses is the 12th house. While 12th house people are hardworking, conscientious, intensely self-driven and can be highly principled, they tend to project their personal fears and defensiveness on to others. They find it difficult to trust and give room to all but a narrow, self-confirming group of close associates. Their political way of working is unlikely to create democratic, broad-based consensus. Hence error and misunderstanding can persist, and being ruled by them can feel claustrophobic leaving little 'room to breathe'.

'12th House Continues to Rule – Let Battle Commence!'
"You have to trust 12th house people, or lock them up"[39] was the focus around which my initial analysis of the 1997 Labour

landslide victory turned. It could not have been more prophetic! Throughout the past ten years we have had accusations of 'spin', 'control freakery', 'in-group sofa government' and just plain 'lying'. We have been told by the media of secret battles (via intermediaries!) between Tony Blair and his Chancellor. The latter has been accused by colleagues of 'personality flaws' and intolerance, the words of which read remarkably like a 'cookbook' summary of 12th house characteristics.

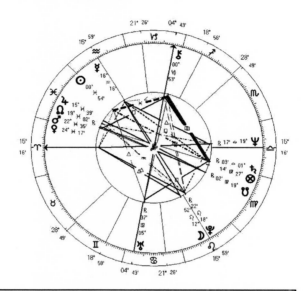

Gordon Brown
Natal Chart [18]
20 Feb 1951
08:40 UT +0:00
Grittnock, Scotland
55°N49' 004°W20'
Geocentric
Tropical
Placidus
True Node

Figure 18 - Gordon Brown's Birth Horoscope

Over the past ten years the 12th house tendency has spread with George Bush, Vladimir Putin and Ariel Sharon all having their Suns there. The consequent obsession with fear of others, the need to defend ourselves against what 'they might do to us' and insistence we must sacrifice our freedom in the service of security is now accepted as inevitable – 'the only game in town'. Looking back to the fresh sunshine of that early May 1997 day, life seems to have become ever more despondent and desperate. Does it always have to be like this?

As I write, it is expected that Tony Blair[40] will announce his retirement very soon and, as you receive this, Gordon Brown will be, or about to become, Prime Minister of Great Britain. How will things change? Intrinsically, the two men are not as dissimilar as it first seems, although it takes an astrologer to see it. The open and initially attractive, 'hail fellow well met', seemingly good-humoured and self-effacing public persona of the outgoing Prime Minister is deceptive. All you are seeing here is an Aquarian Moon conjuncting the North Node in his 10th house. This is his image; not the real driving force. That is explained by a tenacious Taurean Sun and Jupiter, an impulsively belligerent Mercury and Venus in Aries, ruled by Mars in Gemini just behind his ascendant in the same sign. Lacking the maturity of vision to think through the implications of his decisions, but determined to prevail, he has manipulated and charmed his way through ten years in power. During this time much has been attempted, but little been done properly and completed. What financial and physical dangers for Britain and the world in the future have been created remains to be seen. Opponents point to Iraq as Tony Blair's legacy, whereas he himself would like to feel he has left the country's education, health and public institutions ready to become leaner and much more efficient. Others may worry that by his 12th house driven obsession with security and limiting legal rights, he has, albeit unintentionally, prepared Britain to be taken over by Orwellian fascism.

Gordon Brown[41] does not have the 'image-friendly' 10th house Moon and North Node. So, with him, personality-wise what you see is what you get. He is dour because he is intensely anxious, conscientious and hardworking. The Piscean focus means he could not care more deeply. With so many planets in the 12th house, he is intensely private. This explains the awkwardness of his progress toward the top job. That, with such energy, he wishes to be Prime Minister at all indicates great kindness and idealism. He is a man with a mission.

Of course, that does not necessarily make his judgements and policies correct, nor indicate that his approach to government will be effective. The apparent financial successes of his Chancellorship may yet come to haunt users of hospitals, schools and transport systems. The drain of Public Finance Initiatives[42] will continue to bite, as infrastructures age and decay, but cannot be replaced, because we are still paying for them. The cost of housing, pensions, student and more general debt may become far less easy to sustain. For in time the property boom will burst and temporarily cheap Chinese and Indian products and services will no longer be with us. As a nation we are trying and working harder, yet being overtaken by Asia. For these reasons; the 12th house Piscean devotion of Gordon Brown may turn out to deceive him, as well as us. However good his intentions, will the caveats of great Chancellorship that are often placed upon him be his legacy? Or will he be seen as a leader, who projected his own personality of obsessive hard work upon a whole nation and left it exhausted and failing?

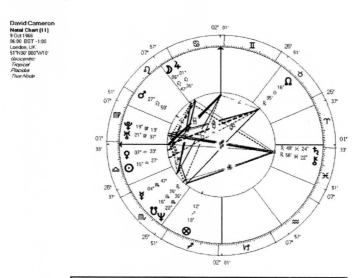

Figure 19 – David Cameron's Birth Horoscope

However that goes now the decks are cleared for a great political battle, which has very much to do with the 12th house. As we observed during the Conservative Party leadership contest[43]; although David Cameron[44] has an attractively friendly Venus and Sun rising in Libra in the 1st house, his Moon and Mars are proudly and imperially placed in Leo. This Mars has now progressed into 12th house Virgo and moves between the natal and progressed Plutos and Saturns during the build-up to the next UK General Election. It will oppose Gordon Brown's natal Mars and

Venus and be applying to oppose Gordon Brown's Saturn too – a critical 'up close and personal' battle in every sense!

When Tony Blair was at this stage of preparation a few years before his 1997 victory, he was dismissed as 'Bambi'. Seeking to dismiss David Cameron as a lightweight publicist with little or no policies would be a similar error. The key question that needs to be asked is whether David Cameron is a manipulative, 'all things to all people' presenter whose actions in office would be as, or even more, divisive and repressive than Labour's? Alternatively, are his often-mocked statements, such as 'hug a hoodie' and 'rewarding the family', expressions of a healing vision that is vital for Britain? If so, has he the clarity and strength of will to apply these subtle insights to expansive benefit; like a homoeopathic political process?

Crucially, has David Cameron the capacity to help heal the psychotic trauma projected on the world by the 12th house paranoia of recent leaders and their policies? Or, with Gordon Brown's progressed Moon and transiting Jupiter about to activate his Midheaven in the coming year, will Gordon Brown mature into a much more open and publicly effective figure in the top job? Will his Piscean familiarity with the failure of fear focus a stronger and more effective healing? Or will the challenges of the turn of the decade be such that they can be no more than *endured*, whoever is in power?

It will be interesting to see how things develop.

Further Reading

Contrasting and complementary approaches to consultation
Darrelyn Gunzburg *Life after Grief; An Astrological Guide to Dealing with Loss*
Bob Mulligan *Between Astrologers & Clients*
Noel Tyl *Synthesis and Counselling in Astrology*
Adrian Ross Duncan *Astrology Transformation & Empowerment*
Prudence Jones (editor) *Creative Astrology*
Babs Kirby *Experiential Astrology*
Tracy Marks *Astrology of Self Discovery*

PART 3

Working with Astrology

Can Astrology Enhance Our Understanding of the 21st Century?

This third section considers whether there would be benefits in returning astrology to mainstream academia. Could it extend contemporary academic theories? Would its capacity to describe, relate and synthesise intrinsic natures ease the contemporary tendency to fragment understanding? Has astrology some service to give to belief systems? Would theorists and researchers in conventional areas of knowledge find that astrological input casts new light and so expands the potential of their expertise?

Of course, it is for the expert in a particular field to answer such questions. The astrologer can only open doors and leave a few pointers. The expert will decide whether to enter, consider in depth and decide if the notion is not as strange as it first seemed.

This book only aims to start such a possibility. It is not complete, but focuses on areas of knowledge that have interested me. Astrology may be helpful in many other areas and ways. As can be seen from the bibliographies at the end of chapters, my colleagues have much scholarship and depth to add.

Before 'rolling up our sleeves' and moving into some specific subject areas, it is important to be clear about what exactly is being attempted. Right now, each subject we study at school or college has a built-in system of concepts and precedents that can be compared and developed along well-defined lines. Within each subject area, there will be definite sub-areas that may complement or contradict each other. Experts are acknowledged by the work they do. Leaders in each field attract followers. Hence sub-areas, trends and contesting theses develop. Because these can usually only be tested and understood in terms of their own set concepts, modern academic subject areas and departments can become separated, even isolated. It is academic etiquette that particular subject areas do not intrude upon each other, except in generally accepted complementary fringe areas. Above all, the basic rule is that you have to learn the language and 'our way of doing things', before seeking to interfere.

Introducing astrology to these worlds of expert knowledge will therefore be a challenging process. We are suggesting that major contemporary knowledge systems have good reasons to look back and connect with a language that has been devised and refined from the apparent movement of the heavens, mostly by people long dead. This language is not that of any specific modern discipline, but it does offer insights into how key elements of most disciplines relate to exactly-measured astronomical observations.

To give this a chance, we should start from the view that we *may* have something to learn from each other and be willing to make allowances and show respect. There is no sense in starting on a journey if there is no chance of arriving. So, however unlikely it might seem at first, experts in their fields must accept an amazing possibility. This ancient knowledge *may* hold clues that *might* explain and even answer problems that exist in modern theories and specialist knowledge systems.

Of course, few astrologers would claim to have expert knowledge, or the understanding to judge contemporary academic subjects. That the reverse is not the case is a curious irony. While no astrologer would seek to judge genetics unless previously trained, there are geneticists proud of never having studied astrology who claim the right to declare it dangerous nonsense. This book seeks a humbler role. It asks permission to stand at the door of some academic disciplines and explore whether a possible connection with astrology can be considered. Finally and hopefully, it asks whether there are problems with the workings of modern knowledge which some aspect of astrology may be able to explain; even answer.

Perhaps the questions astrologers ask and the suggestions they make come from ignorance or naivety, but then perhaps they do not. The specialist physicist, biologist, psychologist and so on will know if there is anything useful in it. If there is, then we can explore how progress can be made. Often astrologers' comments and questions strike chords that answer problems about matters they do not fully understand themselves. There is no threat in that, only clarity and benefit all round. Should we discover radically different but even more valid views of the world, how could the world and we be anything but the better for it?

Chapter 8
Astrology & Religion

As above, so below; as within, so without.
Hermetic maxim

'How can a good God have created such a cruel world?' is frequently asked in our sense-obsessed materialist 21st century, where 'being satisfied' quickly expands from mere expectation to a *right* to be *demanded*. 'Either he is powerless against evil, in which case how can he be God? Or evil is a part of God, in which case how can he be good and kind?' How can we explain mass disasters, such as the South East Asian tsunami, earthquakes, famine, hurricanes; or individual human tragedies, such as being born disabled, the death of a loved one, experiencing painful illnesses?

The 'Fair & Logical universe' outlined in Chapter 6 gives a clear answer. The karmic condition of the mind creates and is attracted to distortions of the truth that can be explained by astronomical cycles. The negativity of past thoughts and actions so sour our minds that we are drawn to points of time and space that reflect them. These generate therapeutic experiences and the chance to learn and purify past negativities. There are reasons why we are born to be eminently kind and attractive, but also to suffer constant adversity. While intensely unfair in terms of one lifetime, maybe serving and suffering are exactly what are needed to learn and purify for all lifetimes.

Astrology on its own is not a religion or belief system. To many serious students of astrology, those who claim to believe in it are as dangerously misguided as those who reject it outright. For both of these attitudes are based on blind superstition. Rather, astrology describes the structure and order of what Christians would call 'God's creation' and humanity's inner struggle to reflect its perfection. Astrology is a systematic tool that examines the relationship between astronomical cycles, our personal characteristics and events on earth. Both the medieval European world picture and Eastern cultures placed astrology between mundane life on earth and the divine absolute understanding of God, or the Universal Mind. The archetypes of astrology were seen as qualities to be developed to their ideal level. They described the struggle within the human personality between its creative, devotional, aggressive, intellectual, expansive and structural dispositions. We come to understand ourselves by identifying our unique way of thinking, acting and organising. The more we understand our nature, the better use we can make of our potential. If we can identify and work to rectify areas of weakness, we can improve our performance.

Religious ceremonies act as therapies to enhance our understanding and actions. Ideal expressions of sound, sight, touch, taste are therapeutic. A piece of music, work of art, colour, tastes, smell, massage and the like inspire us to purify and enhance our behaviour. Religious practices use such understanding to 'stir the soul' and 'improve the spirit'. Individuals react to aspects of ceremony and so become close and unified with the perceived ideal divine nature – the heart truth of a particular religion. Astrological archetypes and cycles can identify and structure such therapies.

Understanding which therapy suits which individuals personalises such experiences of the 'divine'. This personal contact can reinforce religious conviction. For some it can give visions of angels. In Ancient Greek times, the Gods were seen as higher beings, holding the destiny of humanity in their hands. Man could do as he wished, but could not avoid the consequences if his actions railed against the 'will of the Gods'. In monotheistic religions, idealised archetypes intercede between God and man in the form of angels, prophets and saints.

Astrology is an attempt to study in detail the nature and flow of such intercession, whatever the religion. Just as visions of angels and the words of the prophets can be corrupted by the minds and actions of deluded individuals, so can astrological understanding. But, as with angels and prophets, the cycles are the very processes of the divine mind. So, to ignore, misrepresent and misuse such higher understanding brings confusion and severe problems to our lives. Because astrological and other esoteric knowledge can be misused and lead to self-obsession, some religious traditions have urged followers to avoid them. Yet, the priests and advanced practitioners in nearly all religions have at some time known about and used this 'hidden' knowledge for 'higher purposes'.

In the 21st century, the power of ordinary people to change themselves and the material world is so much greater. So, it would be an enormous benefit to have a systematic understanding of the cycles that underlie our feelings, the decisions we make and the resultant outcomes.

Providing such knowledge could be a way of enlightening the limited vision of our relative perspectives and so serving the natural flow of the universe; not usurping the Will of God. As such, it can be most beneficial and appropriate for both the individual and society.

Armed with the greater understanding of and responsibility for our lives, it would no longer be sensible to rail mindlessly against an 'unjust God', as if in the modern fashion, we were desperately seeking for grounds to sue him for compensation!!

The Hindu and Buddhist religions have always enjoyed a comfortable relationship with astrology. As suggested in Chapter 6, they see astrological systems as a way of exploring, understanding and benefiting from knowing the workings of the karmic consequences of our behaviour. Firstly, we accept that it is our deluded, impure minds (not God) that have caused everything that happens to us. Then we seek to purify negativity in an informed, systematic way. This leads to greater tolerance and compassion. Such an approach to life sets beneficial limits on the extent to which we see others and ourselves as competitors – also the way we undertake this competition. The higher ethics and methods of purification in these religions can be practised without blind faith and the struggle of self-castigation for our 'sins'. Guilt and condemnation of ourselves and others does not need to come into the picture. Rather, the individual is encouraged to see the consequences of his actions and take action to purify them. If he fails to do so, he and those close to him will suffer. Once we understand the way karma works, we experience the benefit of greater contentment and happiness. Living life in this way is an empirical, not a judgemental, process.

Hindu and Buddhist practices use astrology to determine the timing of religious festivals and ceremonies. New and Full Moons are times to purify past negativity, not follow base instincts and lose control – so easy to do at such times. Special events are timed to take place at moments from which positive growth will occur; or at difficult times, when focusing on devotion and purification will prevent matters getting worse.

Contrary to first impressions, Hinduism and Buddhism focus on one essential absolute divine truth. Their familiar 'deities' are not ultimate gods to worship in the way Jews, Muslims and Christians worship their One God. Rather, they are idealised archetypes. The Tibetan Chenrezig represents the essence of compassion. By focusing on his ideas, symbols, associations and experiences we become compassionate. In the same way, Manjushri represents and invokes mental exactness that cuts through all confusion. Saraswati invokes knowledge, music, creativity, and idealised womanhood. By immersing ourselves in the ceremonies, pictures, words, music, colours and aromas associated with these archetypes, we make them part of us and purify our inner natures. The scores of such archetypes all emanate from and bring us back to the same universal source. To worship individual gods, absolutely and exclusively only heightens the ego, separates the individual and brings delusion and suffering. For, all are empty of intrinsic nature, no more than devices to cleanse away delusion. To the Hindu, the Atman, the ideal individual self, unifies with the Brahman – ultimate reality. To Buddhists all creation is one universal beginningless mind, encompassing and putting in perspective the illusory nature of all relative experience.

Astrological archetypes fulfil a similar intermediary function and systematise practice that uses the benefits of the idealised deities described above. Each individual birth chart describes the predicaments that confront the incarnating individual. Its progression and transit connections reveal moments of challenge and potential transformation. Knowing this, an expert spiritual friend can suggest which deity and practice of that deity could illuminate and purify the individual mind and liberate true understanding of ultimate reality. If a lack of feeling and sympathy (e.g. maybe the astrological chart shows a potential for selfishness and intolerance) for others is causing patterns of suffering, then internalising the vision and qualities of Chenrezig may help. If communication and understanding are afflicted (e.g. Mercury afflicted, or badly placed), then Manjushri may be suggested. There are scores of other possibilities.

Buddhism and Hinduism come to the same essential conclusion as the monotheistic religions, developed from the Middle East. There is only one truth and pure living and care for others is the way to the permanent happiness of that truth. Whether the way to achieve that happiness is focused on the all-encompassing ideal of the Lord God, the one God, God the Father, or via an idealised intermediary 'deity' that brings us to ideal understanding, the aim of purification and union with one God, or universal mind, is the same.

Middle Eastern originating religions appear to focus and discipline religious practice along what some may consider more narrow lines. They seem to have a more protective approach with regard to their followers. God and his prophets have laid down ideal forms of behaviour that must be followed to be at one with the one God. Because of this, their priests may consider the use of astrology as a dysfunctional distraction that puffs up self-importance and so blocks the path to redemption. Yet all of these religions have a mystical, hidden tradition that knows of and uses such knowledge. Many of the concepts of astrology we use today came from Arab scholars. Indeed, without their scholarship, much ancient astrological understanding would have been lost. Jewish mysticism includes study of the Cabbala and the astrological archetype keys to the Tree of Life. For a wide range of spiritual people, the six-pointed Star of David is a symbol that describes on the one hand the interaction of humanity's aspiration to heavenly understanding; and on the other hand divine purity coming to humanity on earth. Both Islam and Judaism base their festivals on the lunar calendar. Traditionally, the Muslim month of Ramadan commences and ends when the Mullah can see the first crescent of the New Moon in the evening sky.

As described in earlier chapters, the Christian Church's relationship with astrology has been substantially defensive and suspicious. St Augustine's 5th century rejection of astrology is based on such a simplistic misrepresentation of what the knowledge is saying that it has been suggested the comments were inserted at a later date. He argues[45] that it must be false, because a rich and poor child can be born at the same time and place. Then he goes deeper, citing the biblical twins Esau and Jacob, who were born so close to each other that one left the womb holding the heel of the other. In maternal relationships and social achievements through life, their experience could hardly be more different. So how can astrology work? One obvious explanation could be that the first twin was born not holding a heel, but with his heel held!

The 13th century theologian, Thomas Aquinas, deepened understanding, when he acknowledged that the planets exert an influence on the physical world but not on the human soul. If astrologers look for the timing of crucial decisions and turning points in each twin's life and the intrinsic nature of their decisions then; we may find both men subjected to similar pressures and reacting in the same archetypal manner. If both had understood their astrology and been able to objectify their relative earthly situation, both and not just one may have overcome the barriers to spiritual progress. Not only the archetypal, but the actual outcome of their lives may have been closer.

In addition, astrologers would suggest it is more than a coincidence that so much of the main narrative of the Holy Bible is based on astrological symbolism. As Milton describes so graphically in *Paradise Lost*, the scales of justice by which the Lord God judges and casts the recalcitrant Satan down to hell are the sign of Libra.[46] Following on from this, it is easy to seek other connections between astrological archetypes and the key biblical themes. The temptation of humanity by the serpent in the Garden of Eden that opens Eve and then Adam to the irresistible touch of sexuality is one of the essential meanings of Scorpio. Rising up from the mire of self-indulgence to the clarity of heavenly light is the ideal purpose of Scorpio's regenerative power. Redemption from negative entrapment to this regeneration is found by following the word of God and through the intercession of his Son. The promise of this Son of God, a Messiah, and a heavenly king is the symbolism of Leo. Jesus was born of a virgin – Virgo, the sign next to Leo. At his crucifixion, Christ took on the suffering and died on the cross for all beings – Pisces, the sign of the fishes, which was the symbol of the early Christian Church. He was born again and became the Lamb of God – Aries.

Christian festivals follow the astrological calendar. Easter Sunday is determined by finding the first Sunday, after the first Full Moon following the Vernal Equinox (20th or 21st March) when the Sun enters Aries tropically. So the crucifixion and resurrection of Jesus is based upon the time that the Sun moves from Pisces to Aries. Whit Sunday occurs fifty days after Easter. It symbolises the descent of the Holy Ghost, which brings God's message to earth – Gemini. We celebrate Christ's birth at Christmas, four days after the Winter Solstice, the shortest day of the year, because the Sun's descent from the northern hemisphere ends. The 25th December is when the return of the light can begin to be experienced. 'I am the light of the world,' [John 8:12]. The Wise Men were astrologers for a reason – and astrology has a structurally important role to play in Christian understanding and practice.

Religious fanaticism as the root cause of many violent conflicts
Many people have noted the connections both today and throughout history. When considered superficially, they do seem to be explicable in

this way. A closer examination shows it is not the clashing of the essential messages of particular religions that causes conflict, but the institutionalisation of over-simplified interpretations of the messages into movements and churches. Mundane minds impose mundane literalism upon teachings that were intended by the founder and prophets of the religion to be symbolic.

Most spiritual masters correctly advise disciples to focus on a clear path to spiritual understanding and to avoid eclecticism. If you are to find ultimate understanding and fully benefit from Islam, there can only be one god and Mohammed *is* his prophet. Christians *can only* enter heaven through the intercession of Jesus Christ. If you accept a Hindu or Buddhist master as your 'root guru' then *only through focusing on him* will you avert distraction and confusion. Whatever your religion, such advice is correct and essential, but this does not mean that every single incarnated being has to follow the same spiritual path. Thinking in this way sparks lethal religious intolerance.

This is an essential error and not real spirituality at all. It is 'spiritual materialism'[47] – a state of mind where we become attached to beliefs, rather as we become attached to our material possessions or pleasant sensations in everyday life. Followers are so overwhelmed and transformed by ecstatic experience, inclusiveness and purpose that they naturally wish everyone they meet to share it with them. At first the motivation for such attitudes is a kind, generous wish that everyone should be as happy as they are. However, when faced with a negative response, the frustration of such disciples can easily degenerate into seeing non-believers as the root cause of all problems in the world. Non-believers then become the evil to be eradicated so that all 'true believers' can be saved and 'God's will' triumph.

The institutionalisation of religions into rich, self-protecting church bureaucracies means there are millions of followers who can be formed into political or even military movements to fulfil the opinions and special interests of the priests that control them. The role of the papacy in the medieval politics and the Florentine Medici family in the 15th century, the ravaging by European powers of the wealth of South America, indeed most European colonialism, was justified by the notion of the 'superiority' of the Christian word of God. The spread of Islam into Europe, the consequent Christian Crusades and more recent Christian and Jewish intervention in the Middle East remain at the heart of world conflict today. Many attitudes on all sides are so fixed because their heart spirituality has been corrupted and calcified into spiritual materialism.

Such misrepresentations and misunderstandings are profoundly and ironically tragic. For the truly wise and profound mystics and teachers in every religion are enlightened visionaries. They speak the same essential truth and suggest similar good deeds towards that truth. Their styles and cultural methods may be different, but the intention and vision in the end comes to the same place. It must do, or it would not be really true. Different individuals and groups start their spiritual journey from different places. So, each requires different techniques. While those of similar dispositions may work in harmony towards a generally similar spiritual goal, to leap from such common worship to fanaticism and violent condemnation of others is not spiritual at all. It is no more than mundane greed, ignorance and hatred: a false 'spiritual materialism' that turns the vision of heaven into an experience of hell.

In today's global village, such mindsets threaten the very existence of civilisation on the planet. Whereas in the past religious fanaticism led to localised conflicts and at worst temporary destruction to particular areas; today's communications spread such conflicts with breathtaking speed to all areas of the world. We desperately need the means to study, understand and respect each other's behaviour. We need to do this in a culture-free way that cuts through the distortions that can emanate from institutionalised and hence materialised religion.

The brutal climate of accusation and blame and especially guilt make the task of working together really difficult. Each belief system, be it a traditional religion, Christian, Islamic, Jewish, Hindu, atheist fundamentalism, mechanistic materialism, capitalism, various cults of the 'individual', 'democracy', the 'American way', or victory in the 'war against terror' that seeks to apportion blame, judge and punish from its own perspective alone, is responsible for the angst and anxiety that is terrifying our 21st century world. Apportioning blame, allocating *guilt* is the central problem.

For in declaring guilt, we point the finger towards the outsider we do not understand and avoid facing up to our own inner responsibilities. We also help to cause the suffering being experienced on all sides. When we identify and seek to punish others as guilty and see ourselves as whiter than white, we are merely projecting our own inner sense of guilt on to strangers and outsiders. Consequently, we give ourselves the impossible predicament of catching and punishing the entire world. It is far more comfortable, safer and likely to be much more fruitful to interact with others and take joint karmic responsibility. By the law of karma each person is responsible for their own side of the problem – we have all got into it together. This lets no one 'off the hook'. Certainly some are still more responsible than others. Some will have to experience far more difficult consequences, but this is not a matter of condemnation and blame. Rather, we should seek to understand, give support and start reconciliation.

Condemnatory finger-pointing of guilt creates desperate negativity that sours redemption. It produces nothing that is positive, because it is based on separation and superiority. By contrast, if we allow astrological concepts and cycles to describe the true nature of each person and the true benefits and difficulties they face, we can understand exactly how we are working on our karmic challenges together. We will have to pace ourselves. We may have to side-step many problems, but we are far less likely to make matters worse.

When religions denigrate and exclude astrology from their world picture, they cast a black shadow of ignorance that prevents us knowing the essential inter-related building blocks of creation. Ironically, astrology, which is a lower form of understanding than the ultimate truth of any of the great world religions, is the very vital tool needed to help cut through the spiritually materialistic distortions of mass movements.

Astrology focuses and clarifies individual predicaments.
Properly used, it can explain the nature and development our mundane experiences. It can reveal what is left to work on. Armed with this understanding, we are ready to find and follow our right spiritual path with our eyes open; and to tolerate those on other paths. Because we are developing understanding of the one universe, in which we all live, we do not feel threatened – rather we rejoice in the wide range of rich understandings. We realise in that in no way is God cruel or unjust and we find a way of being at one in this best and only universe.

Further Reading

Zev Ben Shimon Haalevi *Astrology and Kabbalah*
Greg Bogart *Astrology and Spiritual Awakening*
Roy Gillett *The Essence of Buddhism*
Goswami Kriyananda *Wisdom and Way of Astrology*
Robert Powell *Christian Hermetic Astrology*
Courtney Roberts *The Star of the Magi*
Rev. Dr. Gordon Strachan *Christ and the Cosmos*
Richard Tarnas *The Passion of the Western Mind*

Chapter 9
Astrology & Philosophy

Do not seek to follow in the footsteps of the
masters; seek what they sought.
Zen Saying

The sensational development of mechanical expertise in recent centuries
has created an assumption in the popular mind that human progress is
linear. When we compare the machines and explanations of the 17th
century to those of today, we see what seems like ever-advancing
development. Yet, if we look at the history of ideas more deeply and
widely, the foundation of our modern society is not just an end process of
natural evolution, but rather the product of particular, impermanent
thought forms that for the moment dominate how we perform and judge
our activities.[48]

As we shall see in next two chapters, advanced modern theories of
physics fundamentally modify the rigidity of Newtonian mechanics. Nor
is the mechanistic linear paradigm new and unique to our 'enlightened
times'? Archaeology describes many ancient cultures with a considerable
grasp of the mechanics needed to construct major buildings and to
explore, conquer and 'civilise'. Advanced Babylonian, Persian, Egyptian,
Chinese and Indian civilisations all flourished many years before the
birth of Christ. Their constructions may have lasted far longer than will
those we build today.

A linear view based on its development and pre-eminence was the
egocentric centre of the Roman state. However, unlike today, an
understanding of how heavenly cycles reflected life on earth that had
been inherited from the Egyptians and Greeks was allowed, if it
supported imperial aspirations. Then in the Empire's declining years it
turned to a view of Christianity that persecuted, repressed and so nearly
destroyed cyclic paradigms like astrology that they were all but lost in
the Dark Ages that followed. In the 4th century AD, Emperor
Constantine's early dictates started the process by
institutionalising the Christian message into a state religion. This
narrowed the range of accepted knowledge and outlawed much ancient
wisdom; even some Christian practices. A Christian Church with very
limited parameters developed out of the Dark Ages into the early

medieval period. It was hierarchical, didactic and claimed a monopoly of knowledge. Followers were required to rely on faith and the interpretations of the priests, rather than empirical observation.

The rediscovery of Ancient Greek and Roman philosophical, political, cultural and scientific ideas in the 13th and 14th centuries seeded a process that led to the Reformation's questioning and the consequent fragmentation of Christendom. Without one source of Truth, the door was open to empirical enquiry and philosophical questioning. From the time of the Enlightenment and scientific revolution of the late 17th century; there developed a struggle between the literal interpretation of world history, as determined from the Bible, and the findings of material science. This continued well into the 19th century. As recently as 1828, Champolian, the pioneering French student of Egyptian Hieroglyphics, had to promise not to discover anything that contradicted biblical history, before he could receive funding for his research in Egypt. Darwin's evolutionary theories in his *Origin of Species* were a source of bitter controversy that continues to attract the counter-argument of the 'theory of intelligent design' from today's Christian fundamentalists.

In the first half of the 17th century, Descartes made major advances in the new human-centred world picture by applying logic to human existence. Starting from scratch, he argued it was necessary to question everything and, when he did, everything except his existence was called into question – 'I think, therefore I am'. From this seed point, all knowledge must be reconstructed in a way that does not allow doubt. He concluded that the mind is separate from the body, the existence of God and the existence and nature of the material world. Because of this a mathematically based scientific knowledge of the material world is possible. Such a view was to spawn a movement that has become known as the Enlightenment. Upon its ideas and consequences our modern society is based.

Although in the 21st century the achievements and benefits of the Enlightenment are now seen and measured in terms of the rational and material; the endeavours of its early pioneers were as much a quest to advance understanding of ethics as mechanics. If discoveries were questioning blind faith in Church teachings, then what was the intrinsic nature of humanity and its governing institutions? What should be the moral basis of our relationships with each other? John Locke held reason, rather than accepting the opinion of authorities, to be the key to deciding the legitimate from the illegitimate functions of institutions. Reason could optimize human flourishing for the individual and society in respect to both their material and spiritual welfare. By following natural law, we fulfil humanity's divine purpose.

The French philosopher, Rousseau, was less trusting. He came to the conclusion that only through a 'Social Contract' in a just society could humanity's 'brutish' nature be tamed. The goal of government should be to secure freedom, equality, and justice for all within the state, regardless of the will of the majority. Voltaire exposed and crusaded against tyranny and bigotry. Tom Paine's pamphlet *Common Sense* was a key influence in establishing American independence and the US Constitution, whose principles remain at the heart of political idealism to this day.

Immanuel Kant argued that both the laws of nature and laws of morality are grounded in human reason itself. The rules and structures of mechanical science are valid and effective because they are based on pure intellect. They are a projection of the structure of that part of the human mind. There is another part of the mind that experiences pure sensation, which can never be subject to the rules of mechanical science. With this understanding of mind, he went on to assert, as Richard Tarnas so succinctly puts it:

> The world exists only to the extent that man participates in its construction. We can know things only relative to ourselves...the mind never experiences what is "out there"...reality for man is necessarily of his own making, and the world in itself must remain something one can only think about, never know.[49]

As we shall see (and dispute!) in the next chapter some 21st century scientists may insist that modern discoveries show that even what Kant felt to be mental sensations and morality can be described by mechanical reason. Whether this is so makes little difference to the essential error in Kant's analysis. While it is brilliantly close to the way things are, it misses a key paradox. The universe we see may be dependent upon the structure of our intellect and our sensations, but we do not create something out of an empty void. Such a nihilistic view cannot be correct. If it were, how could our minds ever have been created? If there is nothing, how can we exist as something, with minds to consider, devise and create so much more than ourselves?

When we try to impose our minds on the universe, anything that falls short and is ignorant in our actions is thrown back upon us for correction. It is by improving and trying again that discovery and invention progresses. Kant's philosophy suffers, because it lacks the concepts of karma, emptiness and compassion. Everything we think, see and do with attachment is a product of a mind that sees cause and effect selfishly. Because such a view is always partially true and dependent upon planetary cycles, what is seen and happens will have consequences along predictable lines. Hence the structure of the mind's intellect, sensation and morality that Kant describes. If the mind broadens beyond a narrow view of self, it will discover methods of sympathetically understanding from ever more possible planetary-indicated perspectives. With this comes greater wisdom that appears to give greater control to choose from a variety of outcomes. However, ultimately, control is irrelevant. For nothing is left but that mind seeing all actions, causes and consequences; all there is to see. This wisdom beyond the illusions of nihilism and eternalism is what the Buddhists call 'the end point of nirvana'[50].

To see compassion and wisdom hand-in-hand melting into a point beyond separate self makes immorality impossible and the quest to explain phenomena by means of mechanical discovery unnecessary – for all is seen and known. To the Buddhist this is the essential nature of mind. From such a perspective, Kant's view of mind is a brilliant analysis of delusion.

In his *Critique of Pure Reason*, Kant stated:

> Philosophy is not some sort of science of representations, concepts, and ideas, or a science of all sciences, or anything else of this sort; rather, it is a science of the human being, of its representing, thinking, and acting – it should present the human being in all of its components, as it is and ought to be, that is, in accordance with its natural determinations as well as its relationship of morality and freedom. Ancient philosophy adopted an entirely inappropriate standpoint towards the human being in the world, for it made it into a machine in it, which as such had to be entirely dependent on the world or on external things and circumstances; it thus made the human being into an all but merely passive part of the world. Now

the critique of reason has appeared and determined the human being to a thoroughly *active* place in the world. The human being itself is the original creator of all its representations and concepts and ought to be the sole author of all its actions. (7: 69-70)

The first error in this key statement from Kant is his assumption that the classical view considers human nature to be mechanical. That humanity is subject to pressures of the 'Gods' (or cycles of the planets) is both limiting *and* liberating. By being attached to where we are, we take on all the opportunities and limitations that are relative to where we are. This is what the enlightened mind would consider the Greeks to mean. Our birth karma causes our minds to be born at a time, date and place and so subject to the cycles of the universe and especially our solar system. This is no more limiting and no less liberating than being a certain height, build, race or socio-economical class. No one would deny such factors make a difference. Yet hardly anyone would claim that circumstances of birth or culture make us machine-like and trapped forever. Kant's second error is to ride roughshod over paradox and make claims that the mind is absolute and its structure inescapable. He chains the power of choice to the deluded perspective of each individual human being. As well as trapping our individual existence and circumstances in hopelessness, such a view dangerously obscures the true nature of morality and values. Without them how can society be fair, pleasant and bearable to live in and, if it is not, how can there be genuine origination and power for its individuals?

Political and social institutions have struggled with such principles throughout the 19th and 20th centuries until today. The ability to find reliable working models of social justice has been problematic – far more so than the ability of mechanical scientists to discover new ways to harness world resources and serve our desires. The root problem lies in the inability of Enlightenment philosophers to find a common understanding of the nature of humanity and to determine the individual's rights within society.

John Stuart Mill argued that the universality of the law of causation is an induction from our experience and does not extend to 'circumstances unknown to us, and beyond the possible range of our experience'. If he is right, scientific method is based on no more than the underlying assumptions of a particular area of study. If this is so, then knowledge acquired through scientific enquiry is by definition piecemeal. As such, it is most unlikely to be reliable as an absolute foundation for social decisions. That our contemporary governments and media appear unable to grasp this is a source of endless popular confusion and misunderstanding. Mill argued that actions are right in the proportion to which they tend to promote happiness, wrong as they tend to produce the reverse of happiness. Yet he saw problems in this. Circumstances may lead to individuals and groups seeing happiness as emanating from contradictory actions. Famously, he cited the moral principle of charity dictating that 'I should feed a starving neighbour' and the moral principle of self-preservation dictating that 'I should feed myself'. If I do not have enough food to do both, then I should determine whether feeding my neighbour, or feeding myself would better serve general happiness. Clearly Mill, as we do today, needed to find a way of defining happiness in an absolute, rather than a relative, sense. This task is impossible when the environment of the analysis is no more than a bundle of mechanical relationships, drawn from fragmentary mechanical studies and subject areas, selected on the basis of no more than the anarchy of individual and group emotions to be found in academic bureaucracies.

Nietzsche radically rejected past philosophies and cut through much adolescent and arrogant optimism in the Enlightenment thought. So, he prepared the ground for our understanding the predicament of living in the fragmentary uncertainty of the 20th century. Less than four years before Neptune and Pluto conjuncted in mutably intellectual Gemini to mark the beginning of a new 500-year cycle between the two planets, his *The Will to Power, Book I*, described three steps by which 'nihilism as a psychological state' would be reached by the ordinary person. At the same time, in *The Gay Science,* he described what he called 'eternal recurrence' – the view that time runs its course and then repeats exactly and infinitely. The absurdities and pains of life must be endured not only once, but repeatedly and forever. Nietzsche imagines that the nihilist would find this thought torturous, but for one who has learned to be a 'Yes-sayer', it should be bliss. From this position, Nietzsche considered the role of the 'Overman'. This ideal and advanced individual can overcome the forces working against him and transcend the mentality of what Nietzsche called the 'herd instinct' or 'slave morality' and create personal values without the influence of social norms.

While feeling a little uncomfortable with the way the German words translate into English, many astrologers would celebrate Nietzsche's philosophical restoration of the cyclic nature of phenomena. They would also confirm the enhanced state of mind of people who understand this. Meditators and mystics may wish he had realised that such understanding demands gratitude, humility and seeing service to others as a privilege.

Unfortunately, his conceptual insight of the Overman was simplified and not developed. Later it was grossly misrepresented by Nazi Germany. That this could happen stems from an essential error at this stage of his analysis, which may also explain why Nietzsche was reduced to insanity in the last years of his life. He failed to look for a deeper morality of compassion as the basic *raison d' être* for a community of *Overmen*. He did not consider that this community could find purpose by serving the consciousness of those in society who had not reached its level.

Existentialism holds that human beings can be understood only from the inside, in terms of their lived and experienced reality and dilemmas (anxiety, dread, freedom, awareness of death); not from the outside, in terms of a biological, psychological or other scientific theory of human nature. Human beings are subjected to an indifferent, objective, often ambiguous and 'absurd' universe without natural order that they create temporarily by their actions and interpretations. Confronted in the modern world by the increasing dominance of mechanistic discovery and its attempts to map and dominate our inner lives, are there still important 'places' that the mechanical (the only real 'reality') cannot reach?

It is not surprising that people were attracted to such paradoxical and apparently unanswerable dualism. Existentialist philosophy became the 'grown up' way to view the reality-without-hope of the 20th century. Indeed, such a 'grown up' view of 'truth' fitted both conveniently and tragically alongside the massive expansion of materialism of the time. Existentialism may be correct in claiming the centre ground for individual experience of life, with its impermanence and difficulty in finding inherent truth. Yet in doing so, it consigned to impotence individual ability to see through, influence and change the delusions of the world. Living for the day, without hope, or meaning became the only 'way of the wise'!

By contrast, the 20th century work of Bertrand Russell and others on Logical Positivism sought a precision of philosophical language that would do no less than establish a non-contradictory language of analysis and bring irrefutable clarity to meaning. They sought a way for values and the individual driving forces behind decision to be as disciplined by language, as were the realities of mechanical engineering. Ironically, Wittgenstein, who Russell encouraged as a protégé, came to the conclusion in his later work *Philosophical Investigations* that the root problem lay in the philosopher's misuse of language! The irony is compounded by the fact that students of Wittgenstein continue to find it difficult to achieve consensus when interpreting his work!

Our root problem today lies in the Enlightenment philosophers' misunderstanding of the intrinsic nature of the human being and the essential driving force behind nature itself. Their theses are contradictory and essentially without hope. If, as Rousseau suggested, man is at heart brutal and needs a contract with society to behave with decency towards his fellows, then from where will he find decent individuals to draw up such a contract? If, as Locke suggested, it is the institutions that need to be tamed, from where do individuals draw the power to do so? And can both be correct?

Certainly, when we consider their ideas in the context of their time, then society has been considerably improved by attempts to implement them. In a modern democracy, for all its shortcomings, ordinary people have more power and live safer and more comfortable lives. Yet problems caused by human greed threaten the very existence of our planet as we know it. The amorality of modern society has created an educational system that lacks, almost fears, common moral values. More and more people are turning to fundamentalist religious solutions, based on beliefs that pre-date the philosophers of the Enlightenment by more than a millennium. To control the people, governments are pouring vast resources into modern technologies that will track, trace and identify more and more information about every individual. If Locke is right about the nature of institutions and authority, we are in serious trouble!

We honour these great thinkers when we see their work in its historical context. Their achievement was to identify root ideas as an antidote to the outdated authoritarian attitudes that had oppressed and emasculated the populace and encouraged divisive religious wars. Their failure was to deny ancient wisdom's potential to give insight into the nature of individuals and the universe they lived in. In seeking to correct the ignorance and brutality the past had brought to their times, they rejected too much. So they left the human soul in ethical anarchy and society at the mercy of ingenious machines. As mentioned earlier, they threw out the baby with the bathwater!

This essential 'baby' was obvious – astrological understanding of the cyclic nature of the universe and our solar system – the cycles of the very earth upon which we depend for our existence. Its rejection haunts us today. Seventeenth century academicians dismissed an art and science that had been struggling to be heard against ecclesiastical fear and prejudice for thirteen centuries. They replaced it with embryonic, complex and contradictory philosophical models that could never be more than 'second fiddle' apologetic justifications for the social consequences of material science. In doing so, they 'cleared the decks' for a brilliantly executed, but fundamentally fatal, rape of the material resources of the planet. The ecological challenges and cultural conflicts we face today are a direct consequence of this philosophical error.

We have now reached a stage in history even more dangerous and schismatic than the 17th century. For now we have the power to destroy not just each other and our society, but the planet itself. Our economy may be intended to give opportunity and ever-expanding prosperity to all, but can we sustain such an aspiration? Is it not an illusion? Is not economic expansion dependent upon ensuring the less fortunate do without to provide for the more fortunate? Even for those who have them do not material goods that constantly fail to create happiness? Worst of all, the principles by which we seek to control our societies are relative and difficult to define. Everyone seeks love, but which of its meanings do we seek? How can we fight for freedom without enslaving the freedom of others? What experiences bring happiness that lasts?

The heart problem in the philosophy of the past four hundred years has been two-fold. Seduced by the material discoveries of the time, it has been ever-eager to reject the mystical and metaphysical, because they will not submit to the same rationality as the observed mechanical universe. Because science can show that the Earth was not created in 4004 BC, does not mean that the archetypal biblical story does not have profound relevance to eternal happiness through pure moral behaviour. In the same way, the teachings of the great world religions can touch, cleanse and clarify individual understanding and answer the predicament of existential alienation. Whether or not Christ literally died on the Cross and was the only 'Son of God', his image of such sympathy for all humanity can be a key to decency in all times, whatever the culture.

Christ's willingness to pay the ultimate price describes how caring beyond self-interest for the truth of the universe and benefit of others is the key to eternal happiness. Mahayana Buddhism trains the mind to see beyond contradictory relative illusory 'truths' to focus upon two key notions – the unity of the ultimate emptiness of all relative phenomena with compassion for all existence. HH the Dalai Lama of Tibet puts it with incisive simplicity: 'If you are looking for self-interest, then care for others. This is enlightened self-interest'. Harming others only brings the likelihood of their harming you.

For indeed, the vengeful mind lives in the fear of vengeance, the hunter lives in fear of being hunted. We are all together in our search for happiness. In seeking to make others happy we train our minds to be constantly happy – an answer to John Stuart Mill's predicament. Such states of mind are not easy to sustain in a world where mechanical devices promise immediate sensual satisfaction. It is far easier to see others as denying what is 'rightfully ours' and the solution to be the eradication of those 'others'. The Islamic teachings of seeing criticism as genuine friendship, giving hospitality to strangers, observing the privacy of sexual intimacy and regular prayer to focus our ultimate divinity; may seem to some as judgemental and 'spoiling the fun' of everyday existence. To those who live that way, it is the *laissez-faire* self-indulgence that dominates our modern world that is the source of a 'hell on earth'. We resolve such conflicts by stepping back from absolute judgement. By seeing through the eyes of others and seeking to help in appropriately acceptable ways. So, everyone moves towards happiness that lasts.

Pure minds and pure actions are possible

With patience and humility, we can start to accept how our own past imperfections have been the cause of our present difficulties. This is the heart message of all major religions and the answer to the philosophical uncertainty of the modern world. Such a view needs to be placed at the pinnacle of our society, without fear or favour even to that we hold most dear. Instead of a few special people or ideas, we prize all existence. Seeing like this will make our material discoveries far less important. It does not deny or take them away; rather, it puts them in perspective.

What we know becomes clearer and more accurate. We restore a holistic balance to our understanding of ourselves in the universe.

The 21st century (as was the 17th) is ready for a radical new thought form – a paradigm that answers our present predicaments. Fortunately, we have much more knowledge and far more ways to discover and exchange ideas than in those earlier centuries. Astrologers would suggest that there is every chance we can discover/rediscover and implement a philosophical foundation that explains and regulates our lives, while retaining the many benefits we enjoy. Indeed, it is the very discoveries of the modern world that enable us to identify and implement the 'mechanics' of morality in a far more detailed and systematic way than has ever been possible before. When to 'be good' it was necessary to follow blindly a religious teaching and rely on priests for its interpretation; the impotency of the people and corruptibility of the institution left everyone vulnerable to exploitation. Today, by using computers with astrology, anyone who wishes can map the behaviour and motivations of the human being – body and soul.

Let us be clear, astrology cannot determine and direct human spirituality and behaviour – to do so would be 'the work of the devil'– but it can describe it. With his eyes so opened to people and situations as they are, the individual will still need an ethical spiritual technique to strengthen and direct his resolve. With both, behaviour can be transformed into actions that spread happiness. Knowing more clearly the nature of others and the institutions they take refuge in, we can be clear and patient with any difficulties on the way. Astrology provides the insight to understand and honour, not feel threatened by differences. When we look through the eyes of astrology, we see a just, understandable and almost inevitable reason for all the relative behaviour it describes.

By opening the doors to clarity, we clear away any reason to fear and develop an antidote to our suffering. If we look deeply with astrology's divine logic, we will understand ourselves as well as the mechanics of the mundane world far better. We will see in detail all the attachments of our relative minds and realise they are the source of confusion and suffering.

By looking like this, we grow to realise we are all one universe that is the same within and without. Like William Blake, whose imagination lived in, saw through and saw beyond the so-called Enlightenment, we may develop a realisation of what that word really means.

Further Reading

Richard Tarnas *The Passion of the Western Mind*

The following two books offer an understanding of the concept of enlightenment from a classical Mediterranean perspective.
Trans. Titus Burckhaardt *Mystical Astrology According to Ibn Arabi*
William Bodri *Socrates and the Enlightenment Path.*

There are many books and teachings that explain the Eastern view. A very simple introduction to the background of such teachings is available in Roy Gillett *The Essence of Buddhism.*

Chapter 10

Astrology, Scientific Method & Genetics

> Hurrah for positive science! Long live exact demonstration! Gentlemen, I receive you, and attach and clasp hands with you. Your facts are useful and real.
>
> **Walt Whitman**

As recently as 1855, with the above words, this great American was one of the first of the romantic poets to celebrate material science, when it was struggling for proper recognition in an academia then dominated by the classics. Now in the 21st century, material science has moved from outsider to being considered by many as the only permitted insider. Yet, in terms of all the knowledge that has been discovered, compared and shared over the billions of years about the existence of Earth and the thousands of years of recorded human history, modern material science could be no more than a phase, even a fashion – certainly not 'absolute truth'.

So it is important to put the natural sciences in perspective and consider not only what and who we value, but *how* we measure the values themselves. Governments, medicine, industry and the general public seem to depend upon on statistical studies as the 'be all and end all of truth'. Does this fundamentally limit and even threaten the freedom and health of humanity in the 21st century? To what extent should we allow it to determine how we live our lives?

The Scientific Method
In spite of the many philosophical developments over two thousand years and more, Aristotle's Four Causes still play an important role at the conceptual heart of Western rationality and science. Yet, has our contemporary culture an unbalanced, partial understanding of the causes – does it understand their implications fully?

By the first, the Material Cause, we seek to understand what something is made of; things happen, because of the nature of their material constituents. The second, the Formal Cause, looks deeper into the essential pattern that makes the cause behave as it does. The third, the Efficient Cause, considers what has made something come to be what it is. The fourth, the Final Cause, explains what it is trying to be.

To Aristotle, the Final Cause was the crucial heart end of a teleological process that explained ends, purposes and goals. The modern scientific method tends to focus more on the first three. So, we discover how things work but live in an anarchy of Final Cause outcomes that we have no means to contain and control.

Of course, Aristotle's philosophy sought to explain more than the mechanical. His interest was as much in the processes of poetics, ethics, metaphysics, politics and dreams, as in physics, mathematics, anatomy and physiology. He saw the notion of *service* as the essential way to discipline the less clearly linear first group. Modern mechanical science sees its discoveries as a service to society in a general sense, but does not have the tools to assess the benefits of such service. It leaves it to political and market forces to control and contain them.

So as we found in the previous chapter, today we see 'reality' in a very material and functional way. What is '*really* real' is decided by a method of scientific enquiry that isolates and tests each element of knowledge, then builds up and adjusts the 'edifice of reality' accordingly. Theses are clearly defined and stated, a set of test conditions are laid down. Then an experiment takes place, is checked, replicated and discussed. If all works as expected and continues to do so, within its clearly defined variables, then this becomes fact. Upon such 'facts' it is considered proper to decide government and commercial policy and form the 'expert' advice behind legal decisions. Provided that a person works within such 'properly established' knowledge parameters then their actions are acceptable. This is seen as essential 'protection' for professionals working in our 'health and safety' obsessed modern culture.

Anyone seeking to challenge such 'properly established' knowledge needs to go through a rigorous process of definition and testing, which requires proper funding. Modern-day scientific research requires expensive machinery, buildings and staff. In today's world, terrorism and commercial profit dominate political and business decisions. So, it is difficult to find funding, unless what is planned has a clear chance of bringing defence, commercial or medical benefits. As a result the public view of standing and status as a scientist is mainly measured in these fields and by the methods that adjudicate them.

Such a system is not only self-confirming, self-fulfilling and, hence, self-perpetuating, but it is also highly exclusive and protective of its privileged positions. Remedies and processes that have been used for centuries may be banned in the light of recent research. If they are effective, attempts to patent and profit from them may be made. It is argued that this is just common sense. We are using the advances in modern science to assess and improve methods from less enlightened times. After all, leeches are no longer the panacea to all ailments. We do not operate in an unhygienic environment without anaesthetic. 'Look at the advances we have made over the past 100 years, as a result of this rational, sequential approach to the discovery and application of so many wonderful cures,' is a statement that it is difficult to argue against.

There is no doubt that the modern world is cleaner, faster and full of powerful methods to change circumstances. The discipline and incredible skill shown by the 'scientific method' is the reason for this. Our ability to heal injury and sickness and to control the spread of many diseases is remarkable. We travel and communicate at enormous speed over great distances.

We know more about the world than at any other time in history, but this does not mean that we know everything. Nor does it mean our prized contemporary 'scientific method' does, or ever could, answer all the needs and explain all the phenomena in our contemporary, or any other, world. It has considerable shortcomings, which we ignore at our peril.

Firstly, although the actual experimental process of thesis, carrying out the experiment, analysing and reporting the results may be perfectly performed, who decides which experiments should be studied? As well as the danger of commercial interests distorting the funding, the interest (even prejudice) of the researcher can decide which experiment will be chosen. For decades, the tobacco industry focused research one way, its opponents the other. When researching the psychological and social effects of the recreational use of illegal drugs, we may ignore the influence of the legal environment. Would we suggest that alcohol use leads to the gun battle slaughter of the Prohibition years? In a way it did but, paradoxically, making alcohol legal prevented the killings. Does applying conventional allopathic research methods properly test the subtleties of naturopathic medicines? Who asks and phrases what questions? Can a researcher's opinion about his study be entirely factored out? Can we be sure that the scientific method is applied rigorously at every stage: deciding to study, early design and during the experiment itself? If not, we may be getting perfectly accurate results that are irrelevant or prove something very different than seemed at first.

Secondly, the simplistic and authoritative way in which such discoveries are presented to the public can imply claims far beyond those intended by the researcher. We are told that 'scientists have discovered' this or that, when they have only come up with a possible statistical connection. Whether and how a finding is announced can depend upon the interest (commercial or otherwise), friendship patterns and even prejudice of the editor or proprietor of the media outlet.

What is 'true' may be only one experiment away from changing. Yet it will remain true until that next experiment is done. The BSE crisis showed the tragic helplessness of this way of using the scientific method. Cattle were fed the food that created the problem. The population were urged by the government to 'eat their meat' for years, because it 'could not be proved scientifically' that this was harmful. When our worst suspicions were finally confirmed by research, public confidence in government scientists was undermined for some time into the future. As a result, the public ignored more useful and valid future scientific advice.

Thirdly, there can be problems with the statistical method used for assessment. It is an ironic paradox that Mark Twain's statement 'there are lies, damn lies and statistics'[51] is so often quoted by the popular media, government and industry, yet they still abrogate authority to a science that is based on these very statistics. Of course, the problem is not the statistics themselves but the lack of controls over the people who use them. We have already seen that certain ways of selecting the studies undertaken and phrasing the questions can critically determine the result. Sampling number requirements, probability quotients, margin of error adjustments and final number reports may be correct in themselves but can be presented in misleading ways. The axis one selects for a graph, or the time period, can give such an incorrect impression that the report is little more than prostitution of statistical methods. Unless recipients of research findings have the means and understanding to assess them, they cannot judge them. They cannot know whether researchers have tampered with their samples and final reports, or even suppressed perfectly accurate results for financial or political reasons.

Fourthly, in spite of these three limitations that genuine researchers would acknowledge as valid; we still place almost total reliance on the pronouncements of 'scientific research'. The material mindset so dominates such research that academic activities not following the narrow 'scientific method' are at best seen as rather quaint and childlike – at worst downright dangerous and 'ought to be banned'. The never-ending quest to discover and refine the 'nuts and bolts' of the universe can become the 'sacred cow' that dominates not only what we can do, but also what we are allowed to believe. It tells how we are allowed to live our lives.

Such an attitude places outside conventional scientific study the experiences and activities that a majority of people feel are what make us human. 'You are just being emotional.' 'Your observation is anecdotal.' Of course both criticisms may be valid, but it can be very dangerous to dismiss intuitive insight out of hand. To return to the BSE catastrophe: in the 1980s it seemed simple commonsense that giving ground-sheep meal to grass-eating cows might be harmful, but there was no scientific proof that it was. It was also commercially expedient to rely upon the practice not being 'scientifically proven' to be harmful. By the time research had proved that commonsense was correct, it had cost human and countless animal lives, many businesses and much scientific credibility.

Fifthly, as we have seen already, we tend to use and exploit the products of science as a means to an end. It is our emotions and mental assumptions that really determine what we do. How and what we love 'stirs the juices' and brings magic and excitement to our lives? Our values make us break our necks to be there, to do that, to celebrate. Our experiences motivate our actions. They cause very practical things to happen, whether it is scientifically sensible or not. Would it not be wise to study the structure of feeling itself?

What effect did Bill Clinton's feelings, on that fatal first night when Monica Lewinsky passed his door, have on his effectiveness to bring peace to the Middle East and Al Gore to the Presidency? How different would the consequences of 9/11 or global ecology have been if Gore had become President? Would more or less people be alive today in USA, Iraq or elsewhere? How many more or less billions of dollars would have been spent? Would Iraq have been invaded? Would fewer people in Britain have felt let down by their government?

However rigorous our 'scientific method', will it ever be able to measure the consequences of emotional decisions, or the way religious and political fanatics exploit them? Will the complex machines measuring electrical brain currents ever be able to do this? Even if they could, could we justify attempts to direct human behaviour by mechanical intervention? Will our brilliant material scientists confine themselves to remodelling the universe as a finely tuned Porsche, with only a dangerous incidental role for the people inside?

So, we depend on 'scientific method' as the factual foundation of our 'free-market' global economy, while the anarchy of emotion and personal preference determines and vetoes its decision-making process. As a result, we have immense and efficient material power, but when deciding what to do with it we are at the mercy of either dramatically conflicting value systems or no values at all. We have failed to study and take account of Aristotle's *Final Cause*.

Is survival-of-the-fittest anarchy our only future?

Is there really no way that cuts through cultural and religious assumptions; that sees and describes logic in human behaviour? As we have seen in Part 2, astrologers insist there is. They claim that a simple comparison between the birth charts of two people can reveal clearly the dangers and benefits of any liaison between them. Everything that happens seems connected with a mass of constantly repeated planetary cycles, and other cycles dependent on them. These are assembled in a unique way for each person and event at each moment of time. By studying what happens during many similar previous cycles, we can make an assessment of what issues may have to be faced in the future.

This helps us decide better and worse ways of handling these issues. If violence is likely, how can we be both strong and conciliatory and so defuse the situation? If things are likely to be against us, can we avoid the worst by keeping a low profile, or putting as little at stake as possible?

Because we are studying pressures and situations, leading to a range of possible reactions, there can be no one specific outcome or cause. What will happen depends upon the passion or intelligence that drives the reaction. This can be difficult to predict exactly. So how do we test the system's validity?

From what has been explained in Part 2, it is clear that the simple and mechanical application of the scientific method is hardly suited to find and treat patterns from the many variables within astrology's archetypal structure. So much depends on individual spiritual maturity. How can a machine measure that?

Could astrologers establish a hierarchy of expressions of, or reactions to, particular astrological configurations? A tense and afflicted Mars can lead to four possible levels of response. With the basest first, these could be:

1.   Blind physical violence
2.   Emotional outbursts, frantic activity
3.   Quick action to save others
4.   Being a still centre of peace in a dangerous situation

The more aware and self-possessed the response, the more mature the person. On its own, this could be measured. However, to do so in isolation might be dangerously misleading. Much will depend on many other factors in the birth chart. To express level 2) may be a positive outcome, or give cause for concern. When we factor in progressions and transits, the same reaction at different times could lead to opposite judgements. Clearly much work needs to be done to identify the various elements and then make a start on synthesis. To recognise, respect and resource those with the experience and wisdom to do the work would not only be of great benefit to astrology, but even more so to 21st century science's ability to serve society.

Pressure, possibility and an imprecise knowledge of the nature and timing of outcomes is accepted in weather, earthquake, financial and even medical forecasting. It is not only reasonable, but beneficial to treat astrology in the same way – to define and test it on its own terms. It would be beneficial because the methods developed could help modern science resolve its shortcomings and fill the gaps that its discoveries have highlighted and created.

Of course, many of its shortcomings mentioned above may be only temporary. Some are not problems intrinsic to material science itself, but caused by ignorance of its true nature by the media and the public it serves. Perhaps the popular view of material science is too simplistic and trapped in an 18th century view of Newtonian mechanics. Education can put this right. What we know today, is not all there is to know. As we research and discover, no area of existence will evade material science's explanations.

While there may be much truth in this, will material science really explain and direct the problem of emotional involvement, personal and religious prejudice in decision-making processes? This is a key issue for biological, genetic and psychological studies of the mind. Are our thoughts and emotions the by-products of chemical and electrical processes of the brain, the structure and dispositions of which are the products of our genetic structure? Would astrology continue to make a central contribution to our understanding of life whether or not this was so?

Consideration of two such key questions needs to be drawn from several scientific disciplines. In this and succeeding chapters we will look at the natural, psychological and social sciences. Let us start in this one by focusing on Genetics.

Genetics and Astrology
Thousands of years before the discovery and charting of the DNA spiral, meditators had looked within and described a similar spiral structure. Tantric studies focused upon inner energies ascending one side and descending the other side of a double helix around the spine. Such practitioners worked out various methods of sound and colour, visualisation and movement to 'raise the kundalini' as they called it. The Earth is tilted at an angle of 23 degrees from its dead centre, as is the human heart from the dead centre of the human body. This tilt explains the Earth's precession on its axis, which appears as a wobble, like a slowing spinning top. It means that a commonly observed point in the

heavens will appear to retreat each year. You can consider this to be the Earth appearing to advance around the zodiac, or the heavens appearing to retreat. Looked at from both perspectives, we see a two-way spiral, each with a focus that moves in the opposite direction to the other – reminiscent of a double helix, reminiscent of the DNA spiral. The two interlocking equilateral triangles of the six-pointed Star of David, described in Chapter 8, symbolise a similar concept. Could it be the nature of life on Earth is the product of, and is based upon, this essential archetype, both within and without everything that is?

The Human Genome Project harnessed immense computing power to map the genetic code that defined in detail what made up each facet of physical existence – shape, sex, structure, health, cosmetic factors, and so on. The Promethean aspiration was that science could determine, control and re-order a life's condition and ultimately create it according to predictable patterns and set criteria.

As the findings of the project are digested and attempts are made to use and exploit them, we shall see if the human condition is as mechanically predictable as geneticists hope. Will we discover that human consciousness does not exist until a mechanical process kicks in, and ceases when the mechanism wears out? When the physical brain ceases to function, does consciousness cease to exist, or is it still there but without speech, sight, touch through which to express itself? Reports from people who have returned from near-death experiences describe temporary departure from the body, looking down, being aware of people around their physical form, but not being able to communicate with them. Astral travellers describe how to 'fly' to and observe other places, but remain attached by a 'golden cord' to the still physical body.

In contrast, research with people who have come out of a coma after several years suggests they have difficulty in accepting that time and circumstances have passed and objectifying what has happened to them. In one amazing incident Terry Wallis, an American man from Arkansas, awoke after twenty years to remember he had a baby daughter, but when talking to her he found it difficult to accept she was now a grown woman.[52] Of course, this may not disprove awareness, but rather the problem of adjusting to the experience of living from a purely three-dimensional, time-trapped perspective. It is still pertinent to ask if memory and understanding cease when the mechanical devices through which they are expressed are damaged?

We may be able to get an idea of the inner experience, as opposed to the outer appearance, of coma victims if we focus on our own waking moments. As a writer and strategist, I often awake with clean clear ideas or solutions to problems. Unfortunately, the distractions of the waking day can lead to their being lost. Ironically, the most clear and total understanding is experienced when I am lying in bed, hardly awake. If I try to record it, my scribble is barely legible - see left and centre columns in Figure 20. The trick is to look at those notes as soon as I am out of bed, and then write a clearer, more sequential version – see right hand column. Now the ideas are safe for a day or so, until I have time to write them up fully.

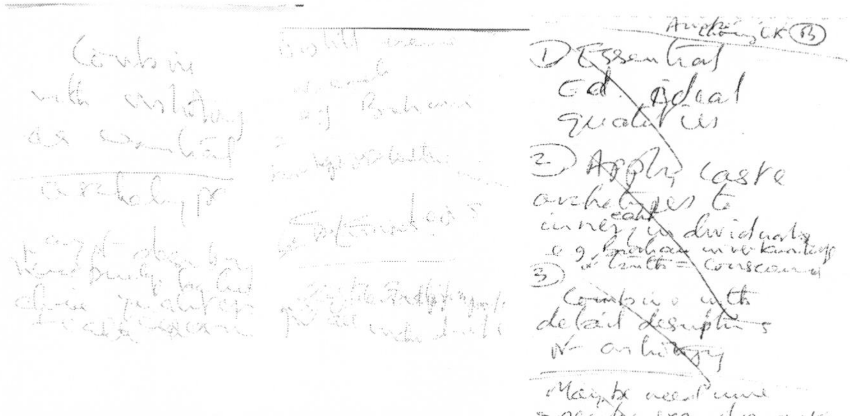

The scribbles in the two columns above were written on waking. Those in the third were written from these, two hours later. A key part of Chapter 18 was the finished result.

Figure 20 – The author's waking scribblings in two stages

The example alongside shows clearly the shortcomings of basing judgement upon external objective observation alone. What is happening for me internally is a 'clear light' experience of immediate absolute understanding, followed by a struggle to hold on to the insight. The final version in Chapter 18 was achieved by rigorous hard writing. This is the most dense and difficult for me. Yet, if I succeed, this is the clearest light for the reader. What I was to write was most obvious when I first woke. The outside observer sees the opposite – an apparently hardly conscious, almost illiterate, person, who then appears to become lively and at the end writes intelligently.

We have a paradox. The more substance and time involved, the greater will be the inner struggle to keep an idea and explain it. The less substance- and time-dependent our circumstances, the clearer our insight will be. Does this suggest insight is independent of the physical body; that consciousness is omnipresent and only becomes limited when attached to the time and place of a particular body?

Richard Dawkins would not think so. In *The Selfish Gene* he suggests that the body is the beginning and end of everything. Life is merely process for the sake of process. We have to be brave and grow up to the 'fact' that we are a minor and very temporary part of a massive amoral process of evolution from which our thoughts and feelings are but by-products of our bodily processes. Dean Hamer in *The God Gene* suggested a genetic mechanism that activates in the brain experience of 'self-transcendence', a sense of wholeness, inclusiveness like the experience of the divine.[53] By this he explains humanity's tendency to empathise and develop ethical principles and even its belief in the divine.

Stephen Pinker's *Evolutionary Psychology* 'proposes that the human brain comprises many functional mechanisms, called psychological adaptations or evolved cognitive mechanisms, designed by the process of natural selection. Examples include language acquisition modules, incest avoidance mechanisms, cheater detection mechanisms, intelligence and sex-specific mating preferences, foraging mechanisms, alliance-tracking mechanisms, agent detection mechanisms, and so on.'[54]

Steven Pinker goes on to suggest that respect for the old and ancestor-worship in traditional cultures was a myth invented by old people to help maintain their dominance through the time in their lives when they were physically weaker. 'One ubiquitous component of religion is ancestor-worship. And ancestor-worship must sound pretty good if you're getting on in years and can foresee the day when you're going to become an ancestor. Among the indignities of growing old is that you know that you're not going to be around forever. If you plausibly convince other people that you'll continue to oversee their affairs even when you're dead and gone, that gives them an incentive to treat you nicely up to the last day.'[55]"

The facts weaken his case. Few, if any, human societies cast out and leave their old and infirm to die or survive on their own. Nor does this natural tendency to care for the elderly seem to be based entirely how their wisdom will benefit society, before or after death. Often family, friends, strangers and state-funded institutions, care for the most helplessly old and otherwise disabled and sick people. Yet, few people in modern society follow ancestor-worship. Is Pinker suggesting that our modern society is suffering from a dysfunctional psychotic, over-secreting 'self-transcendence gland' that is working in direct contradiction to the principles of natural selection?

If not, then perhaps there is something more than crude self-interest and mechanical cause and effect to life. Kindness and decency may yet lie at the very essence of the universe. For, in spite of occasional explosions and collisions, the dominant story of the universe is that the stars, and planets, very survival is dependent upon keeping to their cycles and patterns by *tolerating* and *accommodating* themselves to each other's movements. Darwin may well have cleansed much superstition and ignorance. This is not the same as saying that his theory of evolution understood and explained fundamentals of every aspect of universal manifestation. How could it? He did not know or study everything!

At the same time, what we have learnt from the mapping of the genome is and will be a potent force for our own and future times. Genetic engineering enables crops to be modified to enhance yield, protect against disease, develop preferred characteristics and include therapeutic properties. Plants could become medicines and be enhanced to create healthy populations. In animal and human genetics, it is possible to engineer and correct many qualities and defects. Allied with various artificial insemination techniques, doctors are coming close to creating life. Some even claim to be close to creating the spark of life from a favourable, but still inorganic, environment.

However brilliant these achievements may be, they are no more than fragments that adapt and at times improve the circumstances of life. If we are to advance along this path in a more complete manner, four key questions remain

> ***Firstly,*** *do we and how do we assess fully the consequences of our interference with genetic structures?* What we have learnt from immunisation and the use of antibiotics encourages us to be cautious here. MRSA and other resistant man-created infections could be but very minor problems indeed compared to the effects

of changing one part of genetic structure without fully understanding the co-dependence of many others. Also, we have to guard against creating a protected species, with some beneficial characteristics but others that are lethal.

Secondly, could we ever explain genetically the intricacies of our mental and emotional processes? Hamer, in referring to monoamines that activate self-transference, is dealing with just one important fragment of the rich tapestry of religious experience. Christ and the Buddha may well have identified with all sentient beings, but they also had qualities of mental wisdom, endurance, courage, vision, language skills, objectivity and many more. Above all, such a being would need to have the insight and immense power of will to challenge society. To identify, let alone create, such a being with the right amount of each quality, the scientist would need the stature of understanding of the being he was creating. Quite simply, to create 'God', you have to be God. Without such stature, who knows what monster may emerge?

Thirdly, even if we could, how, who and by what process would we decide what are functional and acceptable thoughts and feelings? If we knew by what genetic process jealousy, kindness, aggression, personal inadequacy and the myriad other facets that determine our human decisions were projected;, some person, institution and method would have to decide what is acceptable. We could focus upon encouraging the most admirable and eradicating the most perverse behaviour patterns, but this would still leave uncertainty in the middle ground. We have already seen that a minor emotional attitude can have a major effect. With all this to consider it seems that, as understanding of genetic detail and consequent intervention develops, we will need more, not less, religious/ethical understanding.

Fourthly, how would we control and discipline unacceptable behaviour? If all this is an irrefutably proven fact, then is it not society's duty to act to enforce correct behaviour? How and by whom would this be done? What new crimes and methods of enforcement would be needed? Would we wish to live in such a society?

To attempt to answer such questions reveals more problems than it solves, because we assume we can only explain our emotions and thoughts by mechanical, linear, genetic criteria. That the exercise seems nonsensical clearly makes the point that material explanations, based on a mechanistic 'scientific method' alone, are unlikely to explain or answer the issues of life.

Before claiming that we have reached a seminal moment in human history, where the human scientist has the ability to explain order and create life, we should re-read the story of Frankenstein. Its lessons become all the more telling and important, because today Frankenstein's aspirations are virtually possible. We have advanced beyond the farcical notion of harnessing of the power of dramatic lightning storms and using body parts dug up from graveyards. Today we know the genome's structure, have electronic microscopes, advanced surgical instruments, sterilisation, refrigeration and other methods of preserving raw materials. There is much we can actually do; yet the shortcomings remain the same. Can we genetically control human decision, desire and imagination? Is the experience of the divine really no more than the pleasant tickling of a biologically identified 'God spot' in the brain? Even if such an area of the brain functions as Hamer describes, does that mean that the experience of God and the conscious unity of all creation is a delusion? Perhaps Hamer is describing how we can observe the higher wisdom of religious experience functioning in the physical brain? The chemistry may not be determinant, but the view from our side of the bridge to another dimension or reality.

If it is possible to stimulate altruism by causing chemical changes in the brain, can geneticists create at will a nation populated solely by Buddhist bodhisattvas, or a St Francis of Assisi, HH Pope John Paul II and the like? Or conversely, in order for the intrinsic eternal kindness and compassion to express themselves in our world is it necessary to have the 'bridge' of a brain with such chemical functions occurring? In any case, by what unit do we measure altruism? In all linear research, there is always a more ultimate question, standing pre-existent to the theorist's 'ultimate' thesis.

When we consider the history of trying to answer questions three and four above, we should remember that the biologist's temptation to intervene and 'improve' on nature is not new. The ghost of Nazi eugenics is rarely absent when the hubris of skilful invention puts God 'in his place'! The advanced experimental methods of material science are good at detailing the steps of manufacture from A to B to C and so on.

They are not so good at ensuring that what is created is more than a cloned replica of the original, or a pale and awkward shadow of full-blooded life.

The mechanical, evolutionary visions of Dawkins, Hamer and Pinker describe a partial 'truth', emanating from no more than a distorted projection of their own minds. Could it be that in seeking to outlaw God from the contemporary world picture, Dawkins is reacting automatically to the Neptune in Aquarius, Pluto in Sagittarius driven contemporary fundamentalism? Maybe he is seeking to create a scientistic fundamentalism of his own. Just as Christian, Muslim, Jewish and Hindu fundamentalists are pulling our world apart by insisting they are absolutely right so are atheistic and scientistic fundamentalists.

For, to separate into right and wrong is dependent upon taking a position from which to judge. Relative truth varies according to the mind of the viewer. Certainly, if you wish to achieve a linear ambition in the material world, you have to take a tight position from which to do it and discipline yourself according to the rules of your aspiration. If you perform perfectly, you are right perfectly within the limitation of the goal you set yourself – that is all. When it comes to emotion and mind, you need to open up to see clearly. This requires a different kind of logic.

Could it be that within all creation is an endless eternal mind that can *be* everywhere and understand everything, before, after and between the manifestation of this and all other conceivable things happening and living? Could there have been times when such universal understanding permeated and enlightened the mundane world far more than it does for most of us today? Could it be that our failure to understand the deeper, subtler inner meanings behind gross material manifestation limits our modern view of reality?

Part 2 showed how astrology can explain, cleanse and so guide emotional involvement and personal prejudice when making decisions. Astrology can give direction and flexible order at the point where genetics just offers dangerously powerful amoral options. Astrology educates the individual about himself, his environment and the people affected by his decisions. In doing so, it helps answer the very ethical and political issues that genetics cannot address.

The cycles of astrology have the disciplined malleability and karmic balance to purify, and so play an important part to link individual experience to the flow of the universe. The mandalas of planetary movement, mentioned in Chapter 3, could be related to our knowledge of the patterns of the human brain, balancing organs and the nervous system. Is there correspondence and relationship? With careful research we may find complementary patterns between astrological cycles and genetic structures.

In order to consider how to explore this, it might be helpful to ponder the questions that follow. These are not necessarily in the order in which they should be studied, but rather in the order that the answers, once determined, should be presented.

* Is there a mind or quality of understanding that incarnates from outside into a pattern of a chemical process that genetics is becoming able to conceptualise?

* Is there a connection between the decision to copulate and cosmic cycles? This is important because, once conceived and then born, an entirely predictable series of combined and integrated astro events will occur.

* Do these astro events have a direct, complementary and modifying connection, or any other association with genetic structure and instruction?

* Does the astrological birth chart help us understand the mapping the genome? If we go deeper into what lies within astrological language and genetic description, this idea may not be as unlikely as it first seems.

* Assume we were able to devote the same amount of resources (especially computer time) spent on mapping the genome to the astrologer-designed studies of the relationship between astronomical cycles and human behaviour. Could what we discover be as beneficial to humanity, as it is hoped the Human Genome Project will be?

To ask such questions, let alone study them, opens doors that require material science to understand beyond three-dimensional, linear, sequential analyses. It asks whether the present scientific paradigm is too simplistic to explain every aspect of existence. The nature of this possibility is considered in the next chapter.

Chapter 11

Universal Paradigms: Past, Present & Future

The hero of Olaf Stapleton's[56] book *Star Maker* goes to the top of a hill and beneath a clear, open sky forces his consciousness to expand, encompass and become the entirety of the heavens. From this perspective, he can focus down to particular planets and places and see different cultures. He describes alternative ways that evolution could occur and ultimately reaches an intuitive and timeless vision of the Star Maker, the creator of many universes.

Such a state of mind is an experience you cannot have an opinion about. For, until you have had the experience, it seems fanciful. Yet, once you have had it, it is too all-encompassing not to be real. Indeed, this sense of reality is so total that even explaining that what happened was as a result of chemical changes in the brain is no more than a by-product of the truth. It cannot diminish its all-embracing existence.

Astronomers concentrate on the power, distances and immense forces of the universe. Then they tell us that all this makes them and us small and insignificant. Astrologers focus on the experience of what holds the universe together – the harmony of its cycles – harmony that comes from understanding, honouring and yielding to the flow of all there is.

The universe appears to be endless, because we separate ourselves from it and build instruments to see it that way. There is another way of looking at it. We can look and *feel* within, not out there, as did blind King Lear we can 'see *feelingly*'. We can focus and check up upon every part of ourselves with 'our inner eye' and get beyond bodily limitations. When we step away and detach ourselves internally; our inner eye intuition can open up and expand 'to see' the whole universe. We can have a sense of all that has been, is and will be throughout beginningless space. Then we can put into perspective all those conflicting, extrinsic partial-truth theories we have been taught and told. All great discoveries started from inner-informed inspiration.

The strong clarity that comes from such an inner way of looking confirms what we found in Chapter 10. However much we spend on however many experiments, three dimensional, linear, sequential analysis is too simplistic a method to study and explain every aspect of existence. There needs to be a deeper way for science to advance. Material theses have too many shortcomings to be the exclusive and essential foundation of all meaning. The basic assumptions of contemporary science need to go through a dimensional shift of paradigm, which is as or even more fundamental than that activated by Einstein's work on relativity in the first part of the 20th century.

There may be deeper understandings of subtle forces and new factors that our assumptions and methods of study have been too gross to fathom before this time. Just as the 19th/20th century discoveries of electricity and the silicon chip (always there, but previously unnoticed and unused) have been critical to our lives today, so may yet unknown discoveries transform our future lives. Who knows that the experience of astrology, which so many sensitive and intelligent people still vouch for after centuries of dismissal and persecution, will not be seen as offering genuine insight into the workings of the universe? Something like Percy Seymour's hypothesis or elements within it may yet be found to have real value and meaning.

In this chapter, we will consider this by looking at astrology alongside the languages of mathematics and the developing paradigms of physics.

Mathematics

The scientific argument that there is intelligent life somewhere else in the universe is based on its apparently infinite area and the number of bodies it contains. There must be a star somewhere out there that has an orbiting planet just like Earth. In an expanding, limitless universe maybe there is someone just like you reading a book exactly as you are now – rather like the '1,000 typing monkeys in the end producing a Shakespeare play.

Enshrined in mystical teachings, such ideas have been around for a long time. Several centuries before Christ, the Buddha went one step further. He taught of a limitless universe of infinite clarity, which our delusion-clouded minds prevent us from seeing. As a result of this delusion, for beginningless space and time we will continue to reincarnate as the child and mother of every kind of creature over and over again, until we realise the deluded nature of the relative mind.

If anything were ultimately possible within the universe, would this mean that anything goes and anarchy rules? Not at all; for immediately we take a position and look from a particular perspective, then a set of consequent relationships 'kicks in'. Mathematics is the language that defines and communicates the fundamental structure of those relationships.

Because of its rigour, exactness and consistency within its clearly defined terms, many mathematicians and philosophers have seen it to be the universal, culture-free language. We assume that all nations and races, even extra-terrestrials, understand and accept it. What is proved in mathematics is proved for all time.

So it is, but only in relation to the mathematical set of rules that emanate from a particularly defined relative position. From a different perspective or dimension of study or paradigm, things may change. When moving from conventional to a non-Euclidean or projective geometry, we may consider the consequences of two parallel lines actually meeting at a point, or points, we call 'infinity'. When we look more deeply into the apparent arbitrary occurrence of prime numbers and move into three-dimensional geometry, we find there appears to be a diminishing pattern to their frequency as the number of digits of the number increases[57]. Will we have to move to a fourth dimension to give absolute, rather than provisional, proof to *Riemann's Hypothesis*? Einstein's Theory of Relativity radically changed the notion of time. It prepared the ground for space travel and splitting the 'core particle of all existence' – the atom.

When we move into concepts and places far removed as to be on the fringes of how we live life on Earth, or deeply down into the nano-world within, then the structures and rules upon which our conventional lives depend fall down. Maybe there is no life after death. If there were, however; the material mathematics of space and time would be of little use in understanding the reincarnation process explained in Chapter 6. The body remains dependent upon the rules of its space-time continuum, but the transmigrating karmic residue is no longer subject to these rules. It moves instantly, as if through a *Star Trek* worm hole, to become attached to an appropriate other point of space and time. Here is a set of karmic learning experiences, ideally suited to this stage in the reawakening process.

For, if there is sense in the notion of reincarnation, then its processes must be based on a logic that transcends the mathematical rules that pin us down to this one lifetime. Maybe Einstein's redefinition of the relationship between light and time moves our rigid minds in this direction. However, this does not mean that no consistent rules would apply. Many astrologers see the movements of the heavens, and the language of behaviour they relate to these movements, is the gateway logic that describes karma and hence links lifetimes – higher mathematics indeed!

Whether we are dealing with our familiar mundane world, or the subtle forces of reincarnation, there is a rule common to all mathematical systems – each must have a logical consistency in terms of its own clearly defined criteria. Therefore $2 + 2 = 4$ will always be so, unless a new factor that reliably changes this and all other directly dependent phenomena is found. Two apples plus two oranges will make four items of fruit, but not four apples or four oranges. Of course, distinctions are not always that clear-cut. For example, would a pattern of repetitions noted every 45 days still be significant at proportionate intervals – say every 22.5 days, or 30 days? If the sub-patterns do not always occur, how weak and irregular need they be for them to be considered insignificant and the result random?

Similarly, we have already seen that human emotional and mental action and reaction may be systematic, but on a broad spectrum of possibility rather than precise mechanical cause and effect. An astrologer may say that an upcoming Full Moon is likely to place overwrought pressures on people. This can express itself within a wide range: mad and reckless actions; struggling to control ever mounting pressures; deliberately withdrawing from worldly concerns to avoid either of these. At each level of reaction we could claim a consistent language of archetypal cause and effect, even though the outcomes are very different.

Returning to mainstream mathematics, our material world is defined and kept in order by the arithmetic, algebra, geometry and trigonometry we learn at school and university. Finely crafted aeroplanes, cars, buildings, factories, armaments, bridges, dams and the vast organisational infrastructure that holds all together are dependent upon this knowledge. None of them would be possible if designers did not have a brilliant understanding of conventional mathematics and the ability to apply it with fine engineering skill. Our modern world is so full of unbelievably ingenious things that it is difficult to restrain ourselves from going that one heady step further – to say that this world, and the way we observe the universe from it, is all there is.

Clearly, conventional mathematics is the language of this so-observed 'universe' and the final arbiter of all *material* things in it. However, to insist that this state of affairs is the only obvious and irrefutable truth in *all possible' universes* – in fact, is the truth of the one-and-only total universe – is a step much too far that I suspect few mathematicians would be willing to take. Yet, many political decisions and power struggles emanate from the mistaken view that one imagined 'practical reality' exists and it is the only criterion by which to determine success or failure.

Certainly, there is great wonder and satisfaction in applying mathematical design to perfect, then to drive the resultant finely-tuned vehicle. Mathematical understanding can give such exact control of output that fragile projects, such as flying hundreds of ordinary people around the world at great heights and speeds or sending humanity hundreds of thousands of miles into alien space, can be completed safely. Understanding mathematics and applying it to the physical sciences and mechanics gives unbelievable power and control over the modern world.

Yet, we have seen already that crucial areas of the decision-making processes of this world ignore mathematics, or distort it to achieve personal advantage. Modern science accepts that there are areas of human emotion and mental obsession but holds them to be illogical and outside science. Maybe, they take comfort in thinking, through education and social development people will grow wiser and more scientific. Hopefully, biologists and geneticists with psychiatric drugs will find ways of locating and treating those parts of the brain that cause this 'primitive' behaviour.

Confronted by such lack of logic in human emotions and decision-making processes and the very real dangers of nuclear cataclysm, Cold War mathematicians developed what came to be known as Games Theory strategies. The key game was aptly entitled 'Fuck you, buddy'. Its main thesis was: since you could not be sure how your opponent would behave, the logical strategy was to assume the worst. Basing your decisions on the assumption that everyone would cheat and lie must be the best logical way. For, if another person did deceive you, you would not lose. If they kept their word, by cheating and lying you are likely to benefit even more.

Such iron logic may be understandable at the height of the Cold War. Unfortunately, like the nuclear weapons themselves, such strategies have not disappeared, but instead have been combined with a simplistic view of Darwinism and genetics to dominate policy and economic market strategy in the post-Cold War world.

More about this and the social consequences of such an inhumane and ecologically flawed foundation for society will be considered in depth in the closing chapters of this book. For the moment it is sufficient to note that such a view of humanity would treat each of us as being intrinsically greedy, cruel and exploitative. Regular surveillance of every citizen would be 'necessary' to ensure no one is engaged in child pornography, theft, murder, terrorism or any other kind of 'lesser' crime that did not fit the accepted mores of the time. Each work task would be designed around the fulfilling of targets, determined by administrators, supervised electronically and stored in personnel records. Who has seen the film *Brazil*?[58]

The fundamental flaw in such a jaded view of nature is that it creates a world where there is no room for charity or surprise. When all behaviour is reduced to the lowest common denominator of greed, ignorance and hatred, we can only expect constantly to face the worst and never hope for anything better. The magic of surprise, the generosity of offering more than is asked for that liberate, that move mountains, are gone forever. To give more than the absolute minimum would be to expose our kindness to being grabbed and squandered in a lolly scramble of dismissive contempt!

Fortunately, such a thesis is the expression not of mathematics, but just one view of mathematics – the mathematics of desperation. The RAND Corporation's Games Theories may be rational in a macabre way, but they say little about logic and more about the conditions of our times and John Nash's paranoid schizophrenia. They are a comment on the greedy self-interest that inevitably comes to dominate a world, which sees the material market place as the only logical way to 'discipline human nature'. In reducing humanity to such a limited and mechanical view, the mathematics and science that dominate our early 21st century fundamentally betray their own origins. They fall far short of the aspirations and *raison d'être* of the 18th century Enlightenment. They also abrogate their right to adjudicate what we do.

For, paradoxically, scientists who think this way are falling into the very myopic lack of logic that the study of mathematics is supposed to protect us from. We have already seen that the rules of mathematics apply provided that there is a logical consistency in terms of its own clearly defined criteria. If the mathematics of the mechanics of the motor car engine cannot be applied consistently to human behaviour and our decision-making processes, we should seek a logic or consistency that could be so applied – not brush aside without proper consideration any possibility of doing so.

Living in this relative part of this solar system in this galaxy makes us subject to particular pressures. If we are all pliant and vulnerable creatures, might there not be a process of higher logic that describes our dispositions and how they might change? Is there a way of calculating their moments and time lengths? Does the calculation of the special relationships between various bodies moving in space and us have any relevance to our feelings and inclinations? If so, would not our decisions be clearer and happier the more we accepted and were in tune with such feelings and inclinations? Could there be a sacred mathematics that helps us understand and fine-tune such feelings and inclinations?

A compromising balance of circular acceptance allows the Moon to orbit the Earth, even though each body would have a linear momentum if moving through space on its own. Might not a study of all such cycles in the solar system and beyond reveal reflective archetypes? Could understanding these enable us to have a fruitful and balanced life on our planet, as well as linking us to the rest of its universe? Perhaps we should look again at ancient mathematical ideas. While these may not supplant what we know already they may give the insight that comes from a fresh perspective in those areas we do not know or understand.

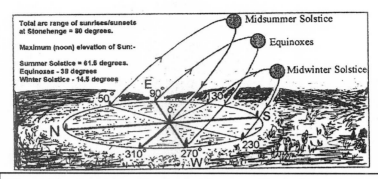

Figure 21 – Stonehenge Sunrise and Sunset at Yearly Quarter Days

England's Stonehenge marks the sunrise and sunset points at the four Quarter Days of the year. Robin Heath's[59] diagram shows clearly how this works. He has shown also that the henge had an outer ring that measured the days and phases of the lunar month and could indicate eclipses. Many books have been written to suggest that the Giza Pyramid was an observatory and much more. A particularly detailed recent theory comes from Charles Piazzi Smyth, who claimed that it expressed time spanning one thousand years.[60] His work is an advancement of Greek, Arab and more recent scholarship covering thousands of years.

Contemporary scientists tend to downplay the connections between major monuments and astronomical cycles, or dismiss them as the misguided superstition of primitive, less enlightened, societies. Yet these societies lasted for thousands of years and left far more evidence of their times than we are likely to do of our own. This includes much wisdom that remains the basis of our culture today. Perhaps we should show a little more respect, ask and consider carefully why these people felt the relationship between the heavens and the earth to be so important.

It is often claimed that such places were 'gateways' between heaven and earth. This is not so fanciful or impractical as it first appears. By living on the earth we are subject to its cycles and the appearance of the heavens tells us the stages of the cycles. The higher the Sun in the sky at midday, the nearer we are to summer. There are other, more subtle cycles. Just one example indicates the vital importance of star-gazing. Due to the tilt on the Earth, certain stars appear and disappear on the horizon at different times of year. When a particular star appears, ancient people knew it was time to plant crops. How the sky looked around that star (hazy, sharp, etc.) might indicate how good the crops might be. This could easily be a sign of the weather conditions around the planting seasons. Whatever the intended human activity, the heavens could give simple practical guidance. Clearly, they were considered to reflect life on earth. If we correlate such ideas with what modern biologists and horticulturalists know today, we will see the clear practical value of such ancient knowledge. Navigating by the stars was an invaluable stage in developing knowledge of the Earth, which is the basic measuring system of today's radar and satellite positioning technology. If we treat the ancient wisdom of astrology with respect, we may discover a reliable structure for the emotions and mental assumptions that rule today's world.

The heavens and the instruments that measured them in ancient times were the basis of all decisions – just as are our modern libraries and computers. This was not because our ancestors were superstitious and deluded, but because they were practical and logical. Why plant in the autumn and harvest in the spring? Furthermore, because their observations between the movements of the heavens and what happened on earth were much more attuned, day-to-day and detailed, our ancestors were much more aware of the value of the heavens as indicators. Life was subject to natural flows, not the product of a particular intellectual fashion, or an individual expert's latest statistically researched reconstruction of 'reality'.

Realising this, we may begin to see why particular religious structures and ancient observatories seem to have a power that people, now thousands of years after they were built, still sense as magical. A pyramid, Buddhist stupa or ancient stone circle was a representation, or a tool of measurement, that reflected harmonious life on earth. As such, all helped people find a natural space for themselves and their activities in their world. So, they seemed to be blessed and to create blessing; worthy of worship. I find this less strange and equally, if not more, useful than our contemporary worship of the motorcar and the mobility, social status and sexual opportunities it provides.

Clearly, being guided by natural cycles has its advantages and disadvantages. Certainly it is invaluable if one's wish is to sustain ecological balance. It would be of far less use if one's aim was to cut a road through mountains to mine and deliver coal to industrial complexes and earn vast billions in profit, whatever the cost to future generations.

The restructuring of knowledge 'from scratch' since the Enlightenment has led the choice between two extremes to seem as stark as this. It is a choice that remains in very few hands; an aristocracy privileged by birth has been replaced by an over-confident bureaucratically-protected intelligentsia. 'Expert wisdom' has severed humanity from interaction with nature; made common sense individual experience fanciful, untrue, primitive, almost something to apologise for, be embarrassed about mentioning! Lack of natural contact with the cycles of the planet, as indicated by the heavens, dependence on the scientific expert's 21st century materialism, constant reconstruction and redesigning of the earth; all have created psychological and ecological malaise. A major contribution to putting this right would be the study and application of a more natural language of mathematics.

Ironically, one key mathematical concept does manifest meaningfully within the natural, artistic and spiritual, as well as mechanical, worlds. The sequential development of the Fibonacci series of numbers, or Phi, indicates the very root of the way life structures itself and expands. By starting from zero and adding two numbers to make a third we demonstrate the exponential process. (For example: 0, 1, 1, 2, 3, 5, 8, 13, 21, 34, 55, 89 and so on.)

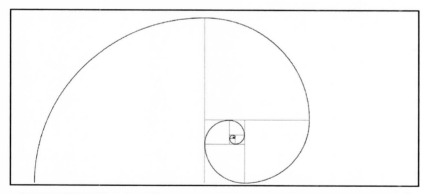

Figure 22 – The Spiral of Life Created from Phi-based Squares

Figure 22 shows how in two dimensions, by making squares of sizes from this Phi numeric progression we create spiral that is seen in shells and plants throughout nature. Closely connected with this idea is the Golden Section derived from the formula $(\sqrt{5}+1)/2$ or the number 1.618033988. It can be applied to a line, where the ratio of the whole line to the largest section is the same as the ratio of the large segment of the line to the smaller. In art, it is a mathematical concept behind the Golden Section that draws the eye to a focal point. In architecture it is a key ratio in the ancient pyramids, the Parthenon of ancient Greece and Notre-Dame Cathedral. More recently, technical analysts in the financial markets have noted that this Fibonacci ratio seems to be a marker for the timing and levels of price movements. This very range of uses, from the most practically functional through art to the arcane, is exactly the wide way that the language of mathematics should underpin, flow through and so unify our lives. Phi is not the only concept with such potential.

Tibetan Buddhist thangka painting and mandala creations are based on geometric linear foundations that relate to human and divine psychology. A framework of squares determines exactly where the key lines should be placed, so that proportion is precise and balanced. Then carefully chosen objects and symbols are placed in the exactly determined places. Appropriate traditional colours are chosen. The finished creation then becomes psychologically effective, as a focus of emotional cleansing, mental relaxation, concentration, compassion and so on. It would be interesting to compare the rationale behind such techniques and the chemical treatments in modern psychiatry. Before we do, however, it would wise to re-read Plato on Ideas and Forms. We are dealing with the archetypes behind such ancient wisdom. We seek the liberation and choice that comes from following the right path in harmony with the universe – not a cure that can be defined, patented and commercially exploited.

In contrast, the brilliant anarchy to be found in modern Western art reveals the dangerous schism between contemporary art and science. Much seems to express a desperate yearning for meaning and personal recognition, or a search for originality of form in an everyday world that is too materially predictable for artistic comfort. Modern art seems to express the crisis of our human need to liberate creative meaning; at odds with a society seeking to be so certain that it becomes unbearably and unbelievably arid. This is what happens to the soul, when mathematics sells out to economics!

At the end of this chapter is an extensive bibliography that considers ancient sacred geometry, building design, town planning and particular number systems by John Michell and Rev Dr Gordon Strachan. Creating balanced and pleasing environments can lead to more considerate and enlightened decisions and relationships. The Japanese and ancient Chinese changed landscapes and laid out buildings to attune the patterns of life on earth with the cycles of the heavens. Today it is indeed ironic that massive industrial developments in both those counties seem to be progressing without regard to the ecological survival of the planet. By adopting both of the key developments of Western rational Enlightenment – communism and capitalism - is China creating this worst of all worlds. In China's future the reflective ghosts of our own imperial arrogance could well come back to haunt us.

In contrast, the more sensitive souls in the West are now exploring the subtle and gentle art of Feng Shui! Branches of this knowledge may have links with geometric structures. Certainly some can be explained by planetary direction astrology. We point to a planet from the centre of the environment we wish to enhance at the time we are ready to do the work, then draw a chart indicating planetary directions. From the meanings, we decide the best placing of objects and activities in that home or workplace. Domestic and caring activities are best placed toward the Moon, the kitchen towards Virgo and so on. Another application of this method imagines the planetary lines drawn around the globe. It has been found that following the line in the direction of Venus can bring love, Mars challenge, Jupiter opportunity, and so on.

Of course, none of these innovations will give us information that will lead to exact mechanical control over the human emotions and decision-making processes – nor would we want them to. Intrinsic in the nature of life is the urge for the space and freedom to choose, and so grow beyond dull, dry, lifeless mechanical interaction. Rather, such innovations give life a naturally ordered direction. From the strict definition of Phi comes the source of infinite variety of the physical, artistic and visionary worlds. In the same way, from the rigid movement of planetary cycles come inclinations that liberate wise decisions. They do this by making clear the limitations we are working within – geometry that is indeed sacred!

This gives us the chance to see clear order in human behaviour – to educate, but not imprison the decision-making process. As the mathematical foundation of modern thought broadens and becomes less deterministic, we will find room for deeper understanding. A higher, more flexible conceptual language will lead to a paradigm more suited to the advances we are making in 21st century.

We will turn away from destructive, obsessive and in the end fruitless attempts to use mathematics to freeze the present into a 'certain' future that we can exploit to our own advantage. We will return to, and then advance towards a mathematics of cyclic possibility. We will experience the genuine indestructible freedom of knowing where we are and having some idea of where we are going.

Physics
For more than five hundred years, increasingly precise and systematic observations of the natural world have intensified. Over these centuries Leonardo's brilliant speculative 15th century drawings of machines and anatomy have turned out to be a remarkable 'prophecy' of our modern world.

The development of the telescope and round-the-world exploration undermined the notion of a geocentric universe, in which spheres of the Sun, Moon, planets, stars and angels – 'God's natural order', circled the Earth. Initially, Galileo's empirical observations suffered religious persecution. Church pressure kept in the minds of the majority of people the idea that God created the Earth in seven days in 4004 BC, until Darwin's work on natural selection in the 19th Century. Even then, his disciples, such as T H Huxley, had to struggle against religious prejudice to prepare the ground for today's view. Now most people accept the perceived contemporary view that life is a product of natural selection and our planet is about four billion years old.

We have already noted the paradox that astrology, which was either rejected or kept at arm's length by the early Christian churches, has suffered more from the abandonment of a geocentric universe than the churches themselves. In a number of *non sequitur* arguments, it was claimed that astrology could not work because it was based on the incorrect thesis that the Earth was the centre of the universe. As we have seen, its study was banned from British universities more than three hundred years ago. Yet, let us say it again; we are still living on the Earth! We are still subject to the same cyclic pressures that have been studied and applied for thousands of years. So, from the perspective of our actual experience, what has changed?

While the experience of living on the Earth remained as before, a lot did change as a result of the discoveries of the Renaissance and those that followed. We had begun to learn about deeper processes that lay beneath the apparent nature of the universe. The genie was out of the bottle. Now we could have more control over the material universe. It seemed we could mould it to our will. The machinery and processes of the modern world are examples of how far we have developed along this path of discovery. However, we still live on the Earth. So surely it is reasonable to consider ancient systems of understanding, based on our ancestors' empirical comparison between behaviour on Earth and the *apparent* movements of the heaven, as seen from Earth.

The invaluable knowledge that has been built up in the field of modern physics over the past five hundred years comes from carefully disciplined observation, checking, testing, applying and correcting, until a consistent, predictable result can be achieved. Only with this degree of certainty, and hence control, can we describe the nature and development of the Earth, build motor cars, invent weapons, aeroplanes, send men to the Moon and beyond. The canon of physical wisdom, upon which all this is based, has been built from scratch – from the bottom up. Newton's apple falls from the tree. He outlines a theory of gravity. We can use this knowledge to work out the acceleration of a falling object and, combined with our many other discoveries, how to bring a spaceman back to Earth. We can measure exactly the movement of the Moon, so that our spacecraft is aimed precisely and the shuttle lands safely. Yet we study the reverse, the Moon's affect on the Earth and its citizens, far less. Even when we do, we tend to narrow down the spectrum of study so tightly or grossly that we miss vital, if subtle, connections.

While the present methods of study may be all we have needed to build specific machines, they are not so well suited to explain the ultimate structure of the universe. To extrapolate what we choose to see on Earth in the 21st century to explain all meanings in the universe limits our theoretical scope. We are like moles seeking to define life on the surface from the experience of burrowing in the darkness of the soil beneath it. The resultant theories will almost certainly reflect the limitations of our knowledge and imagination, not describe the true nature of things. So, in the years since the Enlightenment, theories about the origin and intrinsic nature of the universe have developed radically. They have changed so much that some would claim they follow the passing fashion of human consciousness, rather than show an ultimate understanding of the universe.

As humanity was flexing the muscles of its newly-discovered adolescent power over nature from the late 17th to 19th centuries, the theories were fixed and grossly mechanical. Machines were large and chunky. Science and style were on the rise, the ethereal and magical were consigned to their 'rightful place', as 'superstitions from the primitive past'. Britain ruled the waves and its empire was expanding. Notions of 'good' or 'evil', 'civilisation' or 'primitive savagery' determined colonial policy. The universe was a machine controlled by gravity. The British Empire was the custodian of good order and wisdom; both religious and technical.

The 20th century was destined to be less certain. The immediate build-up to the 1891/2 Neptune/Pluto conjunction and developments afterward meant that the last quarter of the 19th century saw rapid growth of new ideas and discoveries. They were to atomise certainty and even 'atomise' the atom itself.

Alongside the impact of the idealised mechanistic science fiction of Jules Verne and H G Wells came less certain developments. Class and sexual revolution radicalised politics. Imperial hubris and the resentment of defeat fuelled the wars of the 20th century. Further undermining the simplistic optimism of the 19th century, new physics theories changed our understanding of the very nature of reality.

Einstein's Theory of Relativity postulated that, if we could leave conventional time-based earthly constraints, the universe would not look the same or behave as we might first expect. Quite simply, when we looked really carefully, we would discover appearances could be deceptive. The universe was not a fixed interdependent mechanism, because light moved at a constant speed from wherever, by whomever and whenever, it was measured. As a result energy and mass were not interchangeable ($E=MC^2$, where E is energy, M is mass and C the constant speed of light). As well as radical changes in our view of the universe and our ability to travel around it, from this simple key idea came understanding of the nature of the atom and its power for good or ill.

The atom was not split until 1932. However, in a few decades from the first atomic explosion in 1945 until the early 21st century, atomic power has traumatised international relations and the world economy. A small correction to what had appeared to be 'obvious' has entirely changed the world we live in and what we can do.

Yet the popular mind is still to grasp and come to terms with the full implications of such changing circumstances. Rather, it exists and is encouraged to exist in a state of contradictory conceptual schizophrenia. On the one hand is the natural human need for certainty: either a God or at least the concrete classical Newtonian model of reality. On the other hand there is a temptation to test the ultimate, eccentric consequences of Einstein's Theory of Relativity. The result is an illogical assumption that one can travel through time, yet still have the comfort and protection of Newtonian certainty – the *Star Trek* error. More seriously, one can interfere with the structure of matter, patterns of disease and genetic models without being affected by one's actions, or losing control of the outcome.

Even less realised by the general public or even the scientific community are the implications of Einstein's Theory of Relativity for astrology's role in the modern world. Can we still say it was valid to exclude astrology from serious academic study on a basis of a concrete view of the universe, whose most fundamental assumptions were found to be flawed a little over two hundred years later? If a more careful look at the relationship between energy, matter and light can change what we understand and can do in our everyday lives so radically, may not astrology be worthy of deeper study? If we put real resources into looking at human behaviour and events on Earth through the expert eyes of our ancestors, we may well discover explanations that validate their rather arcane astrological methodology. If we accept and use the methodology for the time being, and then investigate, explanations for the patterns may emerge.

We should not reject prematurely because surface appearances do not meet expected outcomes, but look deeper, as do all true scientists. Without tenacity no great scientific discoveries would have occurred – no Archimedes, no Newton's apple, no zero line for prime numbers, even no Theory of Relativity, nor many more.

In fact, the astrological view fits and enhances Einstein's view of the universe rather well. According to his Special Theory of Relativity, two observers within their own respective space-time frames of reference see a given event differently because the speed of light *is* constant. Astrology claims that people behave differently because they are born at different points of time and space and so *see* things differently.

Quantum mechanics pulled the atom and earlier views of its motion apart, developed laser technology in its many forms for good or ill. It came to the ambiguous conclusion that all objects exhibit at times a wave-like nature and at other times a particle-like nature. This centred on the effect of light, or waves, that moved at the speed of light. While the number of electrons moved was increased by a greater intensity of light, the speed of the movement remained constant. However, the frequency of light, or light-speed wave pulses did have a causal effect on the speed of electron movement. In these two ways light can affect photoelectric materials. In the larger world in which we live, developments in photography, supermarket shopping, and the identity cards and scanning cameras of our laser-digital surveillance society are dependent on such discoveries. As a result, what we can do, how we organise our economy and politics have changed dramatically in less than half a century. Studies of the smallest parts of the natural world are having unbelievably massive effects on the macrocosm.

We can now measure with remarkable precision. We have invested trillions of dollars in advanced machinery and research. Yet, the more we discover about the inner workings of the atom and apply and exploit this new knowledge, the more there remains to discover. Vitally, more room for uncertainty has to be allowed at the most intrinsic new-nano level. This is remarkably similar to astrology. We may be able to predict the gross, the archetypal outcome may well be certain, but the precise detailed event is dependent upon too many variables to be sure. Crucially, however, both in astrology and quantum physics, such inexactness does not invalidate larger truth.

So in quantum physics we have two contrasting principles. Firstly, in contradiction to the assertions of classical physics, the precise measurement of very small differences can have enormous mechanical and social effects on our lives. However deeply we look into the smallest matter, adjustments have to keep on being made and it is by applying such tiny adjustments that we gain more power and mastery. Secondly, the accuracy of mechanical processes and outcomes depends on the level of depth and detail at which one is working. For everyday living, classical Newtonian physics is sufficient; for a journey through space, hardly so.

When we know so little about the powerful effects of the most subtle changes in light energy and matter, and are learning more each day, can it be right to reject traditional astrological descriptions out of hand? Could not varying outcomes from those descriptions be based on human experience of the combined effect of planetary interaction? Not knowing the intricacies of the inner workings of the atom and the various invisible waves that have always surrounded life on earth, our forefathers observed regular heavenly patterns on those dark evenings before light pollution. The links may be far more complex than they could have imagined, but that does not invalidate what they observed.

We can only learn from their experience by suspending disbelief. Firstly try to see as they may have seen with their limited understanding, and then, only then, seek explanations from our much greater store of contemporary knowledge. If we place synthesised astrological methods alongside the mechanics of quantum physics, is it not possible that we may discover just why it is that planetary patterns appear to reflect human minds and emotions?[61]

Chaos Theory found that there could be an underlying order to apparently random data, which was so subtle that it could be missed. Lorenz discovered that differences in 4th, 5th and 6th places of a decimal could make a critical difference far in excess of their size. In *The Mathematics of Chaos* Ian Stewart infamously observed that the flapping of a butterfly's wing could so change currents of the atmosphere to be part cause of averting a tornado in Indonesia! The implications of Chaos Theory deeply question modern assumptions about the fundamental nature of reality.

Is manifestation mechanically linear, or does it emerge out of and return to apparent emptiness in accordance with conditions and latent in-built patterns of manifestation? Bernadette Brady's work in progress, outlined in her *Astrology a Place in Chaos,* considers in depth the implications of Chaos Theory for the popularly-assumed contemporary linear model of reality. It shows how the main concepts of astrology fit well with Chaos Theory's mathematical findings of SDIC, phase portraits, Strange Attractors, Hopf Bifurcation, Saddle points, self similarity and scale invariance, homeostasis and Lock-in. Brady's comparisons complement the concept of archetypal predictability claimed for astrology by Richard Tarnas.[62] For archetypes can be clearly defined, but still manifest in a range of ways at the mundane level of everyday living. Tarnas' in-depth consideration of just a few outer planetary cycles explains vast sweeps of historical and cultural change with an irresistible wealth of examples. When we include the full range of planetary cycles, always allowing for archetypal variants, we can achieve a clear mirror-like reflection of what has happened, is happening and will happen.

We bring order to this 'chaos' when we consider the way our ancestors saw things occur and the astrological methodology they used to indicate patterns in manifestation. Merely by giving the traditional interpretations of the Sun and Saturn in the 12th house and Mars being 135 degrees from George W Bush's Midheaven[63], we can anticipate the pattern of his relationship with his father. By looking at his inauguration chart[64] as President in January 2001, it was possible to predict that his Presidency would be dominated by war. The 'decision-maker' sought to achieve through violence what his father failed to achieve. The astrology reveals his unshakeable disposition to manifest a particular and very material outcome.

The notion of a void, a still point, out of which comes manifestation dependant upon clear causes, patterns and rules, is the very essence of Buddhist philosophy. By taking a relative position, one becomes subject to patterns of karmic consequences – dependent arising[65]. At death, or by releasing attachment to one's relative position, the causal patterns in body cease. As we saw in Chapter 6, astrological cycles can be seen as the diagrammatic representation of karma.

The development of theories of physics through the 20th into the 21st century did not challenge popular perceptions of apparent truth; rather they developed and enhance them. The classical Newtonian view of gravity and universal dynamics works pretty well, provided that we do not go too far, or look too deeply. In the everyday world of most people this is fine. If we wish to travel in space, advance our methods of communication and recording, or alter the structure of life; we need tools that can only be provided by a more precise and advanced understanding.

To go beyond our everyday, gross, mundane material world and consider the creation and re-creation of the universe and life itself requires something deeper. How do the gross building blocks of the material world and its waves come in and out of creation? To say mass and energy interchange according to particular rules does not say enough. Does something we cannot yet comprehend stand behind the two? Are there in-built patterns that link both physical and psychological manifestation? What makes us disposed to see, be, or behave in this or that way?

As with all earlier developments in physics, the answers do not need to challenge anything that contemporary science and technology have discovered or applied. Rather, they would provide another dimension of understanding, which may link science and art, the inanimate and animate and show how all comes into being. Physicists seek to explain manifestation by discovering what is called the 'higgs boson', the missing particle that works like glue to turn energy into mass. Could it be that this glue is in fact the state of mind of the observer? If so, it was discovered by Eastern mystics thousands of years ago and called 'ego'! By defining and studying the progress of the grasping human ego, astrology is describing the very process of how and what we create and see.

Re-considering that crucial 17th century decision
When Descartes and his successors dismissed past assumptions and determined to re-start scientific enquiry from the basic phrase 'I think, therefore I am', they behaved rather like a teenager rejecting his parents' ideas and leaving home. Of course, such a moment in life is a vital cleansing that allows the adolescent to reassess phenomena in a fresh light. However, as time passes and teenagers become men and women, it is almost certain that most will come to respect, adjust and then reintegrate their parents' values with their own. So will and should it be with much that the Enlightenment rejected.

By stating 'I think, therefore I am', Descartes took a relative position upon which everything that followed would be dependent. Consequently he enslaved himself and the followers of his dictum to discussion without end. What he forgot was that, however intelligent and articulate we are, there comes a point when we have to stop thinking and talking. This allows our minds the freedom and space to realise the possibility of something more than a three-dimensional linear, mechanistic explanation of the universe. We need a de-intellectualisation process that explores the ultimate consequences of attachment to relative reality. Such a process will open a gateway to the realisation of a higher truth that is of more than three dimensions.

Physics seeks to extrapolate from the brilliant research work that has enabled it to catalogue, describe and control our world so precisely and skilfully and move on to describing the universe and time as a whole. In doing so, it will start us on a journey that physics and its associated disciplines cannot travel alone. By focusing its practical skills on the implications of astrological and other ancient pictures of nature, we may find subtle clues that bring order out of apparent chaos.

We may see that the universe is not only expanding, or even expanding and contracting, as it breathes in and out. It is emerging and returning back to a dimension that the relative mind just cannot find words to explain.

Further Reading

Robin Heath
   Sun, Moon and Earth
   A Key to Stonehenge
John Michell
   The Dimensions of Paradise: The Proportions and Symbolic Numbers of Ancient Cosmology
   The New View over Atlantis
   The Temple at Jerusalem: A Revelation
   The Lost Science of Measuring the Earth: Discovering the Sacred Geometry of the Ancients (with Robin Heath)
Percy Seymour *The Scientific Proof of Astrology* (see also Chapter 3)
Rev. Dr. Gordon Strachan *Chartres: Sacred Geometry, Sacred Space*
Bernadette Brady *Astrology a Place in Chaos*

Chapter 12
Healing the Mind & Body

The word 'health' comes from the same root as the word 'whole'. What does it mean to be whole – to be fully alive in every part of our being? The Chinese have a lovely image of a man moving between the forces of heaven and earth with the goal of remaining in harmony with both.
Jane Ridder-Patrick[66]

The solid imperial power of 19th century factories, locomotives and steam ships, the acquisition of raw materials from afar; and the consequent 'duty' of colonial administration did not bring the certainty and happiness anticipated by the rational philosophers and idealists of the Enlightenment. As we shall see in Chapter 13, this did not surprise many progressive thinkers. They saw the turn of the 19th/20th century as a time of revolutionary class struggle.

Others saw the human condition as universal, whatever the social circumstances and time in history. They sought to look inside and treat individual emotions and mental processes. These people suspected that wealth, privilege or even mere material security did not necessarily lead to happiness or reasonable behaviour. A much more intricate understanding of individual human needs and life experiences was needed to explain behaviour and enable peace of mind. So from the latter part of the 19th century, many people began to question traditional social morality and spiritual explanations for personal experiences and behaviour. With this came a fascination to explore previously held taboos.

There is an astrological explanation – the start of a new 500- year cycle marked by the conjunction of Neptune and Pluto in Gemini (the home of ambiguous and contradictory ideas). It was exact three times during 1891/2. Neptune had only recently been discovered and Pluto was discovered in 1930. Both had cycles far longer than the normal human lifespan. So, their cycles represent experiences and questions that are not easily answered by conventional social assumptions or crude mechanical logic. The previous 1398/9 conjunction, also in Gemini, was an early seed point that led to individual liberation through the soon-to-be-invented printing press, questioning the authority of the Roman Church and the religious hierarchy of ideas during the 15th century renaissance.

Now, at the threshold of the 20th century, discoveries from Egypt, India and other parts of the Empire brought interest in other religions and cultures, which were found to be far more advanced than the early Christian missionaries had suggested. On 11th September 1893, a World Parliament of Religions met in Chicago. The Theosophical Society made early attempts to synthesise all religions into Western culture. The regeneration of astrology in the West by Alan Leo and associates owes much to some Indian astrological techniques. The Golden Dawn magical movement was launched in secret, but soon became public. A metaphysical renaissance seemed to be at hand.

Meanwhile in Vienna

Sigmund Freud was developing psychoanalytical techniques. With these he was seeking to reach and treat the psychosis that developed from the repression of sexual and emotional drives in rigid 19th century society. Freud encouraged his clients to relax, reflect and take themselves back to early childhood. He asked them to remember, talk about and so come to terms with intimate events. These he held to be highly formative of character, personal assumptions and hence behaviour in later life. Toilet training and the overall parental method of upbringing, together with possible perversion in child/parent relationships, formed and could distort personality and behaviour. Only by recognising and addressing such issues could the patient be cured. Psychoanalysis was his method of doing this.

The ingress of Neptune, Pluto, Saturn and Jupiter into Cancer and the subsequent First World War was followed by each planet's ingress into Leo. This led to a breakdown of certainty and a new individual search for identity – especially 'culture- and religion-free' methods, with which to understand ourselves. Because it dealt so immediately, personally, simplistically and self-indulgently with human intimacy, Freudian psychology was ideally suited to take over from conventional religious and social morality. It seemed to cut through what many people felt to be the 'hypocrisy' and insensitivity of previously accepted values. Furthermore, with Neptune now establishing itself in Leo, the popular mood became dominated by fun and fascination with the unusualness of individuality.

Having opened the door to an amoral, and what would be claimed to be a scientific, study of the individual's emotional and mental behaviour; the range of psychological theses and methods of treatment expanded and diverged radically. Freud's psychoanalyst's couch inspired a range of reporting and interactional techniques between patients and therapists. Other approaches were more mechanical. These saw behaviour as no more than a consequence of physical brain activity, which could be trained to give automatic responses. From Pavlov's infamous dogs experiment, B F Skinner developed this Behaviourist branch of psychology. If these animals could be trained to salivate at the ringing of a bell, whether food was present or not, then human behaviour was a reflex action that could be conditioned and so corrected by a particular training, drug or even electric shock 'therapy'.

Such a view of behaviour fitted well with psychology's aspiration to be accepted in the increasingly important scientific community by finding statistical links between observational studies, treatments and outcomes. Combining with anatomists and chemists, psychologists sought a mechanics of human behaviour that could be categorised, contained and appropriately directed by electrical and chemical intervention.

Many psychologists prefer to distance themselves from Skinner's mechanical approach and claim to see patients as individuals. Yet, most tend to treat on the basis of structured diagnosis in very much the same way as an allopathic doctor treats a physical illness. The body of knowledge they rely upon is regarded to be 'expert psychological evidence', which plays an important role in contemporary business, legal and political decisions.

Yet is modern psychological theory based upon as sure an experimental ground as physical medicine? To observe that a motorcar engine works efficiently and goes faster when properly oiled, greased and cleared of corrosion tells us little about the driver, his reasons for driving the car or where he is going. So, does noticing heightened electrical activity, presence of adrenalin or other chemicals in the body and brain tell us more than the efficiency of the brain? To understand motivation and intentions, what is really happening, we need to reach and interact with the consciousness that is 'driving' the brain. To sedate, lobotomise, or intimidate the operation of the brain may restrain negative behaviour, but it is unlikely to understand and get to the heart of what is happening, or why.

Furthermore, the categorisation of what is and is not normal behaviour may be culturally determined. If a mental health system is not 'culturally neutral', it could become an instrument of social control that merely reinforces the conventions of the society financing the treatment. We could even be trapping individuals in a particular 'scientifically' fashionable 'reality'. If assuming a mechanical explanation for every aspect of existence is flawed and deluded scientistic fundamentalism, we are on very dangerous ground indeed. For, if this is so, the essential practice of this kind of psychology is a very lobotomy of truth that forces individual behaviour to fit the interests of those who seek power over the money and ideas of society.

Another problem with over-reliance on 'disease-style' categories of mental illness is that, other than crude suppression of extreme psychotic behaviour by blocking the body's ability to act, treatments rarely get to and answer the root of the problem as the patient experiences it. Rather, mental health patients become institutionalised into sub-cultural types. This leaves them two choices. They over-submit and so confirm their 'illness', become dissatisfied and undervalue themselves in society. Alternatively, they reject their therapist's advice and seek 'solutions' to their life problems that can be lethal to themselves and others.

Events in the development of mental health treatment through the first half of the 20th century showed up such concerns in stark reality. R D Laing's psychoanalytical work led him to claim that what may be considered as mental abnormality could well be no more than a patient's way of copying with family and social circumstances.[67] Every member of a Laing therapy group behaved normally after treatment but, on returning to their previous lives, their original abnormal behaviour soon returned. With the popularity of Ken Kesey's book *One Flew Over the Cuckoo's Nest* and the subsequent film staring Jack Nicholson, mental hospitals in the 1960s and 1970s came to be seen as instruments of social control. They oppressed individual freedom and were organised bureaucratically to serve and perpetuate the self-interest of doctors and nurses and narrow social convention.

In 1972 David Rosenhan's infamous research showed that eight mentally healthy people could get themselves diagnosed with schizophrenia and other mental illnesses, solely by presenting themselves at a mental hospital and claiming to hear the word 'thud'. Furthermore, once they had been admitted, revealing the hoax did not get them released. Only by admitting illness and feigning recovery could they be allowed to leave. When challenged about the fairness of the test, Rosenhan agreed to send more false patients. After several months, the hospital claimed to have discovered 41 presenters of hoax mental illness. However, none had been sent.

This crisis created for psychiatry by Laing, Rosenhan and associates led to a radical re-think with regard to the need for far greater objectivity in the process of diagnosis. In this regard, the advent of the computer seemed most timely. In the last decades of the 20th century, batteries of questionnaires were devised and categorised into specific disorders. Specific drugs and other therapies treat these disorders, and the patient is re-tested to determine progress.

Of course, the very individual nature of the emotions and mental focus behind human behaviour suggests such a mechanical approach may be so dispassionately objective to be dangerously impersonal, even inhumane. Indeed, one American study found over 50 per cent of those studied were 'mentally ill' and 'needed medication'. Another view would be that they were experiencing the normal ups and downs of everyday living, and that to medicate them would be to destroy the uniqueness of their personalities. Furthermore, all statistical studies are generalised and the producers and diagnosticians of 'efficacious remedies' have a personal and economic self-interest in the outcomes of such studies. Could the new computerised questionnaires be as much instruments of expert prejudice and impersonal social control as the opinionated psychiatry that Laing complained about before the new system was instituted?

While it is important to 'shout from the rooftops' to question the dangers of such mechanical and judgemental approaches to mental health, it is also important to recognise that people frequently demonstrate extreme states of depression and psychosis that make them a severe danger to themselves and other people. Also, studying the chemical processes of the brain and ways of correcting the extreme imbalances associated with such behaviour are crucial. Emergency intervention therapies are often the only and best way forward. Their calming potential can create the rest and space that help many sufferers resolve their problems. Also, mental health provision and families can bring great understanding and deep caring. Far from being the problem, the devotion of the patient's loved ones often provides the crucial motivation that drives recovery.

The key problem is that in our modern material world we can devise such powerful treatments that they can become seen as *the only* treatments. This becomes more worrying when we realise the only way of assessing treatments is through statistically assessed mass studies. If a certain percentage of people diagnosed as schizophrenic can return to what is considered to be an ordinary working life after using a particular medication, then this becomes the accepted treatment. It will remain so until a further statistical study shows a better alternative, or dangerous side-effects reveal themselves. Quite simply, the patient is 'at the mercy' of a researcher's decision to engage in further statistical study. No longer a co-creating individual participant in his own life, he may have an additional problem of not responding to a drug that 'most people with his condition' find beneficial. Some have very serious side effects and require other drugs to compensate. Many are blunt instruments.

Another vital problem, similar to that created by an over-allopathic approach to physical medicine, is that the development of a problem is not considered until the symptoms become acute. Quite simply, until the problem shows itself to be serious there is no problem at all. In mental illness, until the patient finally snaps under all the pressure, there is 'no mental illness'. Yet, this 'snapping point' might be the most difficult or even counter-productive time to intervene to address the essence of the problem. As a result the real problem may not be addressed at all. Instead, an emergency chemical therapy is prescribed and the patient categorised and often 'institutionalised' in his own as well as others people' minds.

Clearly we need categories and methods of treatment, but they need to be organic, malleable and non-judgemental, not box-like and mechanical. The treatment should not be so powerful that it permanently undermines the patient's individuality. Hence the statistics we use to assess success and failure need to be inspired, multi-faceted and flexible. They need to be capable of dealing with multi-variant categories and to see many different outcomes as valid. Also, we need to understand human behaviour as an ongoing process and be able to time tendencies, pressure points and opportunities of resolution. We need to be able to define when particular interventions are likely to be more and less effective, and to judge and time those interventions. We should be guided by a profound understanding of the patient's individual condition and nature, not the number of times this treatment has succeeded with a particular group of 'similarly diagnosed' patients. Individual need should become the determining guide of what we decide to do next.

To do this, it is important to see what is happening from the patient's perspective rather than from an 'objective theory of order and disorder'. Children are named in conventional religious societies to focus their mission in life. Krishna is the purely motivated courageous hero; Hanuman the monkey-god provider; Peter is the beloved of Jesus who may deny the truth, but will then sacrifice everything for it. We all like to see ourselves as Robin Hood. Within each of us is a struggle of dreams and aspirations that make much more sense and are far more potent than how much of a certain chemical is running through a certain part of our brains. We see our lives as the playing out of a story or mission. Even those very scientists, who insist the genetic structure is selfish and religion is an enemy of human sense and happiness, are driven by that heart-felt conviction that 'people should not be so silly as to think otherwise'. Business people, who believe that the absolute truth of scientific mechanism is a justification for exploitative energy and arms deals, are driven by dreams of their own imperial glory.

The need for an inner vision, a dream to drive our lives, is as strong today as ever. It shows itself in the obsession with sports heroes and teams, the glorious achievements and falls from grace of celebrities. Major developments in science and technology, including the mobile phone, came from the inventors and developers being inspired by watching early *Star Trek* episodes on television when children. Good stories change the world. They tell us the science we have to discover. If you have the inspiration, the vision, you will find the means to achieve it.

While we like stories that show we can be loved and admired, what especially inspires us are those occasions when success is snatched bravely from the jaws of defeat, when we triumph in the midst of adversity. For this gives hope to everyone, however small and insignificant. Then there is the more mature quality of seeking to do what is right and beneficial, whatever the opinion of others. This vital step in mental health can emerge when we let go at a point of ego-obsessed personal crisis. Religious redemption (objectively observable personality change) often emerges from inner moments of extreme negativity – every Saul has the potential for a Paul-like moment on his or her 'road to Damascus'. Common to mastery in all these experiences, from the most profane to the most profound, is the struggle of various inner visions and assumptions.

Fortunately, studies of such processes have been considerably developed. Carl Jung extended Freud's focus on early life to include what he called archetypal experiences through all ages. Drawing on religious and mythological stories, Jung charted a reservoir of visions that he saw as an intrinsic part of human consciousness – shared 'tribal memories' as he often called them. As we have seen in Chapter 2 and throughout this book, the concept of an archetype is the vital missing key we tend to ignore when seeking truly logical explanations of human behaviour. For archetypes draw together under one heading many understandings and outcomes that may at first seem different, even contradictory. Freudians accept that our attitude towards our mother and father can influence our relationships with authority and our aspirations in later life. Hence, the kind of parents and the way we respond to orders may all stem from the same key quality within us. In the case of President George W Bush, a sense of inferiority and dependence on his father in younger life drew him to experimentation with alcohol and stimulants in his youth, and then to invading Iraq, ignoring the authority of most other nations of the world when President. Experiences that trigger one expression of an archetype can trigger all expressions. If we were looking as he sees reality from inside, we would know why.

This struggle within, between many negative and positive archetypes, means that surface appearances rarely reveal the inside story that is driving the action. Indeed, what appears to be a bad action to the outside observer, when viewed from inside the perpetrator may well be motivated from the best of intentions – or vice versa. George W Bush may feel he is attacking, killing and risking the lives of thousands to make the whole world safe, kind and tolerant for millions. For every apparently good action, all of us have to face and deal appropriately with the negativity of our shadow. A government may invest in security technology to protect us. It may also be motivated by a fear of its citizens and a wish to have information to control them. It lacks the courage to rely upon encouraging ethical values and developing goodwill. When we are obsessed with fear, we project that fear onto the world. When the world and society is ready to fear, it attracts to itself leaders and artistic expressions that create and express a terrorised society.

Defining key archetypes and fully studying the patterns they make with each other could give valuable psychological understanding and guide psychiatric treatments. It could suggest whether and when chemicals might speed up, slow down or block the working of the brain. Crucially it could reveal links that conventional analysis may well miss. Armed with the key archetypes as a means of focus, we could draw together and explain what may at first appear to be highly varied and even unconnected behaviour patterns. A particular smell, sound or even an associate's minor action may well trigger repressed childhood memories and lead to anti-authoritarian behaviour. Our relationships with siblings can determine whether we feel it worthwhile making an effort at school and how we behave in our immediate neighbourhood. To have a chart that tells you when these and many other archetypes are likely to be especially sensitive may prevent misdiagnosis, inappropriate treatments and the wrong conclusion being drawn from a patient's reaction. Astrologers know very well that Pisceans and people with similar astrological archetypes are likely to have hypersensitive reactions to drug therapy and be easily upset by the actions of others. Just knowing this might lead to a reduction of the dose, or increased frequency of treatment and a faster correction of the problem.

Jung drew on a wide range of religions, traditional cultures and their myths in developing his understanding of archetypes and how they express themselves in people's dreams. He and his daughter also calculated and studied astrological birth charts. It is from this area of his work that we see the link between astrology and psychology.

How do astrological archetypes express themselves?
The names of the planets and the signs of the zodiac are derived from ancient Greek myths, which depicted the Gods intervening and directing events in the lives of ordinary humans. Such a view can be misleading – especially to a mechanistic, linear and literalist mind that can only reason in single-concept specifics. Aeschylus may show us that Apollo through the Delphic Oracle 'caused' Orestes to kill his mother, Clytemnestra. However, the key concept of this story is not the idea of divine

intervention but the relationships and duties between sons, fathers, mothers, sisters and those who betray the bond. It is essentially a morality tale about truth and creative responsibility – the Sun and natural order. Greek and other mythologies express the poetic experience, nature, inner struggles and paradoxes between good and evil, action and inaction, courage and cowardice, love and hate; indeed, all the predicaments that drive human decisions.

This book holds that such myths are not absolute fiction or fantasy, but symbolic expressions of very real experiences that are dependent upon the cycles of the heavens. Again, this does not mean that particular planets have particular direct causal relationships; rather that the *combination* of planetary relationships inclines the consciousness to particular archetypal experiences that can lead to outcomes, within a predictable range. By understanding the range, and particularly understanding positive and negative possibilities of that range, we can enhance insight and wisdom and hence heal likely outcomes – or at least help people find the most beneficial possibility. We can turn the inner doubt and anxiety of the negative shadow into a healed, positive experience. The Saul-like journey of intended persecution can be redeemed into a Paul-like life of service. This is the essential healing potential of psychological astrology.

So, as well as giving guidance that improves life experience for everyone, understanding a person's astrological birth chart, its progressions and transits can shine an illuminating light on the generalised 'hit and miss' attempts of modern psychiatry to contain unwelcome and destructive behaviour. It can help at two levels.

Firstly, astro cycles can often predict outcomes if people are behaving in psychotic, self-indulgent ways.

Secondly and even more usefully, astrology helps us understand and touch the specific cause of what they are experiencing. This can give therapists genuine authority. When patients feel deeply understood by others, it is easier for them to be objective about themselves and their situation. So, they feel they are far less likely to feel they need to 'defend'. When people do not feel they stand alone, it is easier for them to be compassionate. From compassion towards others, real change in behaviour patterns and outcomes is possible.

When working with individual patients, the clinical psychologist armed with astrology is in a much more effective position. With astrological insight, he can have a much more detailed understanding of the factors that lead to particular behaviour and life problems. Vitally important, this astrological understanding avoids the danger of labelling the 'sick patient' in a generalised, pejorative way, then reaching for drugs and 'clinically accepted' treatments that will 'heal' the problem. Electric shock/surgical treatments and intensive drug 'therapies' may lobotomise 'unacceptable' behaviour, so it does not disturb social 'norms', but it rarely does much to respect and enhance the individual's potential to grow uniquely and benefit society.

A detailed study of the birth chart of Mark Chapman
The astrology of the man, who murdered John Lennon, illustrates the claims of recent paragraphs very well. An in-depth study of Jack Jones extensive interviews with him in prison reported in his book *Let Me Take You Down* shows him to be a narcissistic, self-obsessed individual – a 'loser', who came to a point in life where he became obsessed with a 'mission' to murder John Lennon. A study of his astrological birth chart explains his behaviour in great detail and depth, and suggests just how much the general availability of astrological counselling at the right time could have helped.

Inspired by the trends of the time, and ironically by John Lennon and The Beatles, Chapman took LSD in his early teens. This drug's hallucinations enhance sensitivity and sensual experience, so the experience is 'super-real'. While the objective and mature mind may be able to observe, learn, grow and become more creative from the experience, the inexperienced or immature user can become obsessed, or even trapped into believing that the 'trip' is the 'real reality'. LSD does not so much *create* illusions, but rather enhances strengths, weaknesses and vulnerabilities that already exist in the personality. At the same time, it can reduce the capacity of the individual to integrate his hopes and dreams with the practical reality of living in the ordinary world. An enlightened society would establish mentoring facilities to guide users through the experience and particularly put it in perspective afterwards. That the distribution and use of LSD was made illegal in the early 1960s prevented such facilities being recognised as necessary and being made available.

Bereft of such support, Chapman was left with his inborn vulnerabilities exposed and unable to put himself and his 'importance' in to perspective.

MARK CHAPMAN
Natal Chart (12)
10 May 1955
19:30 CST +6:00
FORT WORTH, TEXAS
32°N45' 097°W18'
Geocentric
Tropical
Koch
True Node

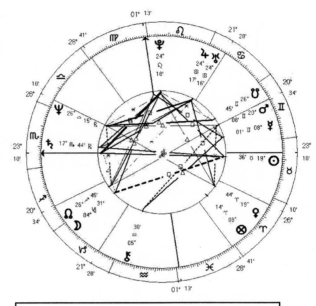

Figure 23 – Mark Chapman Birth Horoscope

His chart is both strong and full of contradictions. Being a Taurus with the ruling Venus in Aries made him both intransigent and impulsive. He would jump to conclusions, be unable to make use of them, but still find it difficult to let them go. With Mercury and Mars in Gemini in the 7th house, he would yearn to share his ideas in the company of others. This explains his friendships and interest in a library and newspapers as a child. In complete contrast, with Saturn in Scorpio in the 12th house, squared by Pluto near the Midheaven, he also retreated into private frustrated desires and an obsession with death. Interestingly his 'happiest moment' in life was caring for disadvantaged Vietnamese children (ruling Venus in the fifth, trining Pluto in the 9th house of foreign travel). Yet, with Pluto in the 9th squared his Saturn he decided to go to Hawaii to commit suicide. His private obsession with his religious mission and the vital imaginary 'little people', who in childhood and at the time of his crime guided his decisions, are explained by Neptune in the 12th house, squared by Jupiter conjunct Uranus in Cancer in the 9th   Crucially, the Moon is conjunct the North Node in Capricorn in the 2nd house. A Capricorn Moon can indicate authoritarian, intransigent and harsh judgements and reactions. The North Node can lead to over-reaching. The 2nd house concerns our personal values – what we are attached to. Putting these images together explains the deluded 'certainties' that so tragically dominated his life.

Before we consider how relating what we know about Chapman's life to these specific astro details could have helped him and maybe even prevented the tragic consequences, let us ask how he could have benefited from conventional psychological analysis.   Freudian psychoanalysis would have attempted to help him recognise, blame and then let go of the influence of his uninvolved and self-centred parents, who left him adrift and unable to find a real place in life. Other methods of interactional therapy might have integrated and educated his inner visions. Maybe after many sessions he would have found more suitable role models than an idealistic rock star and an intolerant, fundamentalist Christian view of his 'personal saviour'.

Maybe this would have tempered his belief that his mission was to fulfil the 'will of God', by eradicating the 'evil' that he saw Lennon to be representing. Yet could any publicly funded mental health system been able to identify and deliver such extensive therapy to such an opinionated and self-destructive person? A diagnosis of narcissistic schizophrenia is more likely to have suggested drug therapy to suppress attachment to his fantasies and reduce his physical ability to act on them. This would have left him dependent upon regular medication, and possibly institutionalisation, if he could not be relied upon to take it – little different to his present situation, but John Lennon may have survived.

Such a desperate 'final solution' emanates from the difficulty of most conventional psychological approaches to guide him through the many ambiguities in his nature and tame the Taurus/Capricorn determination to be 'right and responsible'. The fundamental problem is that our mental health system specialises in treating what it considers to be mental *disease*, where this 'patient's' problem is really his experience of *dis-ease* between what he sees to be his natural self and the world outside. The therapist/patient relationship inevitably disempowers the latter by suggesting there is a *disability* that needs to be corrected, even eradicated, as if it were a gangrenous leg. By contrast, astrological counselling starts from the assumption that everything there is about a person is natural and valid. There may be stresses and strains and poor self-understanding, but these have to be honoured, educated and channelled, not condemned and 'cut out'. A good counselling astrologer encourages the client to make the best of everything he is.

In Chapman's case, the first step would be to work with him to identify the various facets of his nature. Looking at each in turn, we would consider how he could express it in the most comfortable and happiest way. Discussions would emphasise the determined courage of his ruling Venus in Aries, but warn of the danger of his jumping to ill-considered conclusions. Consideration of his Mars/Mercury in Gemini would lead to his sharing the many pleasures he has experienced when helping other people with ideas and plans. He would be encouraged to talk about his achievements at the school library, with the neighbourhood newspaper and with Vietnamese children in later life. We could consider the temporary and contradictory nature of ideas (Gemini) and see how people change their minds. Therefore we have to be careful not to take anything that comes to our own minds to be absolute truth.

Having achieved some comfortable agreement in this area, we would then turn to the more difficult and private area of his Neptune in the 12th house squared by Jupiter/Uranus in the 9th. This would open the door to talking about his 'little people', not so much to label them as 'delusions' he needs to be rid of, but rather as his unique way of finding deeper meanings. I might mention the Preface to George Bernard Shaw's play *St Joan*. Shaw explains his heroine's hearing of voices and seeing visions as 'her way of thinking', because she had a very visual mind. Just as we do not act on every idea, we do not have to act on every voice – such an argument should appeal to a Gemini 7th house. By talking about the nature of Neptune, Uranus and Jupiter in conflict, we would explore the importance of his looking objectively at himself when having these visions. This should help him realise the danger of making decisions on the basis of them.

Such approaches make the client feel the astro-consultant has a unique, intimate understanding and respect for him, in a way few if any others have had before. Once such a trust is established, then it may be possible to make progress on the crucial Moon in Capricorn in the 2nd, ruled by Saturn in Scorpio, squared by Pluto in the ninth house. How this is approached would depend on the strength and reliability of the relationship established. The fundamental point to come to is that it is natural for him to rely upon himself, that only he can make final decisions in his life. Vitally, because of this it is essential that he does not jump to ill-considered decisions. Here we would draw on the easier ground of Gemini and impulsive Venus that has already brought understanding between us.

This would open the door to talking about the Pluto/Saturn square as being concerned with life or death matters. We would spend some time expanding what people understand by death; how it can regenerate and transform, as well as eradicate. Having already agreed that knowledge and ideas are relative and absolute truth problematic, we may move on to how he can best serve society. With all his talent, sense of responsibility and tendency toward inner anxiety, it is clear that being with other people is a much happier way for him. Security-guard work that isolates him in his own private world is not. For, by interacting with as many different people as possible, he can use his inner strength and wisdom to enhance their lives.

This would open the door to talking about *Catcher in the Rye*[68] and encouraging him to read other works that show the unsatisfactory nature of ordinary life has been recognised throughout the whole span of human history. He could explore the many different ways that characters in fact and fiction have coped. The people we admire most are not those who destroy what they disagree with. We prefer those who act in positive ways to help others; teachers in the broadest sense – nurses, doctors, social workers. Tell him this is why he was happy when engaged in social work helping others. Crucially, just as we respect his (Chapman's) unique power to serve, so he should accept and honour the very different way others could serve and educate. Improvement of society and human happiness comes from understanding others, not the simplistic eradication of those we disagree with.

Inevitably in all this, discussing John Lennon's role in 20th century society would arise. Firstly, we could consider the nature of the revolutionary times (Uranus conjunct Pluto in Virgo) of The Beatles' rise to fame. Bearing in mind the didactic, exploitative way Western culture was being imposed and the subsequent East/West conflict, it was inevitable that the younger generation should rebel. The drugs of the psychedelic movement of the 1960s did open minds to sensitivity and heightened insights that only disciplined meditators had experienced before. The Beatles' role in encouraging such experiences could be considered as naïve and irresponsible, but also as necessary in the circumstances. The problems for individuals that ensued were as much caused by the ignorant and ill-informed reaction by the authorities to what was happening as it was by Lennon. To see Lennon as the focus of evil would help no one and confuse many.

The next stage in the process would be to identify possible courses of action. This is where the progressions and transits to his natal chart become invaluable. Our birth natures develop as we progress through life, according to predictable patterns. The circumstances of the Earth at a particular time (the transits) indicate opportunities and difficulties in taking action. Having worked with Chapman to identify his nature and find the best use of his undoubted great ability to serve, now we need to help him make decisions about timing. When, as well as how, should he do what? What reactions might he expect and how would it be best to handle them?

If we study the natal, progressed and transit charts for the moment he shot John Lennon, we can see just how lethal was the absence of astrological understanding and advice. The slower-moving progressions and outer planetary transits indicate periods of strong, growing negativity. The outer (transit) chart shows transiting Pluto about to square the natal Jupiter/Uranus conjunction exactly and approaching his natal and progressed Neptune – clearly an explanation of the 'dark forces'. Transiting Neptune had recently opposed his natal Mars and was applying to his natal Nodal axis. Transiting Jupiter and Saturn were about to conjunct each other just past a square to his progressed Mars (the ruler of his natal ascendant that indicates how he will present himself to the world).

Any one of these factors will occur only once, if at all, in anyone's life. That they should all occur at the same time would be a warning to any experienced counselling astrologer that a crystallisation of his client's fundamental delusions was imminent. On the day in question, the Moon was approaching the same position as Chapman's natal Moon. It was exact less than an hour before the event. At the moment of the assassination, the transiting ascendant was in an exact trine to his natal and progressed Nodal axis and had conjuncted his natal/progressed Pluto just twelve minutes of time earlier. Also, the transiting Midheaven had a few minutes of time earlier conjuncted his natal Sun and progressed Venus close to his descendant. From his perspective, he would feel comfortable with the 'rightness' of the moment. Of course, the Moon transit occurs every month and the ascendant transit every day, but that they should happen so closely together, and when all the other long-term indications were building, is what triggered the event. Rarely can an individual have felt more strongly that his 'appointment with destiny' had come.

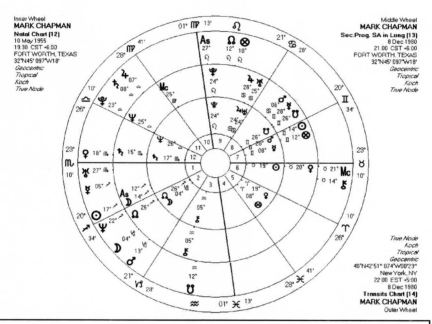

Figure 24 – Tri-wheel comparing Mark Chapman's natal/progressed charts with the transiting planetary positions at the time of John Lennon's murder.

An astrologer working with Chapman should have seen the dangers easily and have warned him of a period when his voices would come to dominate and impair his judgement. He would have been able to indicate a time period when intensity would build, remind him of happier times, and then encourage him to wait, not act, through this negative time. 'Do not believe what seems obvious. Wait. If you still want to act with strong retribution a year later in December 1981, then come to see me again' might be the advice. A Tibetan Lama may advise a period of retreat through such transits. As it was, Chapman had only his own, unguided, inner obsessions to take refuge in. The pressures of what seemed like an endless, building struggle to release tension became irresistible.

Transcending such intense negativity is easier said than done – especially with people who have strong, private Capricorn energy, as Chapman does. They think they know the answer and are reluctant to compromise and follow other people's methods. Success in formal education is difficult for them, because they find it difficult to submit to other people's way of doing things – especially the demands of educational bureaucracy and examination systems. Yet, having such a person, with a gifted IQ of 121 and a heightened sense of belief-driven responsibility, misunderstood and unfulfilled in society is a tragic waste and a recipe for disaster. With the right guidance and just a little less isolation, he could have transformed the power of his obsession and given much that was good to the world; as have many other people who were born close to his birth moment.

Of course, it would be no easier to make available such in-depth astrological counselling to people with Chapman's life patterns than it would be to give conventional therapy. However, consider a society where astrology has an accepted place and is taught at school and university. Imagine a media where astrology is as much a part of contemporary conversation as conventional psychology is today. In such a world, there is every chance Chapman would come to understand himself better and not feel such an outsider. When in difficulty, it is far more likely that he would seek out a non-judgemental astrological counsellor and find a way to become a positive force in society.

Even if there were no cooperation or interest from Chapman's side, then some understanding of the flow of his transits and progressions could be used to identify times of maximum stress and likely trauma. Noting and checking up his handling of such times and giving support might be of great benefit to him, and also protect the society he lives in.

The Terrible actions of Cho Seung-hui
The astrology of the tragic deaths on the university campus at Blacksburg, Virginia, in the USA on 16th April 2007 makes an even

stronger case for its remarkable potential value as a diagnostic, even preventative, tool.

Prior warnings by his English tutor that Cho Seung-hui displayed disturbing behaviour patterns in his writings were a central part of the news at the time. Cho's birth chart clearly reinforces this.

The date and place of birth were clearly published in several media outlets. Doing a Google search for his time of birth on the 17th April, only two entries appeared.[69] One garbled and meaningless, the other was a Chinese language source with just the place and time of birth shown as 'Seoul' and '0300' in Western script. Accessing and then auto-translating did not make the origins of this information any clearer. So I cannot verify the source. The time may not be right, but certainly the birth chart as drawn fits the character we came to know so well from his video during those terrible days.

The combination of Pluto, Mars and Saturn in the 12th house, trined by the Moon in Cancer in 8th house, which built to a Full Moon the day after this birth when it opposed the Sun in Capricorn, would certainly explain the isolated, self-righteous brutality of the man. The strong

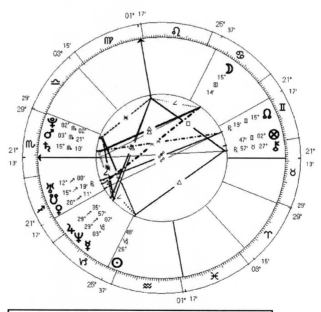

Cho Seung-Hui
Natal Chart (3)
18 Jan 1984
03:00 JST -9:00
Seoul, Korea, South
37°N33' 126°E58'
Geocentric
Tropical
Placidus
True Node

Figure 25 – Cho Seung-hui Birth Horoscope

Sagittarian presence building to Jupiter almost exactly conjunct Neptune, close to Mercury in early Capricorn, indicates just how expansive his delusions of grandeur could become.

These are qualities that any enlightened society using astrology could and should have identified. They could have been channelled into positive expression, or at least contained carefully from quite early in his life. Especially, astrology could have provided authoritative support to his English teacher and also the judge he had been before on a lesser offence. In both case, having the astrological information would have been a timely warning to anticipate and prevent the dangers.

That something was about to burst is clear from the progressions and transits in figure 26. These show that progressed Mars was just one degree before its conjunction to Natal Saturn in the 12th and that the progressed Moon had opposed that position three months before. With transiting Pluto just drawing back from natal Jupiter/Pluto conjunction and transiting Jupiter from his natal Venus (all in Sagittarius), he would have felt that 'time was running out'. He needed to expand and fulfil his deluded fantasy and so assuage the unfathomable 12th house hurt that he had always lived with in utter isolation.

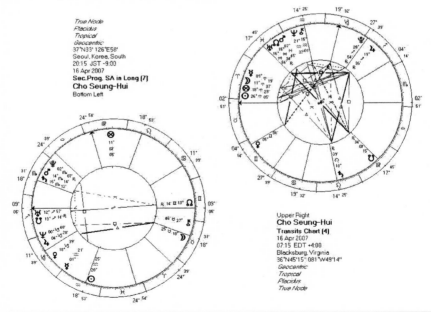

Figure 26 – Cho Seung-hui progressed chart with transits of the first killing

The transiting Sun applying to square his natal Sun, plus the transiting Moon having squared his natal Mercury the previous afternoon and applying to square natal Moon during the day ahead worked together with the background pressure to trigger this day as the one on which he would act. The first murder occurred very soon after the transiting ascendant had crossed Moon and Sun in Aries[70]. Then the Taurus ascendant approaching his descendant took him back to his room, to prepare his statement to the world, which he posted as the transiting ascendant entered Gemini and applied to Venus that was applying to square Mars.

While it is always easy to be precise in retrospect; the underlying dangers and likelihood he would act some time this year could have been clearly seen months if not years in advance. While not advocating a *Minority Report* society[71] with astrology as the key, this case is yet another example of how the authority of astrology intelligently used could save lives.

Mark Chapman and Cho Seung-hui show clearly why astrologers feel so passionately that our society suffers because most people do not know the basic planetary factors that lie behind human attitudes and behaviour.

In today's consumption- and status-obsessed material world, we cheapen and sideline astrology at our peril. With a mind open to the possible great value of astrology, we see the answer staring us in the face and know it makes sense.

The advent of reality television offers an opportunity to put such a big claim to the test. In the *Big Brother* series, several cameras record events 24 hours a day. A preliminary study suggests predictable connections between the behaviour of the participants and the birth, progressed and transiting planetary positions in their charts. Balanced and experienced teams of astrologers and psychologists could work together to discover an experimental design that would reveal the extent of astrology's ability to predict human behaviour and experience. For the nature and value of exactness works both ways. It is just as dangerous to claim causal links that are not possible, as it is to be so inexact as to be irrelevant. It might be just as, or more, useful to study the dimension and range of choices a person is faced with than whether this or that action or medicine will trigger this or that response. Too great a dependence on the automatic (be it allopathically or astrologically determined) may create distorted self-fulfilling prophecies. Knowing the range within which a particular individual is working can broaden understanding of the reasons for their behaviour and hence suggest more exciting and effective solutions to problems.

Paradoxically, rather than restrict options, it is the very describing of an individual's astronomical cycles that gives the freedom of an appropriate range of options. In contrast, labelling a person with a particular mental category or disorder can mark them out for life as failing, inadequate and always in need of corrective treatment and medicine.

Yes it is true, contrary to popular opinion, that astrology really does sets us free!

The art and science of healing the body
It was nearly 2,500 years ago that the 'Father of Medicine', Hippocrates, originated the Hippocratic Oath that is still taken by doctors to this day. When on another occasion he also stated that 'a physician without knowledge of astrology has no right to call himself a physician' he was merely emphasising what was generally accepted as best practice at the time.

Doctors today may feel such an opinion to be strange for a man who is credited with liberating medicine from religious superstition and the notion that disease is the result of divine retribution. Clearly, Hippocrates did not see astrology as a superstition, accepted only by credulous deluded minds. He accepted astrological cycles as observable in nature. The more recent research referred to in Chapter 3, which was summarised by Roger Dobson in *The Independent*[72] may well confirm he was right to do so.

Hippocrates and those who followed his methods were the first to describe many diseases and medical conditions. His treatments were holistic, based on observation, rest, cleanliness and passive techniques to encourage natural healing. In his day, such an approach was far more successful than the alternative diagnostic approach, which depended upon, but lacked, proper anatomical knowledge of the body.

In modern medicine today, while Hippocrates's principles and good practice in treatment are honoured, the emphasis has shifted towards diagnosis and radical intervention – what was known as the Knidian approach in Hippocrates's day. The excellence of research and technological improvements over the past two hundred years has led to 'unbelievable' advances in what is now called allopathic medicine. Drugs, surgical techniques and now genetic and stem cell research have made it feasible for many ailments to be cured, or at least kept at bay for far longer periods of time. In many parts of the world, people are living much longer today than would have seemed possible even a few decades ago.

While all this is a cause for rejoicing, the very excellence of our learning brings with it reason for caution. Firstly, life is not just for the benefit of humanity. Some bacteria cause many illnesses, but only because they want to live. A consequence of their feeding and reproduction in order to live is the harm they do to us. Hence, each time we defeat them can lead to their mutating into a strain that can harm us in new ways. As with the Knidian approach 2,500 years ago; radical intervention with limited understanding can be dangerous and counter-productive.

So, it seems unlikely that mechanical medicine on its own can eradicate all disease. Also, we should not allow the heady power and brilliant ingenuity of modern medical methods to feed the ego of the contemporary medical profession into believing only modern methods should be allowed.

When current practice rejects ancient, holistic methods as barbarian fantasy, patronises them as naïve, and seeks to outlaw them, the pendulum between the two approaches is swinging way too far in the wrong direction. Not that all feel this way. Some allopathically trained doctors see traditional holistic methods as ideal for the first line in a proactive patient-centred health policy. They do not deny conventional allopathic treatments, but reserve them for serious cases – 'horses for courses'. By enabling the two approaches to interact in a complementary way, they can serve more patients more appropriately – usually at far less cost.

Contemporary allopathic techniques tend to see the patient as a passive object that needs to be 'mended, because there is something wrong with it'. Holistic traditional medicine looks at and interacts with the whole person, through eyes, pulse, pressure points and the patient's reaction to questions about diet and experience of life. A self-affirming plan of action is built up with the active participation of the patient. Behaviour can be adjusted in good time to prevent more serious illness later. If this succeeds, the brilliant, but highly expensive, allopathic emergency solutions never become needed.

The tendency only to consider allopathic treatments can lead to patients being over-treated in ways that may lead to other problems. Chemotherapy can weaken the bones and lead to premature ageing. HRT may trigger breast cancer and have negative effects on other parts of the body. Such problems can only be answered by new research. The medicines discovered then take time to be tested. Actual treatments offered can change like fashion. What is in fashion may depend on the stage of the research cycle into particular treatments. It can become very much a 'hit and miss' affair. One patient may be amazingly lucky; another is an unfortunate 'guinea pig'. The patient's ability to control and influence outcomes in such a system can only diminish.

Of course, in the majority of cases, diagnosis and the solution are clear. A powerful, well-tested medicine or surgical technique is applied and the patient experiences an amazing improvement. Yet, the techniques are expensive and might not have been needed at all if an ongoing and inexpensive system of preventative medicine had been in place.

Is there any way that astrology could play a part?
Before seeking to answer this question, it is vital to make clear that we are not considering astrology as a fortune-telling substitute determiner of treatment. On its own, astrology can be of little use. However, if considered alongside a proper qualified understanding of the body and medical theory, we may find advanced medical astrology[73] can be as valuable a part of the physician's armoury, as it was two and a half millennia ago.

By studying the transits and progressions to the natal chart, astrology can predict with pretty precise timing our potential to be under difficult stresses in life. Should such stresses manifest as physical illness, astrology can both support medical treatment and provide radical insights. It can show the illness, then track and put in perspective the progress of treatment. Such knowledge would not normally interfere with conventional allopathic diagnosis and the prescribed intervention, but strengthen patient understanding and co-operation.

Because astrology describes cause and effect on spiritual, mental, emotional as well as physical levels, it offers vital new perspectives into health. Stress does not have to work itself out in the physical body all the time. Indeed, if one is spiritually evolved, there is less chance that it will. This is why attempts to find a statistical link between stress and illnesses, such as cancer, have been difficult to establish. An ambulance driver client of mine has a birth chart that suggests he is severely prone to accidents, but told me he had never had an accident himself. Instead he had earned his living helping other people through their accidents. Having made the spiritual decision to dedicate his life to others, so far he had averted these kinds of problems in his own life. Understanding the astrological cycles can help people channel the tensions of their lives, so that physical illness may not even occur.

Psychosomatic illness studies show how the mind and feelings can be so fraught that real or imagined physical symptoms appear. Cancer comes from genetic dysfunction and consequent breakdown in the male/female balances in the cells of the body and unnatural cellular multiplication. If the genetic weakness is inherited, then it may show itself when comparing family birth charts. It may be environmental or associated with a lack of flexibility and give-and-take in the pattern of a person's life. Either potential may be helped by life-style changes in good time. If we are confronted by a high wall, we could tear our bodies to the bone and die of disease while making little or no progress in climbing it. If a way around the wall is revealed at an early stage, none of that life-threatening energy need be expended.

Perhaps one of the saddest results of the academic rejection of astrology in the late 17th century was that it sidelined major contemporary scholarship into the relationship between astrology and natural medicine. This had been sustained from the time of Hippocrates through Paracelsus[74] and in 1652 Nicholas Culpeper had published his famous herbal guide. It appeared just five years after William Lilly's *Christian Astrology* included detailed insights into decumbiture horoscopes. If that time's early adolescent rationalism had had the maturity to absorb such incisive traditional wisdom, the development of modern medicine may have been more balanced, far less expensive and even more effective.

The relationship between astrology, diseases and medical problems is a detailed and in-depth area of study well outside the scope of this wide-ranging book. To make a thorough start on this path, readers are recommended to read Jane Ridder-Patrick's *A Handbook of Medical Astrology* and then to follow its extensive bibliography.

When considering complementary medicine and natural treatments, it is important to realise that no one is claiming them to be alternatives to allopathic treatments. To say: 'This homeopathic [or herbal] remedy has no measurable active ingredient. It is no more than a placebo' is to miss the point. Would we condemn as useless the smile and gentlest of nudges that eased us away from being thrown down and destroyed by the suction surrounding a fast approaching train? Would we say the danger would have been averted without the smile and nudge, or that only by building a permanent barrier on the station can people's lives be saved?

In the same way, most medical practitioners today dismiss outright the notion of combining astrology with any form of medicine. Yet, in the experience of many perceptive astrologers, there is a correspondence between the development of sickness and the effectiveness of treatment and astronomical cycles, especially if we consider archetype ranges and levels of manifestation.

Because allopathic medicine and modern psychology diagnose illness in a piecemeal way, they are not equipped to consider the notion of an astro-indicator being expressed on various levels –spiritual, mental, emotional or physical. Without knowing the language and structure of astrology, regarding these levels, we cannot see the patterns and connections between an astronomical event and the manifestation *or avoidance* of illness. Maybe a savage transit of Mars, Saturn and Uranus will lead to death, or recovery – much depends on the state of mind of the patient and what he or she has experienced and learned before in life. Yet being able to identify the psychological background to the physical problem and having a method to develop a good mental attitude towards it can play a vital role in recovery. Even the most advanced methods of modern medicine are yet to find a pill that will switch on and strengthen the deepest reaches of the human will.

Pioneering work by Dr Pat Harris[75] suggests a possibility that astronomical factors may be related to successful fertility treatments. She studied the presence of positive relationships of the planets Venus and Jupiter to clients' birth charts at the time of treatment. 'A preliminary study found that 13 of the 16 successful births (81%) had contacts to or by Venus and/or Jupiter when including acutely time-dependent factors, compared with only 19 out of the 86 unsuccessful treatments (22%). Similarly, when time-dependent factors are excluded, again 13 (81%) of the live and healthy births, and 16 (19%) unsuccessful treatments had such contacts. Further, the additional 12 unsuccessful fertility treatments gathered subsequent to the development of the model appear to reinforce it when the findings on these data are incorporated into it.' Her full study 'attempts to validate the model against a new sample of women undergoing fertility treatment' is expected to be available in 2009.[76] If the preliminary study is confirmed, it may be explicable in a similar way to the relationship between astronomical cycles, emotional disposition and financial market price movements outlined in Chapter 15 of this book.

There is much to be discovered and re-discovered. Comparing medical records with astronomical cycles, under the guidance of an expert astrologer who has some knowledge of medicine, can do no harm and may lead to a great deal of good.

Then we may learn how to relate to every patient as an individual. Being able to define and anticipate the development of those differences over time could play an invaluable role in the healing, or even the not-getting-sick, process.

Further Reading

Key books on psychological astrology
Stephen Arroyo *Astrology, Karma and Transformation*
Alexander Graf von Schlieffen *When Chimpanzees Dream Astrology*
Liz Greene
       Relating - The Inner Planets Barriers and Boundaries
       Saturn – A New Look at the Old Devil
       The Astrology of Fate
Michael Harding *Hymns to Ancient Gods*
Thomas Moore *Planets Within – The Astrological Psychology of Marsilio Ficino*

Key Books on Medical Astrology
Nicholas Culpeper *Complete Herbal*
William Lilly *Christian Astrology* [Modern English edition David R Roell]
Eileen Nauman *Medical Astrology*
Astrological Judgement of Diseases
Jane Ridder-Patrick *A Handbook of Medical Astrology*
Graeme Tobyn *Culpeper's Medicine: a Practice of Western Holistic Medicine*

Chapter 13

Astrology, Sociology & Creation

And the Lord God formed man of the dust of the ground and breathed into his nostrils the breath of life: and man became a living soul.

And the Lord God commanded the man, saying Of every tree of the garden thou mayest freely eat; But of the tree of the knowledge of good and evil thou shalt not eat of it: for in the day that thou eatest thou shall surely die.

Genesis II v7, 15-16

Throughout its recorded history, humanity has debated whether nature or nurture is the key influence upon behaviour. Whichever way the pendulum swung, the wise answer has always been the same – neither one nor the other.

The biblical story of the creation shows the muddling of the two concepts from the very beginning. God created the perfect nurturing environment – the Garden of Eden. Then he created Adam, in the nature of his image and Eve from Adam's rib, to live there. However, while God gave Adam and Eve instructions (nature), he also nurtured them with free will to obey these instructions or not. Hence they were exposed to the negative nurturing of the satanic serpent's temptation. Satan's nurture seduced them into falling from grace and expulsion from the Garden. Then God offered an escape from the consequences of following this negative nurturing. He gave positive hope of redemption through the birth and example of a Messiah, whose nurturing they could follow instead. If they did, they would return to their ideal nature. They would sit with the Messiah in Paradise at the right hand of God. The Christian God also introduces the notion of a Last Judgement, when all shall live for eternity; either in the suffering of hell, or in the happiness of heaven. So, he builds a powerful motivation into the nature of humanity to choose the nurturing way that leads to heaven.

Similarly, Plato held that the role of 'nurture', or experience, was far smaller than common sense might suggest. Plato felt that a child began life with knowledge already present within him. In *Phaedo*, Plato suggests that the child does not learn new things but merely remembers them.

As Christian scholarship grew to dominate educational and political life from the Dark Ages into medieval times, a hierarchy of fixed status was established. With expected behaviour and responsibility clearly defined, very little room was left for flexibility. King, noble, squire, merchant, peasant knew their place (nature). They sought a change in the environment (nurture) at the risk of their lives - even their very souls.

The development of the printing press in Europe, translation of the Scriptures and availability of other vernacular books from the 15th century, together with Renaissance travel and discoveries, had an unsettling effect. The Inquisition insisted that questioning the established world-view was comparable to the entry of the serpent into the Garden of Eden. Yet, its most didactic brutality was unable to stem the tide. The new knowledge put humanity back into the driving seat of experience and opened eyes to a vastly different range of nurturing environments and explanations for existence. Several centuries of consequential religious conflict followed. Then Man took centre stage and sought to impose rational humanitarianism as the arbiter of essential meaning. Perhaps we could choose, form and control our nurturing environment – be whatever we wished to be.

The contradictory philosophical explorations of the Enlightenment, briefly outlined in Chapter 9, were inconclusive. Were individuals purely born, virgin vessels to be raised high by the enlightened nature of circumstances, or profoundly corrupted by degenerate ones? Alternatively, were pure and debased environments the product of a person's intrinsic nature? If the pure-spirited, noble Perdita in Shakespeare's *A Winter's Tale*, or Charles Dickens' Oliver Twist, find themselves in low-class or degenerate circumstances, the nobility of their inborn natures not the coarseness of the current nurturing shines through unsullied. Yet in Dickens 19th century writing, there is a contradiction. Even those that at first seem to be the degenerate co-creators of their low lives can have within their nature an ability to rise up and sacrifice themselves bravely for others, like Nancy in *Oliver Twist*, or Sidney Carton in *A Tale of Two Cities*.

Could it be that human nature was intrinsically good and only temporarily brutalised by degenerate environments (nurturing)? Would it be redeemed, if inspired by the right, ideal circumstances? In Nancy's case this was the wish to protect Oliver. For Sidney it was his love for Lucie Manette.

For a while, Rousseau's *Noble Savage* became the epitome of the ordinary man. By confronting the exploitation of indulged and degenerate European monarchies and by experiencing the squalid, unjust and exploitative environments of the bludgeoning early 19th century towns, the rights of man and the notion of the class struggle were born again, stronger than ever. The contrast of life experience, opportunity and legal rights between rich and poor was so extreme that the political struggle focused upon the basic right to survive. This left little room for the niceties of the nature/nurture debate. Because it was so clear that all working people were treated badly in the 19th century, a key question was never asked. Were their intrinsic natures any different to those in power, who were exploiting them? If the positions were reversed, would the victims, when perpetrators, behave any differently, or be just as exploitative?

Not asking that question, Marxist analysis saw the class struggle as the battle to be won and the abuse of the capitalist bourgeoisie, their agents and devices as the enemy to be defeated. Various shades of socialism, at first outlawed and persecuted, found ways into trade unions, political parties and pressure groups. They were to grow ever stronger through the 19th and 20th centuries. They developed from the basic right to freedom of life, happiness and expression enshrined in the American Constitution. From this, and the French Revolution's 'liberty, freedom and fraternity'; grew the notion that the State was responsible for the welfare of its citizens.

In the early 20th century, the focus of Jupiter, Saturn, Neptune and Pluto in Cancer spurred on great movements of social change: workers' rights, women's rights and social welfare. These raised fundamental questions as to the nature, rights and responsibilities of political structure and leadership in the imperial and industrial world. Could unbridled capitalism survive and expand? Started during the first decade of the 20th century and accelerated in spite of the hardships after the Second World War, the British Welfare State was to provide a basic livelihood, accommodation, health care and education for all citizens as of right from the cradle to the grave. In the Soviet Bloc of Countries, this became the 'only game in town'.

The Gemini conjunction of Neptune/Pluto, mentioned in the previous chapter, brought into vogue strange new ideas. Humanity grappled with issues far beyond the capacity of an ordinary human lifespan to understand. What was ultimate authority, and who should have and administer it, became problematic. Indeed, what did we know? What was true and would this always be so? Jules Verne and H G Wells visualised travel to and from space in a future world dominated by scientific discoveries. Einstein was to produce his Theory of Relativity. The manners and facile pretence of a self-indulgent, privileged society were satirised by Oscar Wilde. Their tragic impotence was shown up in Chekhov's *The Cherry Orchard*. George Bernard Shaw's plays asked about integrity, political and institutional morality. His questions remain unanswered to this day.

The notion of family and social order was to face terrible and tragic challenges, as the First World War brought death to millions, unstable nations and the breakdown of colonial imperialism itself. Many subsequent problems continue into the 21st century. Seeking to burst through and replace the Old World imperial privilege of princes, there emerged a curious mix of full-out working class 'democracy' and puritanical fascism, driven by intolerant scapegoating. No longer was it enough to be a patriotic Briton, Frenchman, or German. God was not to be found in such narrow loyalties after all. There were higher values common to a broader humanity, 'provided it agreed with us'. In the 21st century, we still have to learn the implications of how much broader this humanity and its agreements have to get!

In such rapidly changing and increasingly materialistic societies, the assumption of authority by heredity (nature) was broken down. The individual right to enjoy a beneficial nurturing seemed paramount. So a system of academic study that showed how outcomes and experiences related to social circumstances became essential. Was Marxist analysis the inevitable and only way to explain what was happening in modern society? Sociology was born as an academic discipline that studied the effect of social conditions on individual and group behaviour and opportunity.

Potential areas of study seemed limitless. What was the impact of social class background, race, gender, age, parental circumstances and siblings on life expectancy, political opinion, crime, economic consumption patterns, exam success, educational and work opportunities, and a whole plethora of health and lifestyle considerations? How did environments affect performance at work? How do individuals respond to the Kafkaesque alienating effect of ever-expanding self-protective and self-perpetuating bureaucracies in administrative and academic institutions?

Peter Burger and Thomas Luckman in *The Social Constructions of Reality* suggested that knowledge is the product of what is agreed between individuals and institutions within society. Such a view tends to leave the individual as a dependent social construct, entirely nurtured, without intrinsic needs. From such assumptions, or 'realities' (depending on how you see them!) come the phenomena and effects of advertising, marketing techniques and political spin. Perpetuating the consumer society and its mainstream political supporters has become the main source of income for advertising agencies, film producers and media entrepreneurs. The emphasis of sociology has moved on from rescuing the individual from 19th century brutalising exploitation and social prejudice to developing knowledge and techniques designed to enslave him in his own 21st century self-indulgence. Could much contemporary sociological study be accused of reversing its vision, of prostituting itself and enslaving the individual it was born to liberate?

As new sociological theses and statistical studies develop in a world where techniques of amoral psychological manipulation are becoming all the more advanced, will individuals be *'allowed'* an intrinsic nature? Will the nature they are born with be allowed to survive the intrusive nurturing of modern commercialisation? The need for a definition of the intrinsic nature of life and humanity and ethical values in society has never been greater. With the 'right conditions' and nurturing, who knows what each of us can be 'made' into? Are we at a key stage in human history, where nurturing could radically and irreversibly change nature?

In the first half of the 20th century, the crude and brutal hands of Nazi eugenicists claimed the right to decide the ideal human nature and hence each person's right to live. As we saw in Chapter 10, 21st century geneticists now claim to have discovered the very essential building blocks of nature and are proceeding to engineer plants and products. Is this fundamentalist nurturing? We are back to the nature/nurture argument on what seems like a very different and highly dangerous dimension – the creation of life itself. Does the modern geneticist see himself as both the *creator* of nature and *controller* of how it should be nurtured? If so, by how many centuries have we brought forward the 24th century sociological intervention visualised in Aldous Huxley's *Brave New World?*

Before we presumptuously proceed to the ultimate limits of our own self-destruction, perhaps we should check our hubris against the basics of the universe in which we live. 'Is it nature or the gardener [*i.e. geneticist*] who creates the garden?' asks Shakespeare. His analogy of the garden makes a nonsense of even asking the question and seeking to make a distinction between the two. Clearly, a natural drive to grow existed before there ever was a gardener and will continue to exist whether there is a gardener to intervene or not. Just as clearly the gardener has the capacity to adapt and channel these natural drives. If the circumstances are not right, the potential for life will wait. Although the gardener [geneticist] can frustrate the forces of nature, any intervention will never be more than temporary in the universal order of things. Certainly, life will not disappear altogether, but it may disappear as we know and can use it for many millennia.

To astrologers nature/nurture disputes are irrelevant

The description of astrology in this book confirms this. Astrology sees 'the garden' as the universe and the chart of the positions of the planets at birth describes not only inborn nature, but the potential for particular kinds of nurturing as well. The chart develops by progression and is activated by transits. Furthermore, the timing of these progressions and transits can be calculated precisely. So, here we have a predictable pattern of nurturing factors working with a clearly defined set of inborn (natural) dispositions. Or do we? Surely, if the progressions and transits are based on the predictable movement of the planets, then are they not as much a part of natural dispositions as the birth chart? So, are astrologers saying everything is inborn and they are on the nature side of the argument?

Not necessarily! An increasing number of modern astrologers, and even the great 17th century predictive astrologer, William Lilly, believe in humanity's freedom of choice. The renowned classical astrologer Ptolemy, who is better remembered for his technical work, held that an understanding of our astrology could improve our experience of life and even the workings of the heavens themselves. Within a set and predictable pattern of pressures and opportunities, there is a spark of human spirit that can create different outcomes from the same set of conditions. The more positive the motivation, and the greater the clarity of the mind, the more effective the action can be. Astrology has a dual advantage. It defines circumstances clearly and so enables human beings to make more effective decisions.

Knowing this removes much of the confusion about astrology. It is possible to predict outcomes if people are behaving in a psychotic, self-indulgent way. However, if they are using astrology to be compassionate and (vitally important) objective about themselves and what is involved in their situation then different outcomes are possible. Such considerations move us beyond the nature/nurture debate to a higher logical analysis of the human condition and circumstances. *Now we can assess genuine achievement and failure.* Can success, however sensational, be just a lucky chance? Maybe an action was ill considered and only succeeded because the person's astro-cycles were at a 'fortunate' time when she/he could 'get away with anything'. On the other hand, was an apparent failure much more worthy, because the individual behaved heroically in the direst of astro-circumstances?

Such an understanding of astrology puts the role of sociological study, and psychological and genetic intervention, in the modern world into a clear and proper perspective. Quite simply, such studies are commentaries upon, not determiners of, the ultimate cosmic flow. They can only be properly assessed in terms of it. However powerful and potentially critical for good or ill in forming our present social circumstances, sociological and psychological studies is no more than a fashion of our times – an expression of a stage in history. Chapter 5 indicated that it was just a stage in the natural flow for there to be a rapid expansion of communication and media technology because Pluto was in Sagittarius and Uranus and Neptune were mutually receiving each other in Aquarius/Pisces. With Jupiter ruling both Pisces and Sagittarius we would expect such intrusive advances in statistical study to expand into and dominate every area of our lives – to make us aware of many places and experiences. With Aquarius/Pisces so strong it could be expected that material science would over-reach itself in an attempt to solve all aspects of human suffering – the positive justification for genetic engineering.

However, the originality and drive behind this major upsurge will fade, be put in perspective and assimilated into the grand design of all things, as has been every other event and development in history, all of which we have seen to have, or can be shown to have, their own astrological explanations. Everything moves on. Has any garden ever lost its natural disposition to 'return to nature', even in time the scorched earth around Chernobyl?

Certainly, as we turn into the second decade of the 21st century, we will find ourselves asking how effective, beneficial, lethal and long-term will be the skills of the temporarily intervening genetic gardeners, nuclear scientists and their political investors. How much power over our bodies and information about us, our children and their descendants should they have? For, as the rapid acceleration of Aquarian technological innovation fades, issues of control and individual freedom could well shake the assumptions and very foundations of society. The thorough sociologist will seek to track and allow for these cosmic changes in his/her researches.

In 2008, Pluto will have left Sagittarius for Capricorn; in 2010 to 2011 Uranus enters Aries with Jupiter; and then Neptune and Chiron ingress Pisces. Whether we are looking forwards, backwards, or going through these times when we read this, it would be interesting to consider the changes in what we feel comfortable about compared to the decade before. Was much that came during the first decade of the 21st century thrust upon us almost unwanted? Did we ask for it, were we prepared for it, did we understand the implications of it all? Will it leave us free space to explore our own beliefs? How will we react to the dichotomy of enjoying being in computer touch and control of all that is? Will we yearn to struggle back to a past when we were independent and free of constant personal intrusion? Is the development of digital technology and global hysteria causing us to sleepwalk into a highly efficient form of neo-fascism where only increasingly narrow, scrutinised life patterns are acceptable to the political functionaries that spin our lives? Will we welcome or fight against being genetically engineered into fitting such patterns?

Will sociology do more than use its studies in the service of spinning administratively efficient solutions to create and control pliant populations? Or will it take the more enlightened path of wanting to know the nature of and interaction between individuals, groups and contemporary fashion? Certainly much valuable work is being done by independent sociologists, who are supported by commercially-independent funding. Studies of the health consequences of eating, drinking, gambling and addiction patterns in given age, educational and vocational groups are clearly beneficial research.

Much good work is being done, but crucially will it include the astrology of the times, the individuals and groups it studies into its research design? Essentially, do we want to understand people as they really are, so that society can become a celebration of all that is best in all of us? Or do we wish to give the controlling power of sociology research and information technology to commercial interests? Are we happy to give it to power-hungry bureaucrats whose very weakness and vulnerability make them wish and need to manipulate others?

Society has come a long way since the Enlightenment. There has been little time to take stock and put in order the ragbag of old and new philosophies, methods and principles we have half-gathered and/or discarded along the way. We seek to guide our lives by a mass of arbitrary and counter-productive decisions and practices. Suddenly in a hundred years or so, we find ourselves snatched from the certainty of isolated established cultures to a hotchpotch of multi-cultural, contradictory and incomplete assumptions about what should or should not be – as of right! The only thing we are told we should agree on is the obligation to produce and consume. We will burn out ourselves and our planet if we go on blindly like this.

Part 4 considers such economic considerations and the implications for our legal, social and educational institutions Could an understanding of the astrological cycles that underlie the changing fashions of our assumptions about life, values and society help us do better? Could the application of personal astrology help us answer the nature, needs and behaviour of people? If we step back to assess and put our material and social advances in perspective, could we come to respect our planetary garden as an honoured expression of nature? If we develop the humility and wisdom to do that, would we not be far better global gardeners and far happier and healthier human beings?

PART 4

Astrology
&
the Key Institutions
of Society

Introduction

So far, we have shown that astrology is a rigorous system of knowledge. It is profound and could be relevant in the 21st century. Also, it could bring insight and balance to some unanswered questions in conventional academic subjects. Now Part 4 will consider how taking advantage of its wisdom could actually enhance contemporary social institutions and make them much more effective.

While astrological insight could benefit all areas of our lives, for this study we will limit our focus to a few specially selected key areas: finance and business; law; the communication of social values; and education.

Before we start, it is important to make clear the extent and scope of what is possible. Ours is not a quest for an earthly utopia – a heaven on Earth. Rather, we start from the premise that our world is a training ground: a perfect setting for individual and group imperfection to be recognised and transformed. Our institutions should help each of us to identify and heal misunderstanding and negativity. Since beings are at myriad levels of intellectual and spiritual maturity, each of us advances at a different speed. By putting mundane considerations into perspective, we transcend emotional assumptions about what happens, and so see the higher logic and total fairness of the universe.

Each person's progress depends upon the existence of a fertile environment to guide the recognition and selection of wise mentors and leaders. Unfortunately, shortsighted greed and ignorance means we often judge narrowly and so follow the wrong people and procedures. We seek the 'promise' of immediate gain, are exploited and misled. Today's immense material power makes the consequent prejudice and division all the more traumatic and world wide.

To get on the right tracks, it is vital to accept we all have a common dichotomy – everyone seeks happiness, but faces death.

In the words of the black spiritual song, 'Everyone wants to go to heaven, but nobody wants to die'. How can we attain the former, if we cannot avoid the latter? So, how can happiness be permanent? For, if we see what we call 'happiness' as ending, then this very 'happiness' is the root cause of unhappiness. Inevitably, we engage in a struggle to preserve what is unsustainable in an environment that is haunted by the spectre of death; either from constant disappointments and losses in life, or the ultimate end of our own individual lifetime. Desperate to avoid the 'inevitable', we defend our positions and attack others, causing increasing unhappiness to ourselves and everyone else involved in the struggle.

In such a condition we are vulnerable to those who seek to control us by exploiting our present fears, creating new ones and then offering to protect us at a price – anything from an insurance policy to a war against terror! To satisfy what we perceive to be our sensual needs and beliefs; we threaten 'death' to others by defeating them in social, commercial, legal and military struggles. Citing his understanding of modern life as 'the survival of the fittest', Jeffrey Skilling, the ex-CEO of Enron, is said to have used Richard Dawkins' *The Selfish Gene* to justify his company's exploitative manipulation of the energy market[77]. Is the ultimate achievement of the Enlightenment a life and death battle of greed in a free-for-all market place; with occasional regulation for those we catch cheating? Does this mean that we have to see human nature as so base and deceptive that it can only be controlled by rigid, intrusively-supervised targets and regulations?

Such views are anxiety-generated 'gospels of despair'. It is far better to see things as they are, not to be motivated by our fears and depend upon empty hopes for the future. Indeed, our attachment to short-lived pleasures and resentment towards those we perceive to be harming our pursuit of them, intensifies our experience of death. The more we see ourselves losing, the more frequent will be our disappointments and desperation. In contrast, the more we seek to organise our affairs and institutions to provide the greatest happiness for the greatest range and number of others, the less anyone feels threatened. Death at the end of this lifetime is the adversity we all face. To intimidate others with a premature experience of it makes death omnipresent in the minds of all. When we face change together in a supporting community of friends, we see the ends of things as the heralds of new beginnings. Such a view broadens our understanding and ability to handle ever more traumatic challenges. Who knows, there may be consciousness after death. We will find out, if we respect and draw on everyone's experience. In this way, we touch happiness that lasts. So this should be the heart aspiration of the way in which we organise our lives.

We need social institutions that are not about protecting us, but about opening evermore hearts towards such an ideal nature; moving everyone and everything in a kind and positive direction. We stop looking away with fear. Right now and ever after, we maintain a kind state of mind whatever the circumstances. This is the way to see clearly.

By enabling us to cut through illusion and objectify our own and everyone else's thoughts and behaviour, astrology can help us let go of an unnecessary, fear-driven, 'life and death' struggle to dominate and possess. If we can combine such insights with compassion, realising each of us faces some kind of similar predicament; astrology can be an antidote to the manipulative and deceptive excesses of our social institutions. It can liberate us from those tragic and self-destructive traps that come from being focused upon the consequences of short-lived power and revenge.

What is suggested in the chapters that follow is radical and may seem ludicrously unrealistic. That it does reveals just how far our everyday values are removed from ideal principles. Our material mechanistic view of nature has led many people to believe that working for the happiness of everyone is a futile, self-defeating delusion. People proclaim such 'soft sympathy' is a trick to emasculate others in order to gain power over them. Yet, is it not human nature to feel sympathy, even for those far different to ourselves? Do we not admire those who sacrifice themselves for others? Kindness is what makes us feel good about ourselves. While in the court of *apparent* 'self-interest' it may make no sense; in the truth of our experience it is the source of all lasting happiness.

The following chapters show how our key institutions lack the resources to understand social cycles, individual human nature and the principles of trust and freedom that hold all good things together. As a result, they trap us in a continual battle of resentments. Ignorance of each other's nature and the larger circumstances we think we face leads us to an apparently unending, tragic process. We manipulate, marginalise, handle, blame and punish imagined 'enemies'.

These chapters also show a positive alternative. Our institutions, using astrology to understand the intrinsic nature of individuals and situations, may not 'switch on eternal happiness', but will provide a clear conceptual foundation for us to work with. This will be a language that enables ever-broader understanding to educate a healing process. Genuinely satisfied and free, we will be less likely to create ever more problems, but be clearly focused on solving those we have and enjoying the liberation that ensues.

Chapter 14

The Key to Better Economic Planning

To every thing there is a season, and a time to every purpose under the heaven: a time to be born, and a time to die; a time to plant, and a time to pluck up that which is planted; a time to kill and a time to heal; a time to break down, and a time to build up.
Ecclesiastes 3: 1-3

Putting the present economic picture in perspective

On a hot summer's day, sprinkle a good quantity of sugar near the path of a small scouting party of ants. Return an hour or so later to see a massive army engaged in carrying back the 'booty' to their nest. If you can find the nest, note how it expands exponentially. In unhygienic conditions, or where the strength of the human body is weakened and vulnerable, the bacteria and cellular distortions that create illness proliferate just as rapidly.

It is the same in human societies. Throughout our history favourable conditions, inventions, strong leadership and convictions of self-importance have fostered the growth of movements and empires. These have exploited and consumed gentler and less favoured communities.

This driving force for favoured species to expand and then indulge in uncontrolled excess is automatically contained by nature. Perhaps the environment will change, or external forces, other species and cultures will fight back. Also, imperial decline is usually accelerated by the natural tendency for dominant species to degenerate from within. Their self-indulgence leads to 'too much of a good thing'.

Until recent centuries, this ongoing process of growth, dominance, decline and fall has ravaged vast areas of the Earth from time to time, but the planet's natural ability to sustain new life has led to regeneration. Mechanical brilliance and the ability to exploit slavery enabled the Roman Empire to dominate much of Europe and the Middle East. Yet, after a few centuries only fragments of the culture survived to be re-worked by those who succeeded it. To a person living in Europe in the 5th century after Christ, it may have seemed like the end of the world, but only the 'world' as he or she knew it. The ants' nest may suffer destruction from the boiling water poured into it by an irritated householder, but some ants will survive, recover and build anew.

Today, humanity cannot be so sure. Six hundred years of global travel, intensified by 350 of accelerated material scientific discovery and technical ingenuity have led to little of our planet being spared from humanity's control. It seems to be subjected to irreversible alteration and exploitation. The discovery of the steam engine and coal enabled powerful machinery. In the 20th century the development of the internal combustion engine and finding of vast reserves of oil led to a rapid expansion of human activity and a population explosion all over the world. Today, atomic power and ingenious electronics make information about everything ever more available. We have the power to know about and influence individual thought, dispense immense changes, implement advances and destruction at the flick of a switch.

Alongside the technical advances of recent centuries have come economic theories on the organisation and distribution of resources and their products. From the last part of the 18th century, the rights and advancement of the middle and then the working classes became a primary concern. As the absolute power of monarchs and aristocracies diminished, the right of individual entrepreneurs to build factories and transportation systems brought a new kind of exploitation. Against this, the 19th century, abolition of slavery, growth of trade unions, socialism and Marxism led to counter-struggles. More and more individuals demanded control over their lives and the right to enjoy the fruits of scientific advance.

From the second half of the 20th century, the lives of most people in the world's industrialised countries became full of conveniences and an ever-increasing range of goods and foods. Visit a modern macro-market and wonder at the possibilities. There is little food we cannot have, whatever the season of the year or climate we live in. The range and power of technological devices grows ever more rapidly, while prices remain stable, or even decrease.

The driving force behind this 'triumph' of modern commerce has been the dominance of free-enterprise capitalism. Socialist attempts to pre-plan, organise and regulate 'fairly' for everyone were found to fail. They led to inaccessible bureaucracies and potential corruption of the leadership on the one hand and the disempowerment of the ingenuity of individual workers on the other. Dull, incompetent societies were the result. In contrast, setting everyone free to invest, produce and spend as they wished seemed to bring not only freedom, but the greatest efficiency and innovation. The natural law of the survival of the fittest led to the most efficient organisation of society. As we produced more, we became better at it: economies expanded, wages and disposable incomes grew – everyone won!

It seemed that at last the wit of humanity had triumphed over the ebb and flow of nature. More and more people could have comforts, previously the exclusive preserve of a small, privileged aristocracy. Most wonderful of all, we could achieve an efficient and balanced world economy, merely by setting individuals free to make their own decisions.

However, is the G8-, World Bank- and IMF-controlled world free trade economy as total, permanent, ideal and eternally happy as it seems? Have ordinary people really progressed from brutal exploitation, via the dictatorship of the proletariat, to a permanent aristocratisation of the proletariat? Or are we just in the middle of a lucky break? Are we in truth no more than a group of party-goers loaded with alcohol and other 'goodies' to indulge in and gorge on? Is all that lies ahead the jaded awakening of the morning after; to find our resources exhausted and the same old harsh realities of life confronting us?

The notion of economic growth depends upon having ever-expanding raw materials, workers and machinery for production and markets to expand into. Successful market economies of the past always existed in only part of the planet. Labour depended on slavery or low wages. The success continued as long as the raw materials could be obtained and there were more areas of the world to discover and exploit. Today, ingenious machines are our 'slaves' and make the work easier and cleaner for many of us. Since the end of the Second World War, Japan, then Hong Kong, then other parts of South East Asia and now China, India and Eastern Europe have been sources of cheap labour that have kept down prices. More and more people throughout the world have been bought into the production process and so attained the means to become consumers themselves; hence demand increases further and leads to ever-expanding production.

The momentum of expansion is sustained by the investments of banks and financial markets underpinning the manufacturing processes. The opportunity to invest in financial markets has been opened out to more and more people. Today, millions all over the world can trade a wide range of company stocks, commodities and derivatives from their home computers. More resources become available. Wealth increases.

For all these reasons, is our modern economy different to any other in the past? Can this growth go on forever? Can free-enterprise capitalism expand and bring material comfort and happiness to more and more people? Has humanity at last found a permanently successful means of production and control?

Certainly our systems of communication and accounting are as sophisticated as they have ever been. The ability to travel physically, send information and instructions instantly, transport products and track everything we do has never been greater. The most able brains are employed to record and share information, anticipate demand and production costs, then adjust investment and marketing accordingly. International agreements stabilise currency and interest rates and adjust investment and loans to free the flow of world trade. The very fact of competition makes producers and traders examine economic trends, currency rates, GDP, inflation levels, interest rates, employment statistics, government announcements and other economic statistics. These are published in financial columns and available on the Internet from almost anywhere in the world. We have never been better informed in business decisions. So, with the best minds working on it, is the most successful commercial organisation of the planet of all time inevitable?

Not necessarily. If we look more deeply there are essential flaws in the very methods that we use to underpin our apparent success. They start at the core; the kind of competition we hold to be the key to efficiency. Certainly competition can be beneficial, but only if we have a proper definition of what we are competing about. Such a definition would include experiences and activities that offer consistent and lasting success and happiness. However, the present world economy is almost exclusively about competing over material ownership: success as judged by money. We are trying to be efficient about one person's, or group's, ability to obtain more possessions and money than another.

In such a competition, the expertise will be as much about how the rules are interpreted, the costs allocated and when. Fundamentally, the successful individual or company will need the strength to control and manipulate suppliers and customers. To do this they will buy out competitors, or put them out of business. Successful companies become larger. There are fewer and fewer competitors as more and more fail or are taken over. Then the consumer, who for a long time seemed to be benefiting from low prices and efficiency, is now at the mercy of those few distributors that remain.   For the inevitable process of free-trade commercial competition is that producers of the goods receive less and less, but not all of the money saved is passed on to the customers. If not controlled, the end game of free-enterprise capitalism is the opposite of what its name suggests. As in Monopoly, the popular board game, just one middle-person player will hold all the cards and have complete financial control. Then this person can pay and charge what he likes. It may seem very different on the way but, irony of ironies, the end game of capitalism could be totalitarian ownership, without even the 'good intentions' of the Soviet system's social conscience.

Of course, we have monopoly and anti-trust legislation to guard against such an extreme scenario, but can these bodies comprised of appointed insiders really protect the market, or guard against major inefficiencies in the system? Just a few, ever-larger distributors is the way of the 21st century economy as I write. The sheer size of these distributors will give them great influence on governments to regulate in their best interest.

Even the shareholder democracy, theoretically built into the trading of publicly listed companies on the world's stock markets, has been diminished by recent high-profile private-equity buyouts. This removes the company from Stock Market listing. The ownership and decision-making process is no longer by shareholder-appointed boards, but those appointed by rich individuals and investment funds. The purchase can be financed by loans that are underwritten by the company being purchased and repaid from its future profits. The new owners may seek to sell assets and maximise profits.   The general public benefit in such transactions could be questioned. For such arrangements extend the debt exposure of the now privately owned resource and entertainment providers that our 'prosperous' lives depend upon.   Will they continue to exist should market values, our own debt exposure and ability to consume, experience a substantial downturn, as happened in 2000, the early 1990s and 1929?

Because profit margins and other ways of gaining financially are the ultimate aspiration of the company and its owners, it is considered good budgeting to transfer costs to people entirely unconnected with the enterprise. Can they avoid paying the cost of ecological damage, or oblige customers or neighbouring enterprises to cover more costs? They may consider it 'efficient' to conduct activities that may be a nuisance or inconvenience to people unconnected with the company, because it would be too expensive for the people so inconvenienced to take legal action to stop them. Calculations like this abound in the modern business world.

The problem is that people do not engage in business to create a better world or happier people. It is good if trading in a happy climate helps profitability, but that is only a bi-product. The key aim is to become richer and have more and more, whether we need it or not. Such motivation may work well while there is slack to take up. However, because it lacks self-regulation, what appears to be ever-expanding enjoyment of luxury is desperately temporary. Essentially, we remain no better than an advanced colony of ants consuming a very finite pile of sugar. Our methods of economic organisation, however brilliantly researched and implemented, are no more than stopgap ways of justifying unnecessary over-consumption to 'keep the show on the road'.

We can see the weakness of all this when we realise that the core things we need for production are finite. Firstly, underpinning all production are basic energy resources – oil, gas and coal – which are finite. In 2007, the UK is considering a return to nuclear power, whose poisonous waste products can only be hidden deep down in the Earth to decay over tens of thousands of years. Secondly we need basic raw materials. Even if recycled, with ever-increasing production these will wear out in the end. The capacity to find new markets is finite. As recent world trade talks have shown, the world economy remains dependent on the exploitation of the wealth of 'under-developed' areas. Millions continue to starve, because our focus is upon economic expansion and protection of the world's more industrially advanced areas. Some citizens of emerging nations may work for low wages and, in the end, enjoy the fruits of the 'global economic miracle'. Many will be left to suffer without hope, having sold their raw materials below their real value, but found their leaders did not invest the proceeds in sustainable job-creating projects. Then who will there be left for any of us to sell to?

If everyone were to live to the standard of wealthy Western societies, could the present expansion be sustained? To continue to expand production means we will in the end consume all the natural wealth of the planet. In 1961, the UK could support itself from own resources until 9th July each year. In 1981 the time had shortened until

14th May. In 2006, self-sufficiency did not last beyond 16th April. If the whole Earth consumed at the rate of the UK, we would need 3.1 Earths to meet world demand.

The story of Easter Island is highly relevant. Here an isolated society, cut off from the world, consumed all their forests to construct and move statues that were the expression of their beliefs and higher aspirations. In doing so, they lost the animals and birds and their ability to make boats with which to fish for food. The result was war and the survival of only a fragment of the population scratching mere subsistence amidst the useless edifices of the past. How comfortable will our cars be without petrol, and our homes and modern office blocks without gas? Could these things become of no more value than the Easter Islanders' stone statues?

The essential nemesis of our contemporary economic system is the problem of waste. Because the present by-products of petroleum are plentiful, everything is packed and double-packed for ease and cleanliness of distribution. With methods of production so efficient, it is 'economically efficient' to replace rather than repair. Little is made to last. Where, then, do we put what we no longer need? To travel, we burn. To produce, we burn. To dispose, we burn. Smoke, essentially carbon, ascends. The eco-system of the planet, the very conditions we need to survive, is threatened. We are at the stage where there is still enough left to only worry a little bit – rather as the Easter Islanders would have been with still a vast forest on the eastern side of the island untouched. To change our ways would deny the expectations of millions. Our progress over recent centuries has been so immense. We have every reason to expect we will discover new ways to continue to expand and even put right any 'temporary' harm we have caused. 'No need to panic!'

To think like this is to close our eyes to the essential flaw in our economic model – 'Let us continue to enjoy the resources we have exploited so skilfully. Someone[78] will leave out another pile of sugar' said the leader of the ant colony!

An efficient self-supporting economic model
Should not our economy be based on a balanced taking and giving within our limitations to consume and restore what we consume? A good farmer keeps back sufficient seed to plant the next season. He relies upon many generations' experience of good soil husbandry and the seasonal cycles

to know when to plant, harvest and store through difficult times. Certainly, we have developed expert methods of refrigeration, storage and transportation to liberate us from dependence on seasonal cycles to some extent, but no good farmer plans only through and for times of plenty. By an intelligent anticipation of the future, he plans to survive all but the most unlikely events.

An even more fundamental question to ask is to what extent does the present plentiful supply of food and ingenious machines bring human happiness, make us wise and provide political stability? Is it not better to measure wealth not by what we have, but what we can give. This is not to recommend starvation: only the most spiritually advanced can be happy, wise and generous to others if dying for want of food. Yet, does being at the opposite end of economic privilege bring happiness? Do we really enjoy the 'plenty' of being bombarded by the constant psychological manipulation to consume? Do we really want the resultant dissatisfaction, unnecessary guilt, failure, and judgemental atmosphere? Do we want the need to work and consume to dominate our lives? Do we wish to be greedy for advantage and 'good fortune', to gamble and gain something for nothing? We have far more than we need, or our ancestors ever thought possible. In spite of all we have, constant dissatisfaction is all too often at the very heart of modern life. Commercialism even dominates our sport and leisure. How much do we enjoy commercial breaks on television and those constantly flashing pitch-side background advertisements?

Free-enterprise capitalism is a switch of plenty turned full on; a driving force that consumes our very soul. Can we do no more than 'enjoy the ride' while it lasts? Is excess and destruction always the only way of nature, or could we develop a better relationship with our environment? Can astrology help us develop a wiser state of mind and find a more balanced, happy and enlightened way to organise our economy?

Yes, for sure this is possible, but the first step is far more fundamental than astrology. We have to realise that the tragic cause of the rise and fall of each person and all societies is rooted in temptation; the difficult-to-resist appetite that creates, then consumes and destroys life.

When we are hungry, the immediate satisfaction of eating is indeed joyous. How can we sustain that joy? We assume we need to eat more.

While experiencing 'the morning after the night before' may suggest otherwise, we soon find a way of consuming more. The binge-drinker celebrates the opportunity to vomit and quickly get back to more drinking! It takes a little more restraint to hold back consumption and experience the satisfaction of restoring true balance to the digestive system. To eat or drink less can be much more satisfying than eating and drinking too much. It opens space for other experiences that lead to a really rich life. As our judgement considers longer spans of time, we gain more control, are freer and expand our range of enjoyment. Only the fundamentally psychologically damaged will wish to binge-drink into old age. The wise know when to give and take: when to restrain themselves and when to take risks. We develop as individuals by applying what we learn. The aim of life is to expand understanding of how things really are and the way they work; to expand consciousness in a sustainable way. So it should be with our global economic organisation.

If we can accept that sustainable ecstasy comes as much from restraint as indulgence, then astrology can provide the structure and language to help us do the rest. With it, we can step back, put ourselves and circumstance in perspective, explain the past and suggest likely passions and circumstances in the future. So we distance delusional desire-driven consumption, are ready for change and can implement truly objective and intelligent economic planning. The second part of the chapter illustrates how to do this by giving examples from the past and indications for the future. With such wisdom, insight and control we may be able to succeed beyond the point at which earlier civilisations collapsed.

Astrology and economic development from the 18th century

Firstly, we must use astrology to put the economic development of recent centuries in medium- and long-term perspective. To aid the analysis, we will use two major advances that astrology has made, both in spite of *and* because of recent scientific developments. Firstly, three additional planets – Uranus, Neptune and Pluto[79] – have been discovered. Secondly, advances in computer technology now provide precise observation and presentation of planetary cycles. This allows us to trace the unique way the repeating cycles of the outer planets combine throughout the flow of history. Using all that with what material science, history, archaeology and electronics have revealed, it is possible to map and assess the progression and regression of societies over considerable periods of time. Astrology can explain and anticipate the rise and fall of leading civilisations throughout history and into the future. This section will focus on the economic build-up from the 18th century to the early 21st century, and then look at the fundamental issues that lie ahead of then.

Chapter 5 explained how to use the key outer planetary cycles that need to be considered here.

Although not observed until the 1930s, Pluto moved into Capricorn in 1762 and stayed there until 1778. Between 1760 and 1780, some 900 Enclosure Acts were passed. Although enclosure had been an often-disputed practice through previous centuries, it was from this time that it came to dominate and mould the British landscape. By the end of the 19th century, it was virtually complete. This led to a major movement of populations to towns, where numbers increased rapidly. At the same time, Captain Cook and others were mapping the Earth with exact precision. This led to the allocation, ownership and commercial exploitation of land all over the globe.[80]

The key to understanding the 18th century and its economical development, however, was the discovery of Uranus in 1781. This planet symbolises the coming of technological advances, such as steam power, factory production and radical social change. In 1789, following on from the 1776 American Independence, the French Revolution saw such a complete rejection of established order that it threatened the stability of all Europe. Uranus in Leo was approaching its opposition to Pluto in Aquarius between 1789 and 1791.[81] The right of every individual to enjoy 'happiness' became the dominant aspiration for subsequent centuries. Political struggles over the best way to organise society for the greater good expanded rapidly, alongside invention, industrial might and global colonialism. The gross foundations of our modern society were being laid.

The discovery of Neptune in 1846 symbolised the bringing of more pliable, mysterious and 'unworldly' considerations into mass consciousness and economic development. As well as influencing art and spirituality, Neptunian energy symbolised the mysterious, 'magical' power of petroleum, gas and electricity. These new energisers brought greater subtlety and flexibility to industrial development and communication. They were to form the basis of 20th century economies. In 1930, the discovery of Pluto indicated that humanity had brought into its conscious mind the knowledge to atomise the very building bricks of material existence. The scramble for resources and control through these later colonial times led to two brutal world wars. These encouraged massive expansion of ever more sophisticated armament and consumer-based industries.

The transits of Jupiter, then Saturn and Uranus, through Gemini in the 1940s symbolise the rapid inventive innovations that underpin the ingenuity of our modern communication technology. Jupiter symbolises expansion and opportunity in the economic marketplace. Transiting Saturn's sign can suggest problem areas, but it can be a positive force of discipline, regulation, and control. Both help to activate the interplay of the three outer planets.

Kondratieff, the Russian economist, described a cycle that averaged 56 years that seemed to indicate the repetition of technical growth, consolidation and decay. Without considering astrology, he pointed out that, as a particular technical development reached its fulfilment, economic growth tended to stagnate until a new technical innovation initiated a new cycle. He related economic activity to the development of the canals until the early 19th century, then the development of the railways until the 1870s, followed by the development of urban transport and the internal combustion engine until the early 1930s. Since then, we have seen the build-up of armaments and mass production, which reached a point of stagnation at the end of the 1980s. Since then, mass communication information technology systems and especially mobile phones and the Internet have come to dominate our world. This cycle will play itself out towards the end of the 2040s – ready for a new technology, of which we can hardly conceive today. The interplay of Jupiter and Saturn cycles means they oppose each other every 20 years. It is no coincidence that every sixty years the third opposition occurs for a two-year period just a few degrees past the point it occurred sixty years earlier. Clearly technological development comes from the reconciliation of expansion and consolidating contraction that the conflicting opposition between these two planets symbolises.

It is possible to explain everything that happens in our taste and decisions regarding the economy by looking at the interplay of the five outer planets in detail. The process builds gradually and organically, because these planets change sign on different dates. When several change together, or are in tight aspects to each other, the effect is clearer.

When Saturn conjuncted Pluto in Leo in 1947, what Winston Churchill described as the Cold War started. Communist and capitalist countries became locked in crisis over the identity of post-war Germany and Europe as a whole. Also, it was an exceptionally cold winter in Europe as the conjunction was applying at the beginning of that year! When Jupiter in Cancer opposed Saturn, Uranus and Neptune in Capricorn in 1989, the people opposed oppressive government and the Berlin Wall came down. This led to an entirely new economic situation for Eastern Europe, which affected the whole world economy.

However, rather than 'cherry-pick' such obvious examples from the past, it may be more useful to use astrology systematically to anticipate and educate our economic behaviour. What does astrology tell us of the present world economic situation? Answering this question involves isolating key planetary concepts, then overlaying them upon each other to understand the constantly developing situation.

As I write in 2007, Pluto nears the end of its transit through Sagittarius, which it started at the beginning of 1995. The keywords for this are the 'death and transformation of travel, religion and philosophy'. This has shown itself in a range of ways. The number of people travelling by air has expanded considerably, but the development of new aircraft technology has been far more limited than for some time. Perhaps Boeing took astrological advice when they decided to focus investment on shorter-haul innovations and enhancing core technology introduced several decades ago. The European plans for a revolutionary and massive Airbus have certainly been more fraught. We will see the reasons for this when we consider Neptune and Uranus. The expansion of air travel is making a negative contribution to global warming. Incidents of air rage and blood clotting due to long-haul travel have increased. The availability of alcohol has diminished and in-cabin smoking been banned.

Pluto in Sagittarius expresses itself on another level – that of religious conflicts, which lie at the core of the lethal 'war on terror'. The threat of terrorism has led to the tightening of banking systems, the way we do business and the price and availability of raw materials – especially petroleum.

From 1995, Uranus (the constant activator of change) was in Aquarius to be joined by Neptune (the indicator of taste, fashion and belief) in 1998. Then, in 2003, Uranus entered Pisces. In modern astrology, Uranus is considered to rule Aquarius and Neptune Pisces. When two planets are in each other's sign they are considered to be 'mutually receiving' (reinforcing) each other. This means from 1995 until 2012 (the year Uranus leaves Pisces and Neptune leaves Aquarius), invention, change, belief and fashion will be focused upon the inter-relation between technological innovation and universal connectedness. We are able to have almost tactile contacts with people all over the world without leaving our computer screen or mobile phone – what better example could there be of Pluto in Sagittarius combining with the Aquarian mutual reception?

With Neptune, dominated by Aquarius, ruling our religious sensitivity, we have come to believe in technology for its own sake and will be reluctant to stop doing so until 2012. This economic fashion was strongest in the earlier part of the period up to the spring of 2000, when a rare and powerful concentration of planets in the fixed and realistic sign of Taurus burst its bubble and depressed the NASDAQ and general equity markets! With so much time to go in this phase it did not undermine our belief and dedication to technology – just made it more rational. To aid market recovery, ways of bringing more people and their money into the financial markets were introduced as rapidly as possible. Now most people can trade on the web. Digital devices, entertainment, television, ownership of computers, access to the Internet and mobile phones have become the trophies of our contemporary economic belief system. We cannot get enough modern technical devices, but why do we want them? Are we doing any more than responding automatically and unconsciously to a particular stage in the astrological flow?

So it was in September 2001, with Saturn in Gemini (limitation of understanding) opposed to Pluto in Sagittarius (death and transformation of travel) across the ascendant/descendant axis of the USA chart that the World Trade Center atrocity occurred. Pluto in Sagittarius could express religious war against terror. Our new-technology weapons could be tried and tested upon 'offending countries'. Over the next few years, our developing communications and processing power could be used to track, trace and get to know everyone and *promise* to 'make us secure'. Progress in this area of activity accelerated, when Uranus entered Pisces in 2003.

As well as symbolising a world economy that commercialises seemingly endless global conflict, the Sagittarius/Aquarius/Pisces outer planetary cycles have coincided with more opportunity for profit from developments in scientific technology. The mapping of the genome makes it possible to explain and treat illness and personal limitations in radically new ways. It offers a tremendous potential for good, but also the commercial benefit of using patent law to own the very building bricks of life itself. Commercialised research science, allied with massive technological advances, seems to have the potential to 'answer' every human need – except, it seems, to feed the less fortunate of the world! The ability to know and influence the intimate nature and habits of people through the news media and entertainment facilities makes the power of large corporations seem limitless.

However, by looking back over earlier periods in the history of the world economy and relating them to their astrological cycles, we can see that each development is no more than a transitory fashion. What the cosmos presents us with and the attitude we have towards it comes, develops and goes. Although the present explosion of technological discovery and innovation is a remarkable stage in human development, Pluto will enter Capricorn in 2008, Uranus with Jupiter will enter Aries, and Neptune Pisces, in 2011. All we see to be so new and exciting today will come to be seen as old-fashioned and even despised as the cause of many of the problems of that new time.

Yes, it will! Older people may remember how those growing up in the1950/60 saw Victorian attitudes as the enemy. In the 1980s those hippies seemed like out of touch dreamers. The 1990s Stock Market boom encouraged companies to take pension holidays. They did not look ahead. So, in the early 21st century, we curse them for leaving a pension crisis caused considerably by a lack of resources to cover the baby boomer generation in their retirement years. In Britain, many people see Margaret Thatcher's 1980s Neptune-in-Capricorn view that 'there is no such thing as society', as the root of many contemporary social problems and the desperate need for ASBOs.[82]

So, what will happen next? The literal interpretation of Pluto in Capricorn is 'the death and transformation of organisation and political control'. In the light of what has happened in recent years, we can anticipate that the upcoming Pluto in Capricorn period will see us using our capacity to tap into and map the very privacy of each individual's domestic and inner lives. Those in power will have the technology to track and trace all we do and have: our shopping decisions, our unique identity patterns, organization memberships, health, fundamental physical make-up and psychological characteristics will be stored in one central database. This will provide anyone who can gain access to the 'machine' with all they need to decide how we will live our lives and to find and deal with us if we 'rebel'. It is often said that George Orwell got everything right in his *Nineteen Eighty-four*, except the date!

There is another side of the coin – the Uranus-Neptune Aquarian development of advanced methods of discovering and distributing information are widely available to individuals as well. Also, transits of Pluto through Capricorn in previous centuries have had counter-authoritarian as well as authoritarian effects. As a result of Marco Polo's journeys during the 12769/87 transit, trade expanding with the East gave power to the merchant middle classes and led to the growth of towns. In time, it was to spur on more voyages of discovery and questions about the absolute truth of the European view of reality. The 1515 to 1532 transit saw the Reformation. This reinforced and accelerated the process of effective challenge to central Church control, already building from the discovery of printing in the second half of the 15th century. The outer-planetary alignments at that time were uncannily similar to their movements during the development of computer technology in the second half of the 20th century. The 16th century Church wealth in England was redistributed. Through the 1763 to 1779 transit, enclosure and colonialism led to rebellion of the masses, anti-imperialism and hence today's popular culture.

Governments and multi-national companies may have much power, but to date this is dependent on satisfying the very consumers created by these political developments. So in the coming years, it will be difficult for a global economy dependent on mass consumption to contain the growth of human understanding. The media and the advertisers that finance it may be powerful and pervasively manipulative, but the availability of information and global communication will make it difficult to control the populace into the pliancy that Orwell visualised.

Capricorn is the 10th house archetype and the 'managing director' of earthly affairs, because it is strong and realistic. From 2008, the Pluto-in-Sagittarius years could be seen as irresponsibly over-expansive. We may feel we have accepted what our scientists, economists and leaders have offered and told us far too easily. Now, as they feel defensive regarding us, we need to be defensive about them. We need to contain their power, as they seek to contain ours. Keep options open. Be less easily convinced. Stop 'jumping on bandwagons'. Let the best answers emerge by their sheer strength, effectiveness and the sense of long-standing well-being they bring. If we cannot take control and welcome and approach change in such sensible ways, we will develop resentments and prejudices that could tear us apart.

The more we know, understand and work with each other on the human level, the more we develop the wisdom to ignore and reject the propaganda that will enslave us.

It is important we do. For even well before Pluto enters Capricorn, powerful forces are influencing governments and the workplace. Their methods pin down and isolate workers by means of increasingly detailed targets and systems of supervision. Building his ideas from Nash's Cold War game theory strategies, Alain Enthoven developed 'systems analysis' to rid the difficult-to-calculate emotional element from the market and workplaces. It was applied for the first time in Vietnam, where the numbers of Vietcong killed was used to assess soldiers' success. It often led to indiscriminate slaughter of both civilians and soldiers.

Undaunted, British governments (Conservative and even more so Labour) have applied Enthoven's methods to bring 'efficiency' to the British National Health Service, education, policing and the Civil Service, with equally unreliable results and counter-productive systems-and-checks bureaucracy. Minor operations are performed to reduce waiting lists. Insignificant offences are charged to meet targets. To prevent this, targets are made all the more sophisticated and focused. Time spent on bureaucracy increases as forms become longer and more numerous; ever more people are employed to check them. The room for initiative and creative innovation in the workplace is ever more restricted.

Of course, there will always be people who take advantage of loopholes in a loose and incompetent system. However, is subjecting the vast majority of kind and decent workers to ever-intensifying scrutiny the most competent way to deal with them? Might not what most will see as 'petty bureaucracy' mean many more workers will feel forced to cheat, trick, or at least give the minimum they can get away with? Personal commitment in a free and professional work environment allows the space forever-flowering goodwill to emerge. When we genuinely and deeply believe in what we are doing, we do our best. It is a fundamental error to fear and mistrust a workforce. Goodwill can indeed move mountains. Rigid, hardened, bullying regimes build ever-higher barriers that block efficient progress.

So, will Pluto's transit through Capricorn lead to 'colonial rule' of our very souls, or an inner struggle for personal independence by an increasingly enlightened population? It will be both. For Capricorn indicates those that govern and their institutions on the one hand and the reaction of the governed on the other. Pluto in Sagittarius brought a kind of 'death' through travel by an expansion of air travel that threatened both the planet's ecology and the industry's stability. Now Pluto in Capricorn will bring an expansion in the government's power to see and control, but also an expansion in the citizen's ability to see and challenge those that govern. To be safe, we have to keep it that way. Provided that citizens remain wise and independent, we may yet achieve *Star Trek* openness, rather than a lying and oppressive *Nineteen Eighty-four* society.

This is why a wider understanding of astrology is vital. We need the key background information it reveals – refer again to the later sections of Chapter 7. Are the plans of our leaders and our support for them corrupted by delusions of grandeur or a self-interested wish to dominate others? If so, we will become trapped in the lowest expression of the planetary energies and unable to understand the terrible consequences that follow. Nor can we use astrological insight to manipulate solely for personal gain. This is why rigid deterministic attempts to prove astrology are doomed. The manic superstition that drove the horrors at the end of Mayan culture in the 16th century is a savagely graphic example. Unlike them, we need to respect and understand the planet, its people and the place of both in the universe. Then, we will open our arms to all that is good, however strange and new. We will not fear to cut out what is redundant. Seeing ahead in good time, we can create a wise and sustainable future.

The last time Uranus entered Aries from Pisces (the spring of 1927), Neptune was in Leo and Pluto in Cancer. Society was in the midst of dramatic changes in social values and a period of hedonistic self-indulgence. Prohibition of alcohol in the USA was having the reverse effect. The Stock Market continued to boom until Neptune entered Virgo in 1929 – the Jupiter/Saturn sixty-year cycle was in its last few years. All these factors suggest impulsive counter-productive and destructive change.

When the Uranus Aries ingress occurs in 2010/11, it could herald a far more positive process. We will be only twenty years into the sixty-year Jupiter/Saturn cycle. The recent Uranus/Neptune transits in mutually ruling signs have been much more radically effective and have been complemented by Pluto's expansive transit of Sagittarius. Uranus conjuncted and so expanded by Jupiter will this time not be squared (at 90 degrees) by Pluto in Cancer destroying the safety and comfort of traditional family life. Instead Pluto in Capricorn will square it. We will be seeking freedom from centralised government and corporate attempts to coerce individuals into doing what those in power think is 'best for them'. In addition, just a few months after the Aries ingress Neptune enters its ruling sign of Pisces. It will be strong this time, not in fall in Virgo as it was in the 1930s. The obsessively immature and soon-to-be doomed fascist attempts of the 1930s and 1940s to racially purify society are unlikely. Instead, we will struggle over the nature of efficient and comfortable organisation.

So, there is every possibility that the 'new world order' will not be dominated by the paternal imposition of irresistible structures and systems. If we are wise we will be free of them; beyond the need to struggle. The economic market's dependence on consumer satisfaction could force it to liberate and follow human choice. If that choice has the wisdom to confront the finite nature of global resources and manage them more efficiently, then a unique breakthrough in human affairs is indeed possible.

We will need the insights of astrology to help us accept that relying upon new discoveries and the constant expansion of economic activity will not be successful or even desirable. To seek to expand forever can only lead to a destructive explosion. Instead we may have to consolidate and rationalise consumption, using the new technologies to contain it. We may come to rely upon efficient recycling, renewable energy resources and manufacturing longer-lasting products. This is not about doing without, but enjoying something better.

Crucially, why seek to sustain the burden of the frantic mobility of recent times? Why travel to work, when we can do so much more together from where we are? Where travel is necessary, why should millions of people independently make virtually the same journey, each using their own energy resources? Travelling and socialising comfortably together in mass transport vehicles can save them money, other resources and personal stress. Travelling to a limited number of hubs, then taking personal means of transport for the short haul to their individual destination would not only save resources, but reduce the many personal problems that come from the 'boxed in isolation' of our modern world. There are so many ways we could be happier, by working together communally. Neptune and Chiron's transit through Pisces could see great suffering if we cannot understand and implement this.

As well as reducing unnecessary production and waste of resources, such an organisation would enhance the quality of our relationships in modern society. The nuclear family view of social organisation is a very recent development of the Pluto in Leo (1937 to 1958) times. While it seems to provide everyone with an illusion of aristocratic privilege, it isolates us from each other and makes us depend unnaturally on mass communication and opinion, channelled through narrowly controlled media. Ironically, the ability for everyone to own everything for themselves does not liberate, but enslaves and alienates them from each other. It is also incredibly wasteful of resources.

Of course, for society to change in this way would seem to undermine the constant economic growth upon which we are told the 'success' of the world economy 'depends'. Is this really so? Do we wish to be wastefully rich and work longer and longer hours to keep it that way, having limited time for our families and none at all for the community? Will the party 'alcohol and goodies', referred to earlier in this chapter, be available forever? Even if they were, we would soon become hopelessly jaded and worn out. With the outer planetary changes due at the end of the first decade of the 21st century, we will be forced to change our patterns of consumption. We can do this willingly in a humane way, wishing to enhance social cohesion. The only alternative is to follow the Easter Islanders: fight over what is left and live ever more defensively in increasingly protected enclaves.

If astrological cycles had been a part of economic decisions in the 1950s, then it is unlikely the world would be suffering from the problems of the motorcar and carbon emissions. If we had looked ahead to the financial market expansions of the 1980s and 1990s, then financial resources would have been more skilfully managed, the pensions' crisis anticipated – even averted. If we had considered the Aquarian explosion of new technology around the turn of the century, we might have used it to address problems of global ecology, not to exacerbate them. 'Of course, it is always easy to be wise with hindsight', is a customary response. How convenient then that astrology offers this very 'hindsight' we crave in advance of events!

Astrological cycles will happen, whatever we think or do. Fashions and opportunities will come and go, but we do not have to be ignorant of them and so become their victims. We can instead be their beneficiaries. For, using astrology to inform economic decisions does not take away anything we really want and need. With today's wisdom, we do not have to return to the hardship of previous ages, provided that we let go of our contemporary adolescent view of continual *laissez-faire* expansion for its own sake. If we look for examples of waste in our individual lives, and support those business developments that are doing the same, we would soon see that having less and working less may well lead to ever more satisfying lives.

Conclusion

The temptation to boast about our individual success indicates we are about to fail. In the same way, the first sign of decay in any culture is that point when it assumes it has found 'the answer' and seeks to impose it on others. The 'defeat' of Soviet Communism has confronted our modern free-enterprise capitalism with such a danger. 'If only all cultures would accept our view of "democracy", we would have an increasingly perfect world with prosperity for all'. Apparent 'enemies' of such a 'kindly' and well-intentioned view swarm like bees to honey to threaten such arrogance.

The wise see people who challenge their ideas and way of life as friends to learn from. The essential error in our contemporary world economic model is that it is driven by greed, ambition and disregard of the medium- and long-term consequences of our actions. The 'rat race' is all it seems there is to live for. Passive watching replaces family and community involvement. We depend on commentators and 'celebrities' to give us a shared purpose. Sports stadiums become our churches, its stars our priests. We recharge our batteries by knowing, cheering or suffering the results. Yet, inevitable change means success is transitory. We clutch at the straws of possible future victory that we know in our hearts will never last and so are always left empty.

Astrological cycles enable us to see through all that. To see a person triumph over adversity in the sports arena and ordinary life warms the heart. How much more would we appreciate individual triumph over the karmic challenge of a difficult astrological transit or progression?

Using astrological insight in major economic and business decisions makes us better organisers of our material lives, because it provides a conceptual language to know whether the system we are supporting is efficient. We understand and become actively involved in our own and other people's progress. Because we know the people and their circumstances, we trust without needing to check up constantly. We do not just reward the 'good luck' of a favourable transit to a natal chart. Knowing unfair judgements will fall away, we do not allow disputes reach a boiling point of intense hatred and resentment. By such true knowing, we deal correctly and without rancour with the most difficult situations and colleagues.

The most productive part of our life is spent at work, or at school preparing for it. Hence deeper insights and better relationships in our business lives could make us feel much, much better. We may even be able to slow down, do less and enjoy our social and family life a lot more.

In Chapter 15, we will move on from general aspirations and theories to consider how astrology can assist the basic practicalities of our economic lives. Can it really help us avoid the unnecessary and counterproductive in business; make it less of a treadmill? Could it help us make the work we do so effective and pleasant an experience that we could see ourselves almost volunteering to do it?

Chapter 15

Financial Markets & the World of Work

Never work just for money or for power. They won't save your soul or help you sleep at night.

Marian Wright Edelman

The world is moved along, not only by the mighty shoves of its heroes, but also by the aggregate of the tiny pushes of each honest worker.

Helen Keller

As well as informing strategic policy, by giving insights into the broad sweep of economic development, astrology can inform the everyday nuts and bolts decisions of our business activities. We will study how in three main areas: financial market price prediction; the timing and strategy of company foundation, development and promotion; and personnel/team-building decisions.

Financial market price prediction

Trading in stocks and shares, commodities, currencies and derivatives is an intense, highly pressured responsibility. To inform and support their decisions, traders familiarise themselves with the fundamental facts, which they consider will determine the value of the instruments they are trading. Company profit and trading information, assets, cash flows, borrowing, government policy announcements, growth forecasts and employment figures build an understanding of expectation. Such expectation is translated into a price, which is recorded in lists and graph indices of individual instruments, or areas of the market.

Such indices lie at the heart of trading decisions. As the FTSE rises and falls millions of pounds are gained and lost; so traders move their assets to and from stocks, currencies, government and private bonds, commodities and cash. To reduce risk and accommodate dramatic price fluctuations, professional traders purchase derivatives – promises to buy and sell in the future at set prices, or options to do so. Advanced arbitrage studies look for areas of the market where what is in effect the same product is available at a lower price. Some purchase to hold for a long-term investment, not fearing intermediate rises and falls.

Others move in and out of the market several times within a day. If prices go as expected, it is possible to make substantial profit between breakfast and afternoon tea time, just by selling or buying what you started with and reversing the process when the market moves in your favour.

Because instant decisions leading to millions of pounds in profit and loss can hang on a few clicks of a computer mouse, price graphs are constantly before the traders' eyes. By looking so intently, they come to notice patterns in the price movements that give clues to what will happen next. From this, many traders use a system of technical analysis. Particular angles of the graph, the number of days the market has been rising and falling are noted. When the market returns to a previous high or low point, it is said to be 'testing the support of a previous bottom', or about to 'break the resistance of a previous top'. The number of times a top or bottom has been tested can be significant – also the amount of the rise or fall, in accordance with a Fibonacci ratio, can give the vital clue. Because the price movements can be highly news-sensitive, traders employ researchers to scan the media for fundamentals that may affect the value of particular financial instruments.

Even all this detailed material, expertise and knowledge is not considered enough to succeed. Understanding the state of mind, the psychology of the trader is also vital. Prices are often driven by expectation, which can lead to counterproductive greed for too much profit. So, the trader holds on to a position for too long, as the market moves against him and fails to bounce back up as he had hoped. Alternatively, fear of this happening can trigger a premature move and lead to the loss of a profitable opportunity. Unless the mind is calm, expert fundamental or technical analysis of the market indices may be of little help; they may even be counter-productive. There are so many facts and figures to consider that it is always possible to find a 'good practical reason' to support a position that is really based on 'greed and fear', not an objective view of the facts. Separating oneself from such turmoil and objectively understanding the logic that lies behind what is happening is the key to being a successful trader.

The astrologer working in this area of activity may seem to be unable to win, whatever happens. Since success and failure are immediately measurable, if money is not made, the astrologer and his craft will be shown to have failed. Yet, if astrology does predict the markets, some people may say that using such profound wisdom to gain financial advantage over less wise people is immoral.

As is so often the case with astrology; the ethical dilemma is not so clear-cut, because the knowledge has its own built in protection. As we shall see in a moment, there is little doubt that connections can be found between major market movements and astrological cycles. Yet, using these to direct specific and intricate profitable trading decisions depends on the relationship of the trader's chart to the transits. There are many paradoxes. Most traders would deny the links and so not receive the knowledge. Those that do consider astrology may do so at a time when they are not ready to profit consistently. They may ignore the indications, or use other contradictory techniques as well. Making money from the markets is about much more than knowing what will happen. You have to know what to do about what you know as well! So, using astrology to help trade the markets has similar advantages and limitations to using it in so many other walks of life. If we use it with a clean, clear and truly objective state of mind to help others as well as ourselves, we may well be calm enough to read and act correctly on the indications.

The methods and ways astrology can help financial market traders are numerous and often as complex as the markets themselves. The bibliography at the end of this chapter lists titles for further study. Essentially insight can be offered in two main areas.

Firstly, it can provide insight into the strength of a particular company or financial instrument. It can also help individual traders understand themselves and time their decisions to coincide with when they are likely to be clear and objective enough to make fortunate decisions. This is done by a specialist study of individual charts. The approach is similar to birth chart study examples in Part 2, with the focus narrowed down to the areas of the chart and interpretative concepts that relate to money, risk-taking, financial stability and success.

Secondly, astrology can give some guidance regarding market conditions. How long will a general atmosphere of fear, greed, or lack of it create booming, falling, or flat price movements? When might a price change direction? For how long will such a change last?

Here are brief tastes of each of these areas.

In the first area, we would study the individual chart for the foundation of a particular company, commodity market or index.

Our interpretations would be corporate in tone. Here are a few examples. If the natal Jupiter and Midheaven are conjunct, we would expect the company to be a high-profile market leader with considerable success. However, Saturn (structured authority) needs to be strong and realistically placed as well because this provides permanence and control. If it is not, Jupiter on Midheaven could be deceptively over-optimistic. Things may appear much better than they are. If Saturn is in the 2nd house, only by properly structured control of the company/individual's assets and especially cash can the apparent success be achieved. Alternatively, Saturn on the Midheaven may suggest an appearance of dullness and hardship, but look more deeply. If there are signs of good management in the rest of the chart and Jupiter is well placed, then this could be a cautious sensible enterprise and so a good candidate for long term investment.

To see how the company may develop and evolve, we could consider the progressions. The transits can help us anticipate how it will fair in the market place at any particular time in the future, or what happened in the past that may be of significant in the future.

Transiting Jupiter and Saturn can indicate when times of expansion or contraction are likely. Saturn about to leave the 10th house, when Jupiter is about to replace it or is well-place elsewhere, could suggest the share price is undervalued. Now may be a good time to invest for the medium to long-term – buy low now, sell high after Saturn has moved on.

These are just a few obvious examples. All the planets can be included in our studies from an inception, progressed and transiting perspective. It is remarkable how like their company's activities and developments most of their charts are.

Knowing the financial trader's birth chart and development can caution against over-optimism and temper the greed of inappropriate gambling. A major profit on a strong transit of Jupiter in the 2nd house cannot be relied upon next time. It would be a particularly bad idea to continue taking risks should that Jupiter move on to conjunct Mars and square Saturn in the 5th house. It is remarkable how astrology can help the trader identify and rectify doubts and obsessions that are clouding trading judgement. When applied to individual company or market stocks, it can reveal what lies behind incomplete or inaccurate news reports and profit forecasts.

In the second area, by studying the patterns of planetary positions and relationships, we can anticipate the general mood and atmosphere of human interaction on a particular day. Will people feel positive, defensive, foolhardy, cautious or inclined towards risk? Can we see extremes of panic or excessive optimism that could indicate a bear or bull surge? We may also be able to anticipate public taste. What experiences or objects are likely to find favour? Days when the inner planets complement the kind of historical economic trends outlined in Chapter 14 may be when lots of people are drawn towards fashionable products. Be ahead of the flow by supporting those companies that seem most ready to exploit and profit from the trend.

Financial astrology researchers have found links between planetary cycles and price movements of particular stocks, bonds and currencies. The cycle of Venus has been associated with T-Bonds. Since 1980 the Dow Industrial Index has flattened to coincide with the biennial retrograde station of Mars on all but three occasions.[83]

Predicting a major price or trend change in financial markets is particularly easy when many astrological factors combine to give complementary indications. Study the three charts on the following pages in careful detail. The charts show the price indices for three sensational turns: the Japanese Nikkei in 1989, German Bund in 1994 and NASDAQ in 2000.[84] In each case the planetary positions are listed alongside. The 1989 Nikkei turn (Figure 26) occurred with a rare number of six planets in Capricorn, opposed by Jupiter in Cancer. The down-pointing arrow indicates the date of the planetary listing against the price graph.

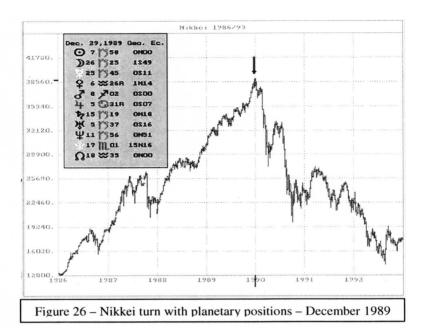

Figure 26 – Nikkei turn with planetary positions – December 1989

In January 1994, the bond markets and especially the German Bund led what was to be for them, and equities, a particularly bearish year. Figure 27 below shows that this time *seven* planets were in Capricorn. The 2000

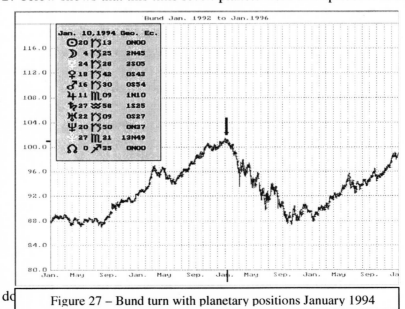

Figure 27 – Bund turn with planetary positions January 1994

in technical stocks was competing with strong contrary pressure from Uranus and Neptune in Aquarius that had been driving the Internet bubble upwards.

Early 1995 saw a recovery of bond markets and the beginning of an exponential rise in the equity markets. After a poor performance in 1994, the market bottomed into the winter as Jupiter (the planet of opportunity in its own sign) and then Pluto entered Sagittarius together. Mars retrograded back into Leo (the sign of gambling) to trine Jupiter exactly on 9th March 1995 – the day the market took off. Save for an anxious autumn 1997, generated by over-heated Far East region markets, prices continued to rise until 2000. Then, as can be seen in Figure 28, seven planets in another earth sign, Taurus, brought the reality of a severe downward correction to the markets.

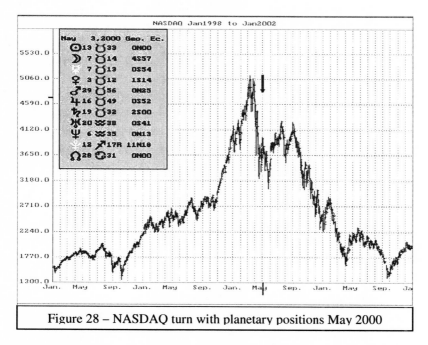

Figure 28 – NASDAQ turn with planetary positions May 2000

These were major turns. To have known them in advance could have led to substantial losses being avoided, or profits being made. By noting the unusually strong concentrations of planets in earth signs, the similarity to the 1989 Nikkei turn, plus some astro-events in the 1929 crash chart, astrology was used to predict the 1994 and 2000 events in advance.

To understand and study the intricate field of financial astrology for short-term trends and individual investment, start from the work of the experts listed at the end of this chapter.

Timing company foundation, development & promotion
The essence of a good business plan, be it for a new company or a strategic development of an existing one, is the creation of a well-researched, insightful and disciplined structure. It is necessary to identify clearly the product, the nature and readiness of its possible market base, the most efficient means of delivery and realistic price and profit margins.

In our modern free-market economies the starting point for a new enterprise or the development of an existing one comes from the experience and ingenuity of the entrepreneur and his research team to identify a 'market need'. Then the aim is to structure production and promotion to match and satisfy the projected demand as tightly as possible. At the heart of such preparation are a good accountant and lawyer, who can select and combine each element in the plan to answer the commercial and legal demands of the marketplace. Their efficiency will reveal possible pitfalls and ensure suitable adjustments are made. An understanding of present and likely future material, labour and distribution costs, plus the likely interest and purchasing power of the intended market, is vital. If the sums do not add up, then good entrepreneurs will not risk capital investment and only the costs of the feasibility study will be lost.

Yet, for all this care and the studied economic expertise, starting and running a business enterprise in the modern world remains very much a hit and miss affair. The plan can be littered with false expectations, hidden inefficiencies and disappointments, which an understanding of astrology could alleviate.

Heading a genuine and sustainable trend in the public's taste for an innovative new fashion is nearly always more profitable than rushing to catch up with the crowd when market interest is nearly exhausted. In the early to middle 1990s, a company that used knowledge of the Uranus and Neptune transits through Aquarius to anticipate massive technological acceleration would have the confidence to invest billions in gaining G3 licences. By 2007, it is clear how justifiable such capital investment was. At the end of the 20th century, developing small Internet companies from scratch made fortunes for a few. Being blinded by the fashion of the times and investing indiscriminatingly in *any* Internet project would not have been skilful. If the value of 'our company' was over-inflated, advanced knowledge of the 2000 Taurus stellium could have guided a sale in good time. Yet, knowing Aquarian transits were to continue for ten more years, the wise financial astrologer would have seen the Internet was entering a mature stage and reinvested after the fall. The Internet was here to stay and would change the *way* we do business. It would not, however, change the intrinsic reality of the relationship between capital investments, profit and loss!

With Piscean transits becoming stronger in the first decade of the 21st century, investment in the software that works with the new technology is likely to be more profitable than the production of the now well-known Aquarian hardware that runs it. With major changes in the outer planetary positions as we reach the end of this decade, great care will be needed when attempting to build on the business experience of the past. As a result of enhanced global communications, delivery of production and services may be organised internationally and electronically. However, can we be sure of the social cohesion and reliability of the technology? We rely less and less on paper records, but are we prepared for a breakdown in the Internet and other communication networks? Will societies and international relationships remain stable? Of course, business will adjust and survive anything less than a total global collapse, but many enterprises that have not looked to the future will fail and fall. With all the outer planets changing signs, the end of the first decade of the 21st century is a very uncertain time – not one in which to take the recent past for granted.

Having used the outer-planetary trends to assess the economic climate, the astrologer can look for a particular date and time to launch the business. While doing this, the timing of various lead in and out stages can be considered. As with a human birth, the chart for the beginning of a business enterprise or development reveals the strengths and weaknesses of what is planned. We have seen that astrology can indicate whether a cycle is at a potent growth stage or near the end of its time in fashion - if the 'bandwagon effect' is over. A chart for the start or development of business can answer many questions. 'Does what is planned come from studied insight, or impulsive optimism?' 'Are other events and activities likely to complement the promotion?' 'What kind of promotion would be most suitable?' 'If our plans are timely, are too many other people likely to have the same idea?' 'How can we stand out and succeed against them?' A skilful astrologer should be able to give answers to these and many other questions.

Fitting the enterprise into the natural flow of social fashion and readiness does not only benefit the self-interest of a business itself. By improving timing and making approaches more efficient and suitable, astrology can help the enterprise to improve the world we live in. The business does not succeed at the expense of the community, but rather its success enhances the community. This ability to use astrology to indicate mutually beneficial relationships between business profitability and social enhancement makes it even more vital than conventional economic decision-making instruments.

Most business plans devised without astrology have an intrinsic flaw. They have no reliable way to assess this public interest. Instead, they seek to succeed by narrowing down focus to serve self-interest and find legal ways to protect the company from the consequences of its actions. As mentioned in the previous chapter, when budgeting, only those costs likely to be carried by the company need be considered. The effect of noise, pollution, pressure on public resources, inconvenience and even danger to the other users is unlikely to be included, unless a law or regulation exists that cannot be avoided. Even if one does consider these effects, advisers will ask if it would be less costly to lobby to change the rules, or obtain a special dispensation.

Such approaches give the impression that to be realistic and successful in business one has to be selfish and uncaring. It is considered one of those unfortunate necessities we have to accept, if we are to live, prosper and have what we need. We have to master 'hard-nosed' reality.

To assume business can only be conducted in such a selfish and self-seeking atmosphere has dangerous and counterproductive consequences. The atmosphere of 'cut and thrust', 'all people for themselves' means that successful business people have to be tough, dismissive of the needs of others (if there are no commercial implications) and must constantly protect themselves from the consequences of their actions. Their self-seeking motivations may attract contempt and cause them to be viewed as 'fair game' to cheat and steal from and to sue for damages. Anyone who has suffered from the effects of major business developments will be inclined to celebrate any setbacks faced by the main players.

It has become common practice to see business in this way, because accountants, lawyers and promotional experts are the sole business decision-makers. While their expertise is essential to clear obstacles and manage an effective enterprise, without astrological insight serious shortcomings and dangers of poor public perception, natural and social disasters may be ignored.

A bad public image of appearing to be rich, uncaring, an exploitative employer and insensitive to human health is an ongoing issue for fast-food outlets. Much more traumatic are those incidents when accidents and natural disasters appear to occur as a result of putting business interests before those of human need. By giving advanced warnings, astrological insight can lead to improved practice that might avoid major accidents entirely. It can guide enterprises towards procedures that minimise damage. Early guidance can be invaluable. Unexpected disasters can threaten the company and its products, not only in the medium term, but could undermine its very existence.

The astrological background to the 3rd December 1984 Union Carbide disaster in India illustrates these issues very clearly. The events are outlined below.

> In the morning hours of December 3, 1984, a holding tank with 43 tonnes of stored MIC overheated and released toxic heavier-than-air MIC gas mixture, which rolled along the ground through the surrounding streets. The transportation system in the city collapsed and many people were trampled trying to escape. According to the Bhopal Medical Appeal, around 500,000 people were exposed to the leaking chemicals. Approximately 20,000, to this date, are believed to have died as a result; on average, roughly one person dies every day from the effects. Over 120,000 continue to suffer from the effects of the disaster, such as breathing difficulties, cancer, serious birth-defects, blindness, gynaecological complications and other related problems.[85]

Such a dramatic tragedy inevitably leads to accusations, statements and legal hearings for many years after. Accusations of cost cutting, the siting of the plant so close to a large population and the lack of a proper warning system were discussed interminably. A good astrologer could have warned of the urgent need to act well in advance the event. For the symbolism of the planetary transits to the natal chart describes exactly what happened.

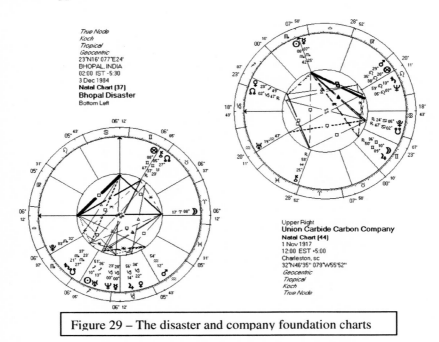

Figure 29 – The disaster and company foundation charts

On the incorporation chart, in Figure 29, Pluto/South Node are opposed by Venus applying to the North Node on the Cancer/Capricorn axis. This suggests the enterprises are likely to be dangerously self-serving and resistant to correction from outside. Any major transit to this point could trigger karmic consequences. During the year of the event, Neptune had been in hesitant retrograde, but now was in strong forward motion in Capricorn and applying to oppose the natal South Node and Pluto. It will only do this every 165 years. On the morning of 2nd December 1984 Mercury had already entered Capricorn and just before 9 pm IST had conjuncted that Neptune and both were conjuncted by the transiting IC at 0135 IST just as the disaster was commencing on the 3rd. This was the trigger indicating the day and time of the tragedy.

The keywords suggest clouds of mental confusion bearing down on the karmic vulnerability of the company. Transiting Mars will oppose natal Saturn exactly 35 hours later. It is also due to conjunct Uranus in less than a fortnight. Together the two suggest aggressive technology challenging authority and creating dramatic upheaval. This is a three-day-window trigger. Since all these transits are known long in advance, an astrologer employed to consider the Union Carbine chart should be able to give warning and guidance several years ahead. He could point to a specific danger during the weeks before and after the event. The strong possibility of the event itself could have been foreseen within a margin of a few days and a warning issued. As the IC is so exactly involved, even which of the company's sites was exposed may have been indicated. This may not have prevented a major upheaval of work and employment in Bhopal. However, instead of a horrific disaster, the site may well have been closed and dismantled in preparation for re-siting in a safer location with better plant and protection. The consequences then for Bhopal may have been loss of earnings and poverty for some years, but tens of thousands would have avoided death and injury. An area that remains polluted to this day may have been saved, along with the standing of the company.

In another well-documented case, astrological insight *was* offered, but ignored. In his book *The Cosmic Loom* Dennis Elwell explains the astrological reasons for the 1987 *Herald of Free Enterprise* disaster, of which he warned the operating company in advance. In addition to these sensational examples, many day-to-day business developments and events can be explained and often anticipated by careful astrological examination.

While a large company may be able to use legal strength and the power of its nation to survive, their standing in the public mind and the marketplace is more difficult to repair. When its reputation is in question, it subjects itself to scrutiny and hence extra expense, from which it may take many years to recover. If they are perceived to disregard social and ecological consequences, the benefits of the most fundamental enterprise can become jaundiced and counter-productive. Yet, in the white heat of commercial competition, driven by the prime aim of maximum profit, such dangers can be ignored. In all these circumstances, standing back and applying objective astrological judgement, and so seeing and acting on likely dangers well in advance, is an essential tool that helps ensure continuing business success.

Of course, most business decisions are less high profile and go unreported, yet the success and benefit of any enterprise and the public interest can go hand in hand if astrology is used. Just as notable short-lived excesses such as the late 1990s Internet boom-and-bust bubble and even Enron may have been avoided or limited; many smaller, unknown deluded and over-optimistic endeavours might not be attempted if the astrology of the people concerned, the company and the timing of the enterprise were considered.

Astrology's value is not confined to warnings of dire consequences. Because it will reveal the risk you are taking and the strength or otherwise of those taking it, some high-risk business breakthroughs can be calculated and negotiated successfully. Sometimes almost foolhardy courage is needed. The key question is 'Are the time and people suited to carry through the project?' The astrology may show that they are, and then offer methods that are suited to the people involved. By taking advantage of this clarity, a most difficult challenge can be carried through to success.

Personnel/team building decisions
Choosing staff and especially appointing leading individuals and their teams in a business activity can be an agonisingly uncertain. Considerable unreliability can be hidden within the conventional indicators most firms use. Qualifications, references from previous employers and claimed experience may appear more promising than works out in practice. References often cloud the truth. The theoretical knowledge indicated by qualifications may be of limited practical use on the job. While previous experience can be a key to the success of similar future enterprises, a fine art of deception can surround anecdotes about previous projects. When judging their success and failure, the power, position and ability to 'spin' of the person in charge may make it impossible to learn from what went wrong and allocate responsibility. If all went well in the past, success may have been the result of good fortune, or even the exceptional work of support colleagues. If these do not receive proper credit, they may be excluded from future projects that fail as a consequence. Social, cultural and friendship acquaintances may be selected for the wrong reasons. Close personal relationships can distort judgement.

To develop objectivity and eradicate distorted judgement, psychologists and educators have devised conventional aptitude tests. These assess personal qualities and technical ability. While practical tests may give a good indication of skill, many that test mental attitudes and dispositions may be less reliable and objective than they first appear. They may not account for that day's state of mind of the person being tested. The kind of test chosen may be inappropriate for the work to be done. In large companies, where people in power feel the need to 'cover themselves' by relying on established guidelines, managers may rely on contemporary fashion in personnel selection. If anything goes wrong, no one can say they failed to use established procedures. Since such fashions are based on research established from the past, they may not be up to date and relevant in the future. Even if they are, it cannot be certain that they incorporate an intricate understanding of specific projects, other people the employee will be working with and the circumstances of the times through which the work will be done.

Astrological insight can cut through all these deficiencies. From what we studied of the working of the horoscopes, progressions and transits of individuals and organisations, it is easy to see how such knowledge could show whether personnel are suited to particular projects and ready for success. Most important, it can indicate the likely balance and relationships within the team. By comparing each of them to the transits of the period of their work together, we can see how easy and difficult the task might be, and so suitably time its development. Astrology can help us decide whether the project should be discontinued earlier, or continued further than intended, because a positive outcome indicates persistence will be rewarded.

Using skilfully focused further questions at the interview stage to compare what the candidate says with his birth and development charts could reveal the truth and value of responses, or give clues to hidden talents or weaknesses.

When team-building, astrology can suggest the mix of appropriate relationships; how the individuals will inspire and support each other and how they are suited to the nature of the project in hand. A powerful leader may attract too much support and acceptance from the team he/she selects, but resist challenging personalities that will enhance dynamism. For other projects, close cohesion and little conflict may be more suited. Discussion of this in advance, with the executive choosing the team and the team leader, will help find the very best people, but also ease relationships during the undertaking. Using astrology can cut through the 'games' people play, when seeking work or advancement.

For such studies to be really successful and ethical, the whole team have to know that astrology is being used and to accept this. It would be counterproductive and wrong to seek to manipulate work teams and employees by insights secretly gained without their knowledge. It would deny their power, confuse their focus and undermine their motivation. The active involvement and commitment that comes from taking full advantage of self-knowledge is what 'makes us tick'. It brings positive life to everything we do.

The possibilities for creative combinations of people in effective teams are numerous. However, it is theoretical and so best seen as an experiment at first. It would be interesting to use astrological insights alongside more conventional approaches to team building on similar projects. Does one or the other improve the productivity and profitability of the project? Then we will learn if it makes good business sense to use astrology to help people work more effectively with each other.

Maybe a very good reason for the above business success will be that using astrology helps create teams that are a more satisfying experience for the people involved. Pilot studies should be carefully planned and explained to all involved by the astrologer and the leaders setting up the project. Does it reduce the number of teams with personality conflicts, low delivery and even failure?

Beyond the vital business benefits, there is an even greater prize to be won from the success of such experiments. It would move the business environment into a much higher and more positive dimension. Making work a more cooperative, friendly, open and family-like experience may well bring benefits that integrate the worlds of work and our social pleasure. The 'harsh reality' of the dichotomy between 'work' and 'play', the 'firm' and the 'family' may ease into a more flexible and friendly synthesis. The successful person's life may no longer be a 'life and death' struggle for survival on the one side and snatched moments of indulgence and the fulfilling of 'responsibilities to the family' on the other. Instead, we may begin to enjoy our lives. We may begin to feel that our best talents are being squandered during those highly awake daytime weekdays. We may find it less necessary to struggle against and cheat each other, easier to give and receive a helping hand – make up for and fill in the gaps.

In the next chapter we will go one step further. Could a positive use of astrology transform the ways we resolve our disputes? Could it bring clarity and deeper resolution to the processes of our civil and criminal legal systems? Could it even help reduce prison populations?

Further Reading

Graham Bates & Jane Chrzanowska Bowles *Money and the Markets*
George Bayer *Turning Four Hundred Years of Astrology to Practical Use and Other Matters*
Arch Crawford *Crawford Perspectives*
W D Gann
> *Forty-Five Years in Wall Street*
> *How to Make Profits In Commodities*
> *Tunnel Thru the Air*

Bill Meridian *Planetary Stock Trading; Books I and II*
Ray Merriman *Beginning Principles of Psychological, Mundane and Financial Astrology*
Grace Morris *How To Choose Stocks That Will Outperform the Market*
Christeen Skinner *The Financial Universe*
Georgia Stathis *Business Astrology 101: Weaving the Web Between Business and Myth*
David Williams *Financial Astrology*

Chapter 16
Law & Justice

... we hold that compassion, mercy, healing, sanction where appropriate and forgiveness leading to reconciliation lie at the heart of a fair and just criminal justice system. Even the worst of offenders remain children of God, redeemed in the blood of Christ. It is our opinion that victims need to be more actively engaged in the criminal justice system, *provided that healing and reconciliation are the focus of such engagement.*
Creating New Hearts Moving from Retributive to Restorative Justice **New Zealand Bishops–August 1995**

Skeleton Outline

When traumatised by terrible things (be they civil torts or criminal offences), what we want most is something to take it all away – 'If only we could get back to where we were before'. Failing this we feel the need to identify and 'deal with' the cause. From these two fundamental human needs the intricacies of our justice systems develop.

We are caught up in technicalities from the start. What are the facts? What is the correct way to present them? How do we define certain acts? What compensation or right punishment is deserved? By what process do we categorise and decide? Having decided, how do we treat those in the wrong? Do see seek revenge, or to rehabilitate? Are some people innately and unredeemably evil? Should we feel sorry for them, or condemn out of hand? What is the best way to help the victim?

The problem with a mechanical system of practices, rules and procedures is that it is only as efficient as the knowledge and skill of the people who administer it. While the processes aim to create balance and fair play, the more you know the system the more likely you are to succeed when using it. So, the outcome may have more to do with an ability to work the system than justice. In some cases, victims may feel even more victimised by a trial. In other cases an accused may be unfairly punished because of a misleading testimony; at another time wrongdoers may be let off because of a technicality. Lives can be scarred as much by the justice system's attempts to put things right as by the event that caused the problem in the first place.

So, how could our justice system be better equipped to correct wrongs? In its present form it is missing an essential ingredient – a system of reconciliation. When wronged, everyone needs closure. When perpetrating wrong, we need to face consequences that will ensure we will never offend again. Genuine reconciliation will achieve both. Whether the offence is civil or criminal, it does not help to seek winners or losers; to avoid the consequences of our actions or gain unfair advantage. The simple solution we all seek is to feel that the truth and 'some good' have come out of it.

While the present justice system can offer a level playing field to all who understand its procedures and many checks and balances to correct errors of judgement, it has two limitations. Firstly, it lacks a truth and reconciliation procedure where the parties can put their grievances informally to a trained listener. As a result, an adversarial process kicks in immediately any action is filed. So, keeping a careful eye on the rules and avoiding 'legal traps' takes precedence over reaching an understanding. Secondly, identifying winners and losers, rather than putting the truth in perspective, can all too frequently lead to the feeling that someone has 'got away with it' or been 'unfairly treated'. Worst of all, in criminal cases, we may just be punishing for the sake of doing so. Minds do not change. Matters have only been made worse. So the payments of damages grow higher and higher, prison populations expand, more people than ever feel wronged or frightened, and there is an ever-growing sense of 'not being able to do anything about it'.

Problems in our relationships come from a lack of understanding of each other – especially how we judge privilege and disadvantage, cause and effect. The heroin addict may feel it essential and right to steal in order to gain the money to buy drugs. Is the root cause of the problem the weakness of the thief, something in the behaviour of the victim or carer that exposed them to such abuse, or the nature of narcotics laws that create a need to steal? Such questions need to be answered before any effective action can be taken to achieve genuine closure for the criminal, the victim and society. Yet they rarely are.

If weakness of the thief lies at the heart of what happened, the judgement must have a good chance of being effective. Will a prison sentence or rehabilitation in the community work best? The court should work with the criminal until a clear action is found and implemented.

This may take time and new procedures, but would be less expensive than long and repeated prison spells,, and the wrongdoer re- offending

It can be argued that nothing happens to us for which we have not created the cause. Hence the victim may well in some way have something to learn from the experience. This does not take away the guilt of the perpetrator; rather it focuses the victim away from the self-image of an 'outraged innocent, who deserves retribution as of right'. Of course, in many cases, it is very difficult to support such a suggestion; some acts are so despicable and victims so kind or innocent. Even in these cases, it is far more helpful to see good reason in the situation, rather than bay with retributive zeal. Are we really dealing with an absolutely evil perpetrator? Is there no good that can come out of this? Is there nothing great and special that can be done that will bring benefit to some people somehow? Even if you are the most innocent relative of the most innocently wronged victim; to know some kind of benefit has come out of a situation honours your loved one far more than knowing that 'the bastard will die or suffer in prison for the rest of his/her life'.

Then there is the law itself. When something terrible happens, knee-jerk reactions are so much easier than getting to and addressing the root cause of the problem. 'If crime is increasing, then increase the punishment – problem solved'. Of course it is not, and to think and act like this insults the victim and condemns society to ever more crime and social breakdown. For tightening the law brings more pressure down on the institutions of detection and enforcement. Legalising some actions does not necessarily mean we are giving in to crime. It may mean we are weakening criminals by removing their ability to benefit from a law that vast numbers of people disagree with. Every action forced on a criminal to 'teach a lesson', or 'deter others' creates division. Every person in gaol crowds our prisons with seething resentment. This means increasing spending on the 'security' of holding society at arm's length. We do educate others or ourselves. We terrorise and are terrorised by our fear.

We could cut through this soul-destroying impasse, enable understanding and turn division into genuine redress, if we had culture-free ways of assessing people and their circumstances that was even free of a lucky break on a fortunate day. Astrology is such a way.

The British system of justice

The British system of justice is based on a rich and ancient tradition that has influenced and so assisted the maintenance of good order in many parts of the world. At its heart lies the ideal of everyone's right to be heard equally, without fear or favour.

It has developed organically from the interaction of three main areas of input: a system of procedural rules emanating from the development of common law over many centuries; laws passed by democratically elected parliaments; and the precedent created by previously decided cases. The procedures allow anyone to bring an action and be heard at a summary stage. If it is shown there is a case to be answered, the facts and rules of the matter are presented and argued in detail by each party. Judgement is given by a judge, who is independent of the legislature branch of the government; or a jury of peers, guided by the judge. To ensure full and fair consideration, several stages of higher courts can be appealed to, until the matter is finalised and the order that follows judgement can be enforced.

As one studies the system in detail, one is struck by the intense interdependent intricacy of the procedural details that can be argued. It is designed to maintain fairness, speedy and clear resolution and the opportunity for errors to be corrected. Yet by its very complex nature it can have the opposite effect. There is so much to know that a lay person is almost always obliged to employ and become dependent upon professional lawyers. These lawyers have a first duty to their client in what is an adversarial process. Everyone having the right to have an expert on their side can create a number of problems.

Because lawyers need to protect their professional position, their advice is nearly always given from a conservative view of their client's best interests. This can create what to a layperson may appear to be artificial, even unnecessary gaps between the parties that it seems risky to try to bridge. Hence, a flexible resolution can be difficult to find. The high stakes involved in the final outcome, plus the degree of intelligence, knowledge and experience needed to advise clients efficiently, means lawyers command high fees. The consequent high costs can overshadow and distort the search for truth in the legal process.

Civil procedure

Fighting a civil case can seem like a sporting contest, where the rules are there to be tested to the limit in an effort to 'win at all costs'. The natural temptation is only to consider an opponent's perspective in order to gain advantage; not to understand, sympathise and seek resolution. Should only one side wish to fight, they can pick on every detail and make the process into a 'trial by procedural attrition'. Then costs can spiral alarmingly and become a barrier to many people proceeding, unless they are willing to act on their own behalf. Civil procedure rules have been re-focused to take account of the behaviour of parties and so prevent the injustices so tragically satirised in Charles Dickens's *Bleak House*. Yet to take full advantage of these new procedures, expert attention is still required.

In most civil cases the existence of a conciliation procedure, before the highly regulated civil procedure process 'kicks in', would solve many problems. Extensive compulsory non-binding arbitration should always precede a summary hearing – at present it is a voluntary option in some courts only. If this does not resolve the dispute, then the arbitrator's report could be sealed away to be shown to the judge when the case is concluded. If a party did not succeed substantially in excess of the arbitrator's recommendation, any award could be lost and costs, even extra costs, suffered by anyone who had refused the arbitrator's recommendation.

Such arbitration would take account of all the factors involved. This is the opposite of what tends to happen in the adversarial situation. Here, in spite of the obligation to disclose, the facts are selected and presented to take maximum advantage of the rules. The real heart motivation or misunderstanding that laid behind what happened is rarely considered. Yet to know what really happened and what is fair, it is vital for everyone to be open to sharing information and be committed to the truth, whoever it favours.

It is at this new arbitration stage that astrology could play a most illuminating and reconciliatory role. Looking at the birth charts, progressions and transits for everyone involved at the time of the matters under dispute would not only give a neutral view of what happened. In addition, it could help each party to see the problem from the perspective of the other side and move beyond the need for a punitive outcome. For what genuine happiness is there when one side wins at the cost of another's resentment and hurt? If our actions harm others, we should be anxious to put this right, whether these actions occur before, during or after the legal process. If we do not get this right, the ensuing misunderstanding leaves everyone feeling hurt and vulnerable. It is easy to be paranoid and feel excessively exploited in an atmosphere, where good intentions seem foolhardy and naive.

Indeed in the harsh combatative world of adversarial litigation to suggest that everyone should 'make up and be friends' might seem ludicrously impractical. That this is so reveals an essential flaw in the way that our legal system has developed. It is also a telling comment on the ethos of the society in which we live.

In the present legal climate, guarding against the danger and expense of litigation prevents an increasing number of voluntary activities. It also leads to excessive costs for private and public bodies. For, nowadays, when things go wrong we do not wish to understand or sympathise, but to blame and punish. We are unwilling to consider the possibility that in some way or other we create the cause for everything that happens to us. Instead, we seek to distort and manipulate the facts to persuade some referee or judge to confirm and reward our 'absolute rightness'. We justify such rigidity by telling ourselves it is our duty to benefit and so protect others like us in the future.

In fact, the opposite is the case. Less harm will be experienced by people in the future if we open up and reveal all the facts. With full knowledge, we can heal situations and ensure everyone does everything in their power to implement positive change. This is the really safe way to make sure negative things will not happen again to us or anyone else.

Within the highest levels of our judiciary one senses the presence of a priestly idealism that does bring justice without fear or favour. Like a jewel it shines reassuringly amidst the confusing distortion, obstruction and extravagance of the everyday legal process. If the civil law was organised to make it easy to pour out the truth from all sides and permit flexible outcomes, then redress would indeed always fit and resolve what has been done wrong. Then how much happier would we be? We need a method that is focused around the high, objective and flexible priestly wisdom of a good judge from the beginning, not just at the end.

Bringing this into an arbitration process near the very beginning and delving into and clarifying the issues by studying the astrology of the events and the people involved is such a method. However unlikely this might seem to those who have not used astrology to see through and behind obstructions, let us try it just once and see.

Crime and punishment

Let us start by reminding ourselves that to have a large prison population is a sign of the failure of law and order, not its success. Astrologers will appreciate the irony that Britain has grown to have the largest number of prisoners per head of population in Europe, at a time when its leaders have had birth charts dominated by planets in the 12th house of imprisonment!

Being tough in response to crimes is of little use if we have no understanding of how to stem the causes that lead people to commit them. To increase sentences and build more prisons, without addressing root causes, will only create the space for more crime and the need for more and more prisons – just like putting another lane on a motorway! Clearly questions of cause go beyond the criminal justice system, although perhaps not that far beyond the social and educational considerations studied in the last chapters of this book. At the same time, we do have to question the effectiveness of knee-jerk changes in the law and political recommendations. The level of re-offending, the atmosphere of prisons and the fear of ordinary people is so great that we have to ask if the way criminals are tried and sentenced has any effect on their behaviour, or any benefit for the victim. Until both crimes and prison populations decrease radically, we can never feel we have succeeded. Could astrology help to clarify this terrible social problem? Let us consider the present system before trying to answer this.

When a crime has been committed, the present system seeks only to identify, try and punish the wrongdoer. It does little to heal the victim's suffering, or make the offender 'pay' in a way that clearly balances and compensates individuals or society. Instead it puts everyone to more inconvenience and expense. Our prisons are overcrowded with people, the majority of whom will offend again, because their minds are set in notions of injustice: 'them and us', 'getting caught is the risk you have to take in my game'. The victim is left covering the costs of sentence enforcement and prison accommodation that ensures the person who harmed them 'pays for their crime'!

Let us say again, when we suffer unfairly, we need closure: the restoration of balance and belief that, however bad it was, 'something good must come out of it'. To know that the offender is 'suffering for his/her sins' gives very limited relief. A criminal in prison may protect society, but does not heal the harm that has been done or enhance social cohesion. The protection is truly temporary. Would it not be better to focus on methods that make the crime the beginning of a process, where the criminal really repairs the damage? Could not redress by the criminal be performed in a way that brings comfort to victims and their families and genuine benefit to society?

Contemporary methods of community service are dispensed as a form of punishment. They are too distant from the original offence and those involved to be reconciliatory. Both the offender and the public are likely to see them as soft, almost 'let off' options. Undertaking unpleasant tasks for the general community is likely to be merely humiliating and so counterproductive, if it is not accompanied by genuine regret from the offender and forgiveness on the part of the victim. Until both are achieved the problem remains and more crime is most likely.

To succeed, all concerned must be committed to rehabilitation that redeems. Then there is a chance that a real heartfelt change has occurred. While it will not be possible to do this in the most extreme of cases, many more people isolated from society by their crimes would respond. How much happier to find ways to enrich society and also avoid living in deep resentment at its expense. If enemies can become friends, the negative becomes positive and fear diminishes.

Sometimes a particular crime is so outrageous that to find the perpetrator and punish him/her is all that seems to be required. The media can so whip up public hysteria and pressure on the authorities that injustice is always possible. In criminal proceedings, the division between the interests of the prosecuting and defending parties are total. The financial ability of one side to find evidence and expert witnesses can lead to injustices that may take many years to correct, if at all. In recent decades judgements in respect of a number of high-profile terrorist bomb outrages attracted emotive news coverage when first given, but subsequently were found to be profoundly flawed; false accusation, the unreliability of too-easily-accepted evidence and forced confessions led to injustice. Frequently too much credibility is given to expert testimony (such as the notorious cot death cases in Britain). Entirely innocent people have spent many years in prison and have their lives ruined.

Confronted with such occurrences, it is not enough to change police interview rules, or ensure that professional bodies discipline the failures of their members after the event. Even enhancing forensic skills and surveillance technology leaves room for error and distances us ever further for that human contact that can identity and heal problems. Such improvements will always be piecemeal answers to failings in the system. They may give future protection to some wrongly accused people in specific isolated circumstances, but we need more. We need a process at the very heart of the legal system requiring everyone concerned in a judgement to come to an intrinsic understanding of the motivations behind and causes of the crime – especially the essential nature of the people involved. Then we need them to be satisfied with what was decided by way of resolution.

Lack of such intrinsic understanding can be disastrous. Sometimes the criminal justice system is undermined by the ignorance of the officials involved. The case of the Rochdale families, suspected of black magic, whose children were taken by police and social services in a surprise dawn raid, then isolated, examined and persistently interviewed about things they did not understand shows the need for this clearly. Subsequent studies have shown that the social workers involved were basing their decisions and recommendations upon doubtful information from a USA pressure group, sensationalised news reports and a failure to talk intelligently and sensitively to the families. It took months, even years, before the wronged families were reunited. A boy of six, whose infant fantasies were fundamentally misunderstood by 'experts' who should have been trained to know better, will carry heavy memories for his whole life. The absence of a process to bridge the gap of understanding between accuser and accused is the key reason for this tragedy.

All too often our system of criminal investigation, legal processing and punishment is no more than a series of desperate clumsy attempts to 'keep the lid on' the consequences of individual greed, social misunderstanding and dissent. Such a society emanates from the assumption that, while it is good to care about each other and the world in which we live, 'with so much evil out there self-protection is the first priority'.

We need a radical method to cut through the morass of such emotional gut reactions, prejudice and whipped up hysteria. We need an exact and genuine understanding of with whom and with what we are dealing. Vitally, we need to see things getting better: victims finding genuine resolution; enemies becoming fewer; crime and prison populations falling; society feeling safe through enhanced friendship and concern for others.

The revolutionary suggestion is that here again astrology should be used throughout the investigation, as well as prosecution, of criminal cases. It offers a vital language to objectify the circumstances and find a beneficial outcome for all concerned; the victim, the offender and larger society itself. Although this might seem a strange and bizarre suggestion, anyone who has worked extensively with clients, their charts and life circumstances will know a highly effective process could be devised. Below is an outline of how the process might work.

In the first instance, studying the astrological charts of the time of the event and the victim(s) could help investigation from the moment the crime is reported. In special cases today, the police informally consult psychics and astrologers to find missing people and objects. They also use psychologists to profile likely offenders. The detailed study of the horoscopes of Mark Chapman and Cho Seung-Hui in Chapter 12 shows how effective such knowledge can be in understanding the offender and the timing of his actions. If such methods were applied more generally, a body of prior experience could be built up that could cut through deception and indicate fruitful approaches when suspects are being interviewed. The present system of investigation is burdened with the self-interest of the suspect and the police need to secure a conviction. So, how the evidence is collected and presented can be chaotic and arbitrary. The wrong person may be accused and the actual offender escape. In contrast, the horoscope and its progressions and transits can suggest ways to test what is being said; they can suggest new and fruitful areas of questioning. They could be invaluable in determining and testing a motive.

Such an astrological report could go with all the other facts of the case to the Crown Prosecution Service who, once they have determined there is a case to be answered, could commence a process to recommend the likely punishment and recompense that would follow a guilty plea. If agreed by victim and the offender the matter would go to the court for approval. If this did not succeed, then the case would go to trial, which would be based on examining the facts in dispute. While the astrological background could be valuable at this stage as well, it should be incorporated into the conventional trial procedures very gradually. Only after a body of reliable experience of astrology has been confirmed from other areas of the criminal process would it be reasonable for astrological and legal argument to be heard together.

It is at the sentencing stage that astrology would be especially valuable. The crucial aims of any sentence are: to send a message to others planning to act in the same way; to put right the harm that has been done to the victim; and to transform the criminal from being a liability to society to benefiting it. In many cases, the deeper knowledge of the offender that astrology gives may lead to a more severe sentence. This could be especially so if it were clear that the criminal had not learnt from what has happened and would offend again if given the chance. In other cases, with the acceptance of the victim, an original but highly appropriate method of redress might be devised. At present, there are set punishments for particular crimes, which the victim plays little or no part in determining. If he seeks compensation, he has to do so in a civil action. Combining the two would save court time and further suffering and expense to the victim.

If the offender were to accept jointly agreed compensation and embark upon a supervised process of redress that he accepted as just, the chance of his re-offending would be much reduced. Whether the sentence was custodial or compensatory; astrologically-based reports could be used to assess progress at each stage until the sentence is completed. This could continue afterwards should the offender wish. It is very difficult to pull the wool over the eyes of a good astrologer.

Conclusion
Nothing that is suggested above is intended to change the fundamental basis of legal traditional and statute – rather to introduce an investigative and diagnostic tool that is culture, and special-interest free. The aim is to introduce a method that cuts through the errors, injustices and ineffective awards and sentencing that undermine the progress of justice and crowd the prisons in present-day society. The benefits could be immense. In civil law, the majority of cases could be settled prior to court proceedings. As this is achieved, ways of incorporating astrological understanding into the legal process itself could cut through delay. In crime and punishment, the method could improve the detection rate,

reduce wrongful accusations, increase the number of guilty pleas and so prevent extended hearings. It could lead to a much more effective sentencing policy from which everyone would gain.

As well as reducing prison populations, it could devise ways of prisoners working out redress in the community – benefiting society rather than being a drain on it. Because such arrangements would be mutually agreed, they are likely to be very different and much more successful than present Community Service Orders. All this might mean that the time and resources devoted to detection, law and enforcement would be reduced, but only to the extent to which the new innovations were effective.

Dysfunctional, socially unhealthy societies that do not address the causes of crime have more and more laws and ever-expanding prison populations. In a truly healthy society, law and order has to be enforced far less, because it is gladly accepted in the heart of every citizen.

The genuine deep understanding that comes from astrological insight would reduce fear, give us the wisdom that strengthens courage and so bring a new positive climate to society. It would move us on from a 'them and us' view of life. It would help us understand people whose circumstances and attitudes are radically different to our own and help us work together towards a common good. It would advance us from our present 'rat race', 'every person for themselves', and 'survival of the fittest' search for personal benefit over others at any cost. Instead, a community of increasing friendship would develop. The trust which that brings will obviate any need for fear.

Chapter 17

The Shortcomings of 21st Century Society

> Education without values, as useful as it is,
> seems to make man a more clever devil.
>
> **C S Lewis**

On numerous occasions throughout this book we have contrasted the material success of contemporary society since the 17th to 18th century Enlightenment with the fragmentary uncertainty of its purpose. Chapter 9 showed that without a central spiritual focus or agreed descriptive language, philosophy becomes piecemeal, contradictory and ultimately defeatist. Without a focalising core of values, 21st century society and its citizens live in a state of ambiguous anarchy at the mercy of their own and each other's basest natures.

The heart aim of this book has been to show this has been caused by fundamentalist mechanistic rationalism increasingly being accepted as the only possible foundation for an 'enlightened' modern world. This chapter will explore why we consider such a limited and pessimistic view to be unavoidable. It will show the dire consequences for ourselves and our descendents if we continue to do so. Chapters 18 and 19 will explore far better alternatives.

The 18th century Enlightenment searched for rational morality as a basis for social values. It was a reaction to what was perceived as the moral bankruptcy of the Christian tradition. Centuries of schism, conflict and Church corruption had essentially emasculated its role as custodian of society.

The vacuum was filled by a new faith – the belief in scientific discovery, its technical development and the expectation that its very rationality would inevitably provide a *natural right* of happiness for every individual. Unfortunately, while scientific discoveries gave great power, they offered little or no direction, only more and more research into ever-developing possibilities. At best, science could be no more than neutral on the moral choices surrounding human happiness. By its very nature, it allowed power to whoever could seize it arbitrarily and so control the commanding heights of the economy.

Vast technological progress and capacity for mass consumption in the 20th century has expanded our society 'on the fly'. We feel powerless to do more than base organisation on stopgap economics and inconsistent values that seem to be picked out of the air to serve immediate interests and demands.

Contemporary cultural values and their institutions

Moving ever closer to becoming the 'spiritual' heart of this materialistic, self-indulgent 'freedom' we seek to spread to the whole world are our commercialised cultural, entertainment and media systems. The accelerating progress in communications technology during the past half-century places it at the core of every detail of our lives. It has a critical influence on how we communicate ideas and enthusiasms to each other, our values, the joys and sorrows we share, and the joint enterprises we embark upon. These consensus vehicles that define the society we live in are experienced through the news and entertainment media.

Totalitarian societies control public taste and opinion by controlling the media and artistic expression. In contrast it is assumed that democratic societies allow and encourage individualism by ensuring that no one-group interest can do this. In Britain in the early days of broadcasting, this was certainly the case. The British Broadcasting Corporation was established to be independent of government and commercial interests. So, it offered a wide range of expressions without fear or favour. Even when commercially sponsored television was introduced, procedures were established to maintain a separation between editorial/programming and advertising decisions, as is done in the print media. Because viewer numbers and categories determine the price of advertisements, careful regulation was needed to prevent lowering of standards and prejudicial reporting.

In recent decades commercial pressures have built up like a log jam about to burst. The development of multi-channel digital broadcasting, interactive modern communication techniques and product placement in programmes is now blurring the distinctions even further. Phone-in voting and comments can finance a reality TV show or sporting event. Paying high prices for exclusive sports coverage can enrich a few stars and clubs at the expense of the many. Such extreme exposure can build to a point where public attention and taste is held in an iron grip by unimportant and artificially created spectacles of doubtful quality. Sport has become the religion of the masses.

The ability of powerful owners of print media to influence public opinion and taste has been well known for many decades and tolerated, provided that the complementary balance of an alternative prejudice is on offer. In the USA, prejudiced presentation is spreading into television news. Even when its aim is objective, coverage seems to be driven by particular cultural assumptions. Although modern technology allows more instant reporting and several 24-hour news channels, the similarity between the news outputs from these channels is remarkable.

The values encouraged by commercial advertisements play a key role in forming the taste and expectations of the public. From an early age, children are encouraged to nag their parents to buy what they see on television and in magazines. As we grow older, particular products and practices are creatively presented to become lifestyle pleasure objects, symbols of taste and status. Even more insidious and invidious can be the assumptions about what is important in life: killing insects; being smart, sexy, or even drunk, avoiding some aromas; but encouraging others.

In order to save the payment of direct licence or entrance fees, over the past fifty years we have created a system of paying just a teeny bit more for products to cover advertising costs. This finances programmes that benefit commercial interests by persuading us to buy what they wish to sell us. Skilful scriptwriters and programme-makers mould the public taste far more effectively than the Soviets or Nazis ever could. We have sleepwalked into and are becoming increasingly controlled and made impotent by narrow, hedonistic commercial-serving totalitarianism: a deceptive, valueless system where most people appear better off – at the cost of their souls.

Small wonder that we are in the midst of a mania of ever-expanding consumption that is bringing us to the point where we will eat our planet alive. We can hardly find the time to halt our indulgence to question our actions – save to grab a quick fix and hurry on our way! Slowly we realise it will not be that easy. As we approach the end of the first decade of 21st century *The Inconvenient Truth*[86] of global ecological disaster increasingly dominates the news, underlining the concerns whose astrology was explained in Chapter 14.

While material science now largely accepts the global warming consequences of its actions, mainstream governments are at a very early first stage of identifying and acting upon this root cause of our problems. As if we were children or adolescents who have been warned frequently about the consequences of bad behaviour, our leaders now tell us all will be well 'if we promise to be good in future'. Cut carbon emissions, even just trade them, and invest in a new generation of nuclear power stations. Then we will be able to carry on expanding our economies, indulging our desires and living life on the superficial margins of disregarding the feelings and ways of others.

As we have already seen, it will not be that simple. The chaotic condition of our contemporary society is the calcified product of the absence of a coherent spiritual heart in our culture. Until that heart is restored, healed and pumping the spiritual nourishment of kindness and understanding throughout the fabric of society, any number of piecemeal mechanical solutions will lead us out of one set of horrific outcomes into another.

Having mined and pumped in little over one century a heritage of coal and oil that took hundreds of thousands of years to create, we are now considering replacing it in the Earth with nuclear poison that will threaten future generations for 50,000 years. How much lower in spiritual degeneracy can our modern world and some of the scientists that serve it sink?

Quite a bit lower, it seems! For rational economics has now reached a view of human nature that separates such notions of 'heart' and 'feeling' from calculations in the economic marketplace. When he wrote *The Calculus of Consent*, James M Buchanan had very positive reasons for seeking to liberate ordinary people and the economic marketplace from well-intentioned 'zealots'. This is the term he used for those politicians and public officials who sought to control and direct policy according to their view of 'the public interest'. In fact, their actions were based on their own bureaucratic self-interest. Only by removing their restrictive regulations could individual expertise and enterprise be free to develop to maximum efficiency. After what was seen as several decades of failed government intervention, his thesis was to become the dominant answer to everything. It opened the floodgates to change, consumption and intensive speculation in an international free market.

Like so many good theoretical ideas worthy of a Nobel Prize, in practice there was an unexpected price to be paid. Political intervention was to be limited to just a few regulatory bodies, comprised mainly of insiders from the area of the economy being regulated. If these were almost entirely independent of the democratically elected government, then how was the public interest to express itself? Quite simply by individual consumers' reactions to what was being offered. Did they like and were they willing to pay for it? This implied a rather narrow view of the human beings, their relationships with the market and each other. Quite simply, all decisions were to be made on the basis of 'giving the public what it wants'. Based on such a fundamental concept, what was good, bad, and desirable or not was determined by what was profitable. Even more disquietingly, this could be taken one step further: what could be *made* profitable by promotion and spinning the minds and attitudes of the public?

So, what had been intended to set people free from the elitist impositions of paternalistic 'zealots' had been replaced by the manipulative skills of marketing experts and their psychological advisers. A system that had been intended to give expression to individual choice had trapped people into an ever narrower view of what was possible, in order to serve the financial interests of their exploiters. A new meritocratic aristocracy with a subjected peasantry had been established. Like the peasantry of the Middle Ages, it was based on the master's ability to control minds, so they would make those limited choices that served the master's interests. In a final irony, the 'democratic' political system itself, originally designed to express the political will of the people, became a creature of spin and distortion to serve those in power. The 'zealots' had returned; this time more functional, openly cynical, with little or no pretence of values and principles.

Is this the individual happiness and freedoms visualised by the philosophers and campaigners of the Enlightenment and the USA's founding fathers? We have come to this, because relying solely on a mechanistic paradigm is inadequate. We need to look again to restore a pure heart of spiritual tradition and a language, with which to describe and assess human interaction.

With current social and cultural circumstances so total and overwhelming, how and where is it possible to start? Children's education is dominated by the mechanical functionality that serves commercial interests. Schools are judged by test results – values are only studied at the margins. How does this prepare our children to see and heal the world they will grow up into?

Values and rational education in the 21ˢᵗ century

In every child's life, there comes a moment when he /she starts to take on the experiences and responsibilities of an adult. In traditional societies the culture is very clearly defined and protected. During adolescence the boys and girls are taken away and introduced to symbols and experiences upon which the beliefs and ways of the adult world are based. In this way, separate cultures maintain their distinctive natures and roles, and respect within each culture is clear.

Global conquest and commerce over the past centuries, and especially since Pluto entered Cancer in 1911/14, has led to radical change in the nature of individual cultures. In addition, migration has led to the establishment of a range of different cultures in previously monocultural countries. The exponential expansion of international travel and communication in recent years means it is very difficult for cultures to exist in isolation and ignorance of each other.

So we face a crucial question: in a multicultural world, full increasingly of multicultural nation states, into what basic values do we initiate our young? What do we wish them to take refuge in? For hundreds, even thousands of years, the priests of a society's religion have taught its essential values. Since the American and French Revolutions in the 18ᵗʰ century, and especially today, this is not seen as an acceptable option. Instead, with so many religions seeking to tolerate each other's differences, excluding religion from the educational process altogether seems to be the best solution.

Or would it be more accurate to say that we have really exchanged several alternative assumed beliefs systems for just one? Have we set aside traditional religions and (except in faith schools) left them to be taught and practised optionally at pupils' homes, but legally obliged *all students* to follow an agnostic and narrow 'rationalist' approach to knowledge?

The knowledge taught has become dominated by functional material cause and effect information. Occasional *laissez-faire* creativity is included as a token counter-balance. Rules of behaviour are confined to the convenience of disciplining the pupils into the mechanics of the process. Almost by default, certainly without proper consultation, it was decided to make rational secularism the essential 'belief' foundation of state education and to initiate future generations into it! The consequent uncertainty of values within our schools and society is now plain to see.

For, into what values do we encourage our children to take refuge? When we are expecting them to stay in school until eighteen and that 50% will continue on into university, is it really satisfactory for the education system to remain morally neutral as it is at present? Provided the child does not cause too much trouble, or rock the organisational boat, schools do not have to consider what their pupils actually believe to be their business. Good academic results are the benchmark for assessment!

Nor are the schools and universities to blame. Taking such a dangerous amoral position in core values is the product of the increasingly utilitarian way that education is viewed by society. We have to develop the highest standards of reading, writing, mathematics and scientific skills so we can succeed in a competitive global marketplace. In Britain, children's progress is tested at the ages of 7, 11, 14, 16, 17, 18, and 21. Their teachers' promotion and salaries and the school's funding can be considerably affected by the pupils' success and failure in these tests. Education is seen as little more than a preparation for the job market. So, commercial interests play an ever-larger role in the funding and organisation of schools, universities and research. Ronald MacDonald comes with gifts to tempt primary 'kiddies' from under five years old to become his customers. Businesses are encouraged to found and fund specialist secondary schools. Commercial interests establish medical and software research 'centres of excellence' at leading universities. As a result, pure education takes a back seat to applied commercialism. Government sees this to be a way to pay the bills. Nor do we need to build or own our schools; private finance will do that for us – at a price we will keep on paying long into the future!

How does all this appear to the pupils at the receiving end of this initiation into utilitarian materialism? Crucially, what kind of values and expectations does this build into their characters, when this process and value system is all they experience during the best hours of most of their days from the age of 5 to 18?

Unless the children attend faith schools, what can parental cultures alone do to teach the difference between right and wrong? Government policy encourages most parents to work. The provision of nursery education means that children could be cared for from as young as one year old or less. When families are together, it is often over TV dinners at the 'fag end' of a hard day, or increasingly in separate rooms, playing and chatting on their computers. Short annual holidays tend to have more to do with extravagant indulgence than intimate, mature guidance and relationships. Even if the parents' religious convictions are clear and strong, such a timescale is hardly suited to teach and inspire fundamental values.

As a result, the patterns of upbringing most children experience emanate from in-fashion role models in the sports, music and other entertainment media and each other; especially when they reach teenage years,. Where educational failure and social opportunity is low then gang culture and anti-social behaviour is the natural consequence. So, governments enact laws to punish and imprison more and more people for more and more crimes. We never consider whether it might be the society spawned by those governmental assumptions that should be 'in the dock'.

Commercialised materialistic society and media further undermine the ability of parents to correct and fill the gaps left by the amoral imbalances in our educational system. Promoters depict us as 'one happy family' of consumers and the parents as there more to supply the resources that feed sporting and celebrity images. The possession of material things becomes a very important symbol of status and hence social security. So, although on the surface the school and peer-group leisure systems seem to be at odds with each other, their essential values are complementary. The school is there to offer the 'tricks of the trade'. We will need these to obtain resources and so continue to purchase and enjoy the material goodies of the adult world when it is no longer proper or practical for our parents to provide.

Is this the essence of the values that we wish and intend to inculcate into our children? If so, the valueless and degenerate nature of our society should not surprise us. With consumption as the very essence of our economic *raison d'être* and success, is it surprising that our children move from toys they do not need, to cigarettes, alcohol, electronic goods, DVDs, music CDs, motor cars, houses, DIY? We seem to have a desperate need to use and waste more and more energy. Then we spend excessive amounts on health, so we can live and carry on the indulgence ever longer. Is it any wonder that our society seems to exist to avoid change and challenge (except in stylised sporting contests)? Is this why we seek to avoid anything that confronts us with the consequences of the impermanent nature of existence?

Initiating our young into such a system of 'education' is essentially flawed. For, it can so easily alienate us as individuals from each other. It can make us feel indulged by, but impotent and unable to change, the world we live in – 'welcome to the machine'! There may be 'loads of money' to be had, but little if any wealth.

Worse still, when serious conflicts of interest occur, negotiation becomes little more than a game of spin and nerve for the in-power players. The manipulated majority becomes frustrated and outraged 'losers' or 'naïve idealists'. Certainly, good people express humanitarian principles and genuine generosity at every level of international and national politics. Yet each stage in the process is so peppered with the unprincipled that rarely, if at all, will the really good triumph over profit and expediency.

Ironically, the lack of deeply agreed values is not even 'efficient realism' in its own material terms. It does not eradicate extravagance and waste. With no ordered core values and principles, emotions can ride roughshod over essential economic realities. Believing in a cause can lead to excessive spending, be it in sport, on a white elephant project, or even a war that serves our fears and prejudices. In a world of conflicting values, administered by the economics of what you can manipulate and get away with, several groups 'spending up large' to fight each other can create a continual Oceana/Eurasia Orwellian nightmare.

By brutalising the 'truth' our commercial, media and political leaders set examples that brutalise the generations that follow them. So much thuggish violence is no more than an immature reflection of the selfish ways of adult societies and the marketplace that we are taught to aspire towards.

Children growing up in the 21st century can only be lost and confused about the world their parents have created for them. The tragedy is we all wish to do the best we can for our children and leave them a world in which they can be happy. How can we put it right?

The next two chapters will seek to answer this. Before this, however, we need to understand the history and causes of the present condition of the educational system that serves our contemporary materialistic market economy.

Educational values – ancient and modern

Ironically, the early traditions of British education held its ideal and central aim to educate the student to have intrinsic values of cultured understanding, principle and service. Yet it is the loss of such values that explain the malaise at the heart of our system over recent decades.

Although originally intended for the children of merchants and middle-ranking officials, whose means were too limited to employ a private tutor, the British public schools[87] became a private system, designed to give special advancement to a privileged class. As such, it became the core training ground for the officials who cared for Britain's colonial responsibilities, as they grew from the 18ᵗʰ century. Its core principles became classical academic excellence; privilege and service to one's country, its traditions and responsibilities; and sporting rules of courage and fair play. The teaching methods and conventions founded the skills that administered the British Empire and the modern world that was to develop from its influence.

The process of initiation into these principles infused every aspect of an almost entirely male and largely residential educational culture. Academic achievement was important, but not the principle quality to be prized. The classics and arts dominated the curriculum. Style and quality of behaviour, 'good Christian practices', responsibilities of leadership and being an example to 'those less fortunate' were far more important that the material functions of 'new money' entrepreneurs and artisans. Public schools were principally a preparation for the army, the church, or colonial administration – maybe banking, or other senior business positions.

Education for all people developed quite separately in Britain from the late 19ᵗʰ century. Initially, basic skills of reading, writing and numeracy needed in the workplace were taught until 12 years of age. A few able children of the working class were able to advance by entering middle-class grammar day schools. Evening class facilities extended opportunity further. Then the 1944 Education Act sought to open full education to all children, through a system of selection the eleven-plus at 11 years old. With all children staying at school until 15 (no longer 14) and most of the 25% selected for grammar schools staying until 16 and encouraged to continue until 18, clearly schools were now intended to play a new and major role in children's social advancement.

The social and what-values-to-teach implications of this were not addressed then and have hardly been since. Grammar schools for day pupils had existed alongside the public school system for some time and largely adopted the latter's values. Although grammar schools were expanding to include a wider range of social classes and the British Empire was being disbanded, the new intake received a watered down public school disciplined initiation and a high academic standard of teaching. The cultural initiation of the remaining 75 per cent was arbitrary.

There were three main problems with this structure.

* Values suited to initiate governing elite drawn from privileged families may not be appropriate for a far greater number of bright children being prepared to administer a materialistic consumer society in a country destined to have ever-decreasing world power. Much of what was being taught might seem to be socially inappropriate, abstractly academic and irrelevant.

* Science and technology were to play an increasingly important role in society and hence education but, unlike the arts and classics, their methods were mechanical and essentially without moral principle. Hence our educational system was to become increasingly functional and amoral.

* Selecting children at the age of 11 was premature and gave unfair advantage to those of a higher or educated social class. Vast numbers of able children were being denied the opportunity to do much better.

A major debate over the third problem developed through the 1960s. Selection at 11 years was largely abandoned and comprehensive education was established. As the new large schools struggled to accommodate a wide range of abilities and aptitudes, the other two problems were left largely unaddressed. We may have created an ideal space, where equality of opportunity was possible, but opportunity to do what and for what reason was not entirely clear.

What was the essential purpose of this universal comprehensive education? Recovering from the critical anarchy of the mid 1960s (Uranus conjunct Pluto in Virgo) into expansive, accommodating idealism (Neptune in Sagittarius/Pluto in Libra) through the 1970s, a child-centred approach, emphasising that the Latin *educare* means 'draw out', became the fashion. The teacher became the provider of resources for individual discovery, group and course work. Standards, purpose and values became lost, as kind and generous educators rushed to keep up with 'pupil demands'.

Inevitably, with Neptune in Capricorn and Pluto in Scorpio in the late 1980s, order was imposed by a National Curriculum, backed up by a system of standard assessment tests at various ages. The world economy and Britain's role in it had changed dramatically in the intervening years. The Soviet Bloc's totalitarian systems were collapsing. In Asia, low-cost production was expanding rapidly. The freeing of world trade had already undermined traditional British industry. In the coming twenty years, advanced Western cultures were to face massive commercial competition. The only solution seemed to be to prepare a highly motivated and functionally educated workforce. To achieve this, ever more standardised tests and opportunities for functional education were employed at every age level.

Schools in the 21ˢᵗ century are confronted with demands forever-increasing levels of pupil performance in a materialistic world, whose values they may well be the victim of, but have had little or no role in forming. This, and the new trend encouraging businesses to create schools directly, suggests exploring ethical values in more than a rudimentary functional way is unlikely. Questioning lifestyle choices, enhancing our relationships with each other and developing communities are unlikely to play much part in the initiation of our children. Through neglect, competitive anxiety and greed we have allowed the brute force of mechanical, amoral materialism to gain and dominate our schools and hence the high ground of our lives.

Conclusion

In this way our schools confirm and reinforce the ethical bankruptcy of the adult culture. As individuals, we may know what *feels* right and decent and only wish that others would feel the same and act accordingly, but our lives are caught up with immediate demands. So answers have to be quick and easy. Ideally it would be 'easier' if they were suggested and implemented by others. 'Solutions' become piecemeal reactions to events. They build up a fragmentary collection of ill thought out laws and regulations that public servants struggle to implement. When they do, we find that the freedom of action and choice of people who have never had anything to do with the problem we were supposed to be addressing is often threatened. Yet the problems these new rules were meant to solve remain as bad as before.

Without core principles of respect and fundamentally fair behaviour that bring out the best in each of us, our social experiences are destined to become ever more beleagued. The three chapters that follow suggest ways to identify and restore such an essential core in our society and education, and so create a positive vision of our future.

Chapter 18
Identifying Essential Values in the 21ˢᵗ Century

> Problems cannot be solved with the same
> consciousness that created them.
> **Albert Einstein**

In the previous chapter, we saw that the very heart, built-in flaw of 21ˢᵗ century society is that its laws, practices, rules and regulations are becoming based on an ever-diminishing lowest-common-denominator view of human nature.

As cultures have become more mobile, societies more fragmented and economies more materialistically competitive, misunderstandings and fear have proliferated. Media-fuelled reaction to crime and terrorism drive government knee-jerk reactions. Behaviour is reminiscent of the frontier lynching mentality of the American Wild West. We have seen how free-market models have been combined with geneticists 'survival of the fittest' descriptions of human behaviour to justify economies based on money, possession and mistrust of fellow human beings. Ever more details of our everyday private lives have to be known. We need to be watched and supervised, even spoken to by cameras. Detailed achievement targets dominate our working lives. Room to decide and give uniquely from our own hearts is being narrowed to the point of extinction. To be sure we are safe, it seems we need to submit to a system that ensures we will never be surprised – not even by joy!

Wait now, is that true or even fair? Compared to everyday life in the 19ᵗʰ and earlier centuries is not our modern world far less brutal and much more accepting? Britain and many other countries do not have capital punishment. We are far more tolerant of minorities. Consider the millions who died in the wars of the 20th century. Unlike colonial times, we care about and seek to understand and help communities less fortunate than ourselves. What about Live Aid, the movement to release Nelson Mandela, fund-raising Telethons?

Certainly, the surface quality of life in many parts of the world has become much safer, more comfortable and plentiful. Publicly we express less prejudice. We are interested in a much wider range of foods, places and experiences. However, to what extent are such improvements and our expressions of charity the product of plenty? Does plenty obscure a less principled underbelly? Would the same old aggressive intolerance return should ever the 'chips be down' again? The self-interest that dominates issues and the level of political debate in modern material democracies suggests a pessimistic answer. Certainly, the marketing experts we considered in the previous chapter feel they know those points that trigger fear, maximum self-indulgence and self-justification. Is there an antidote to such manipulation?

Transcending fear and finding reliable values
By way of contrast, all mature, regenerative, healthy and successful individuals, groups and societies focus around a central paradox that applies whatever the belief system and time in history – how they think about security. The paradox works like this. To experience security it is vital to develop the courage to live with insecurity. For anything we do to make ourselves feel secure is subject to failure and so will make us feel insecure. On the other hand, if we learn how to accept and live with insecurity, we will never be in danger of losing it. So we will always feel secure.

The ancient mysteries have a deep way of showing how personal courage lies at the heart of ecstatic liberation. In the Cabbalistic Tree of Life [88] between the Sephirah of Tiferet (beauty) and Keter (heaven) lies Daath (the abyss). The fastest way to heavenly understanding is courageous devotion to the beautiful. With it we fly over the abyss of self-doubt and so find ourselves in heaven. Doubt, with its constant need for protection, will slow the clarity of our momentum and so plunge us into the abyss of fear, from which it is hard to escape.

That the answer to the insecurities of life is the proactive embracing of insecurity is much more than a clever play of words. It is heightened symbolism that shows how courage leads to a genuine experience of liberation. By clearing away all those nasty, haunting, imaginary horror and obligation mental cobwebs of what might happen, it frees the mind to focus only on what actually *is* happening. This leaves lots of space to take control and deal firmly and practically with what we actually face. We become strong by casting aside unnecessary compromise and the constant experience of failure that comes from *imagining* what may happen.

So far so good, but wait a minute! Is this any more than a blasé *laissez-faire* avoidance of responsibility – a way of living with the anxiety of doing whatever we wish and brushing aside the consequences? Without a framework to describe knowledge of our circumstances and ourselves and without selfless principles, this may well be so. If it is, we could be in for quite a shock.

We need a framework. What could it be? We can start to find it by looking back to that key mistake we keep referring to. The thinkers of the Enlightenment felt that the possibility of developing their inherited framework of values into something better was unworthy of consideration. Now, a little over three hundred years later, the starting-from-scratch science that the Enlightenment sired and fostered instead has reached the stage where its mathematics, economics and most psychological theories of mind have decided that the only efficient way to order human society is to assume the worst. Far from being a 'noble savage'; we must treat each person as a cheat, whether they are one or not. Because of this, we need close systems of control and supervision in public places; rigid targets and centralised regulation of the workplace; and drugs to help us cope with the stresses of such a system. By knowing and controlling so much, we merely intensify our fear of what we cannot know or control.

Is there no other way? Yes, if we can accept a malleable system that is not cast iron, but does provide clear concepts that clarify and explain human behaviour and social phenomena. We may need to accept predictions that are not mechanically exact, but we will be relieved of the anxiety of constantly seeking and not finding certainty. Instead, we will become ever more secure in our ability to understand, explain, accept and improve any outcome that does arise. Open in this way to tolerant learning, we will find we are far less surprised by outcomes than we expected; moreover, when we are, what happens is most likely to be better, not worse, than expected.

This was the intention behind the world picture that pre-dated the Enlightenment. In those days, priests and scholars sought clear cultural values, ways of assessing individual behaviour in terms of those values and, for the wise, an astrological language to describe and explain such behaviour. Of course, many religious institutions misused their power by corruptly treating the spiritual as a commodity to be bought, sold and brokered for earthly gain. This hypocrisy and the in-built self-righteousness of 'one way' religions led to intolerance, religious wars and immense human suffering. The tradition of astrological understanding had been largely lost and persecuted for 1,700 years. It was yet to receive what it so clearly needed - the clarifying benefits, calculation and display power of 21st century computer technology. If reform rather than absolute rejection had been the way of the Enlightenment, we may not have come to the desperate amoral vacuum that threatens our very existence today.

As it is, we denied and removed traditional inner values that had guided and strengthened our ancestors through life's uncertainties for millennia. However inadequate they were, we have put nothing in their place. So, modern science puts humanity in a crisis of valueless anarchy and castrates the very essence of our psyche.

This chapter seeks to suggest ways to rediscover, restore and enhance such vital heart values. If combined with the discoveries of the modern world, they are values that could bring about in the 21st century the greatest advances yet in human history.

Astrology's important role in regenerating core values

By offering knowledge of each other and ourselves in the past and into the future, astrology provides genuine insight into what we face in the present. Paradoxically, this study of all time gives universal clarity that can set us free every time. It opens us up to possibilities and pleasure. We do not close up tight in a struggle for rarely attainable sensual desires that would not satisfy if they were easily available.

Throughout this book, we have seen many specific practical benefits of astrology that help us understand and work with individuals, the economy, business and the law. Here we will celebrate how astrology, when used in a tolerant and positive way, can enhance the very atmosphere of society as a whole and our experience of it – so much more understanding, patience and effectiveness!

However, while the knowledge offers efficacious tools and insight, it cannot make our decisions and do our living for us – that remains our responsibility. With astrology we can know ourselves, the karmic challenge we were born to confront and transform our understanding of the people and circumstances we meet. We can describe clearly the behaviour of other people, institutions, events and their perpetrators. We can anticipate and assess outcomes. We can even access the likelihood of the worst or something better happening by judging what phenomena is manifesting against the larger historical background cycles. If kindness and selfless devotion to good practice lead to good outcomes in difficult circumstances, times we most fear may yet turn out to bring blessings.

When it comes to matters of right and wrong, however, astrology will play an ambiguous role. As we have seen, our ability to observe and develop advanced insight into the flow gives us power over the level at which that archetype will manifest. So in theory we could use our insight for good or bad purposes. People have attempted to use astrology as an aid to seduction, to win wars, to avoid the consequences of rogue trading and many more selfish endeavours. The deluded pore over horoscopes, transits and progressions in desperate attempts to attract their lovers, succeed in business, find what they have lost, and even lose what they do not want. One can try to use astrology to become as greedy, hateful and ignorant as is possible using any other system of analysis and insight.

However, there is a difference. Since astrology is a way of describing the actual flow of the universe, the mechanics of that universe oblige that everything accurately observed must occur in some way. If you seek to distort that flow, you cannot avoid the consequences. If motivation is negative, then attempts to destroy and gain are likely to bring destruction and loss to the perpetrator. There may not be an immediate consequence. It will come at the time when negative karma is appropriately indicated in your chart. We have already seen that Hitler succeeded with Jupiter on his Sun, so when Saturn followed it he could not resist going into Russia and sealing his ultimate fate to fail. The result was vast destruction and the death of millions. The invasion of Iraq and associated events described in Chapter 5 provides a similarly misguided example.

Clearly, we need values to place alongside astrological insight to prevent the worst happening, when the cycles are difficult. We need values that develop standards of human excellence all the time. Such values should encourage kindness, compassion and tolerance that lead to our celebrating and working well with each other – even when conflict is most difficult to avoid. Within the heart of each religion, when stripped of its institutionalisation, are the key ways to encourage such values. Compassion and defining the relative nature of all judgements that separate us from each other are the keys that bridge understanding. When we look deeply with compassion into another person and their culture we cannot help but see as they do. We feel pity for their suffering and never wish to be its cause. So barriers break down and happiness between people and peoples grows. In contrast, when we consider only ourselves, we multiply exponentially our needs and consequent dissatisfactions. Self-obsessed, we see only problems that cloud our eyes from happiness.

With compassion and the illuminating language of astrology, we understand so much more and see clearly what needs to be done. This is the restorative essence we seek – the convenient truth.

Only an ecclesiastical hierarchy, that spiritual materialism in each religion, stands in the way of such wisdom and seeks to fight with another religion or offshoot. Pure religious convictions are too divine for mundane struggles. Religious wars are between ecclesiastical institutions and the prejudiced cultures they create and sustain; not between holy people and their deepest holy beliefs.

At the Enlightenment, religions were judged and found wanting, due to their behaviour. Ironically, religions survived, because they were essentially secular in a world that was becoming increasingly so. It was the light of the holy essence, the compassionate jewel in each religion that was all but lost. It is this essence that must be distilled and restored if living in the world is to be a purifying and healing experience.

Common core spiritual values in the 21st century

So how do we clear away conflicts and establish cross-cultural core values for a decent, kind, healthy and happy 21st century society and planet? How do we clear built-in intolerance and didactic conflicts? Idealising sacrifice for a particular belief, rather than developing understanding of others' convictions, narrowing authority and fundamentalism are dangerously counter-productive. They stop religions from purifying understanding and bringing happiness.

Problems between religions emanate from considerations of authority and the desperately vital importance that devotees place upon their methods of ensuring and enshrining particular moral principles, 'facts' they think of as 'absolute truth'. To avoid self-righteousness causing resentment, it is vital to realise that strong religious conviction is felt for the very best of reasons. Particular practices and teachings have so changed lives for the good that, from pure and loving hearts, devotees wish others to believe and so have the same benefits. Looking in this way, we can see that the most fervent fundamentalist may be acting from the kindest of intentions.

Of course, such good intentions are often misguided. Religion is not a 'one size fits all' phenomenon. It is an internal experience, easily misunderstood from the outside. For this reason, mature cultures tolerate many individual religious choices. Other cultures feel less comfortable with this. They insist upon orthodoxy, feeling paternalistically that, without the clear guidance of established paths of moral divine understanding, ordinary people will remain flawed, deluded and hopeless in the face of temptation. Confronted with an amoral modern society, such anxieties seem to have some force. For today, as many people turned their backs on the authority of the religions, they are left with nothing reliable to put in its place.

Few religious leaders would disagree over the fundamental reasons for our contemporary problems and the principles needed to address them. Whatever else they disagree upon, most would agree that more than at any other time in human history our society needs common fundamental values. They would wish that our media and political institutions identified and institutionalised core values, rather than encouraged more wealth creation and material consumption.

So, instead of concentrating our energies on what divides our religion from another, why not concentrate on organising societies that are focused on everything that unites us – the core values we agree upon? We can do this, while at the same time supporting each one's right to practise and believe in their traditional way. Recognising this is the first step to happiness.

The pursuit of happiness in the 21ˢᵗ century

At the heart foundation of the key rational society of modern times the American Declaration of Independence preamble states:

> We hold these truths to be self-evident, that all men are created equal, that they are endowed by their Creator with certain unalienable Rights, that among these are Life, Liberty and the pursuit of Happiness.

In whatever way we are functioning and from whatever culture we come, the one thing that every one of us seeks is happiness. When we let go of our prejudices about other people's beliefs, we can see that the heart purpose of every belief system is to help people lead a happy life. Hence to organise all societies with the wish for the greatest lasting happiness for the greatest number of people will be the easiest course for everyone. The mistake of our contemporary world is that it focuses on the material as a source of happiness and leaves emotional and mental unease to take care of themselves, or to be sedated if they cannot.

Instead we should put the emotional and mental first, by seeking methods of achieving happiness for the greatest number of people. We achieve this by being compassionate towards others, whatever their tastes and circumstances. Within all but the most psychotic minority cultures and religious traditions are teachings that are designed to take the first step towards universal happiness by making everyone feel at home. This simple, almost prosaically obvious wish links together the moral teachings in all the Eastern and Western religions. It is a two-way process whereby the host offers hospitality and the visitor always shows respect.

In Muslim communities and countries, giving hospitality to strangers is a key part of daily practice. In Christian communities the words of the Apostle Paul are central: 'And now abideth faith, hope, charity, these three; but the greatest of these is charity[89].' Mahayana Buddhism's central teaching extols the benefits of dedicating our lives for the benefit of others. Indeed, most traditional religions and cultures institutionalise the value of looking after newcomers.

In exchange, it is traditional for visitors to respect the customs of the culture they are visiting. At times the hospitality is too easily taken for granted and the visitor shows insufficient objectivity and self-control. For in an alien environment it is so easy to do the wrong thing, or allow a curious mix of good intentions and arrogance lead you to offer, even seem to impose, solutions to other people's problems that are not welcome. So in exchanging ideas about values with people from different cultures and beliefs in our community and its schools, it is important to respect differences and cut through to a common core upon which we all can agree.

To generate happiness for the maximum number of people, all religions encourage basic moral tenets. These emanate from the essential common sense that if we do not harm others there is less likelihood of their harming us. So, if we do not kill, injure, steal or lie, we are less likely to find ourselves in situations where such things will happen to us. Indeed, are there ever situations where the common good allows us to do such things? Exploring the essential morality of such decisions at every stage of our educational and adult social lives will make us less vulnerable to simplistic propaganda. Chapter 16 showed that seeing the astrology of people as individuals and in social/generational situations can only lead to much more responsible and educated decisions being made about crime.

So what principles of morality might all religions accept? In the early 1980s the Tibetan Lama Yeshe urged his pupils to look beyond Buddhist dogma, to seek out what he called 'Universal Education'; principles that all religions could embrace. After his death, his pupil Lama Thubten Zopa Rinpoche continued this work under the heading of 'Essential Education'. Schools and other projects have been established. In 2006, an important development was the launching of *The 16 Guidelines for a Happy Life*.[90] This grouped and explored commonly held ideal values in four categories.

* *How we think* – humility, patience, contentment, delight
* *How we act* – kindness, honesty, generosity, right speech
* *How we relate to others* – respect, forgiveness, gratitude, loyalty
* *How we find meaning* – principles, aspiration, service, courage

The commentaries on each area and concept are enhanced by narrative. We can see how certain eminent people epitomises that quality. Desmond Tutu is a living example of forgiveness; Mahatma Gandhi, principles; Wangari Maathai, courage; Mohammad Yunus, honesty; and His Holiness the Dalai Lama, kindness. 'Basically, the Guidelines make everyone respect other people and stop harming them. They bring the human life into good shape. They take care of everybody and bring peace to the whole country – even the whole world[91].'

The more our societies honour such principles and set them above the seductions of greed, indulgent false judgement and condemnation in their cultures, entertainment and education, the happier we will be. Problems are not impossible to resolve if we are tolerant and approach people from very different cultures with such common standards. We will learn how much we share and agree upon; then feel secure enough to celebrate our differences and bring spice to our lives.

Knowing the astrology of our group and the individuals involved can be a key tool that defines and puts in perspective the myriad varieties of human experience. Combining this with the guidelines offers total insight into everything that is happening. Because we understand, we do not need to judge and punish, but can rather celebrate and experience rising enhancement in life. By contrast, generalised, narrow-minded preaching for and against others from a 'safe' distance of ignorance only brings suffering. Broad and varied societies do not have to be unprincipled 'hotbeds of immorality'. By recognising principles/guidelines and developing compassionate insight into each other's differences, we take care of society. So we will diminish social problems and reduce the feeling that we need an expanding range of punitive rules to resolve them. It is all a question of respecting and working with each other. Chapter 19 will show the benefits of developing such a process as our children grow up together at school. It should be the central part of their initiation.

What should we aspire toward in the modern world?
So, enlightened guidelines, tolerance of variety, hospitality, an absence of harm, and compassion for the needs and feelings of others are the prized core ingredients of a healthy society. If we use astrology with these to understand the individual karmic nature and challenge that each person, group and enterprise is working through, we will already have a much healthier view of what is and is not important in society. Next it is important to consider contemporary ways of identifying what is admirable in other people and whether there are better ways to develop our own self-worth?

Today's sporting-, entertainment- and wealth-obsessed culture seems so facile because it celebrates an undefined commodity-type concept called 'celebrity'. This seems to be determined by arbitrary media selection dependant upon disjointed details about specific people's lives. A person may be admired for being born in. or because they are receiving, privilege. Others may show likeable qualities in a reality TV show, apparent high achievement in sporting contests, or move millions by their singing. Once well known, they become vulnerable to the infamy and soap opera of disgrace, due to the particular actions or lifestyle choices they may make.

The reasons for such rises to and falls from fame are arbitrary, because they are not defined or consistent. A footballer may have the enthusiasm, ambition and boundless energy of youth and a lucky day. So, he scores goals that lead to great success. As a result, he is offered immeasurable rewards, but becomes injured and never recovers his form. A year or so later, a nightclub scuffle triggers a downward spiral in his public image. In the meantime, his poster image has been worshipped on the bedroom walls of millions of impressionable young people, who have projected personal hopes and fears upon him that go far beyond his game skills. Now they energetically blame him for being a bad example. Yet it was our media that gave iconic status to an energetic, immature boy's lucky few days.

Clearly, there is much more to real celebrity that this. We need widely understood guidelines of sustained excellence of character. Knowing the potential in the astrological cycles is a real measure of specific achievements. Only then can we consider celebrating other people's success and condemning their failure? In addition, it would be helpful to the 'celebrity's' motivation for doing what they did.

The distinctions of the Indian Hindu caste system might seem unlikely to be relevant today. Certainly, the idea that individual families perpetuate their class level through birth that has fixed Indian society for centuries and perpetuates gross exploitation and injustice to this day would be entirely unacceptable in a compassionate world. However, the symbolic conceptual archetypes, upon which this system is based, offer ideal principles and roles that it may help us assess how we value others and ourselves. For these ideal principles suggest criteria of respect that apply at many levels of society and can be honoured, whatever our religion – whether we have one or not.

❋ *The highest (Brahmin) role in life* is our spiritual connection with the natural flow of the universe. It is eminently scientific to put this first. The Brahmin is the pilot of our spiritual progress, custodian of values, prayer and dedication to the highest principles. Without devotion to such things, how can any society or individual feel free and happy and have the clarity to find and follow a moral way? Without at least acknowledging the primacy of doing so, our society is in amoral chaos.

However much we distract ourselves or struggle against the inevitability of it, in the end we are totally alone; without any material support, be it family, friends, vocation, standing or status. At this point, there is no one to kid or lie to, only our own conscience and knowledge of things as they really are 'for me on my very own'. Putting off realising this, pretending it does not matter denies the very essence that defines where we are. It severs our link with the universe – the only certainty that does not fail.

Knowing the astrology of our time, date and place of birth and experiences as we pass through life is vital if we are to identify and transcend the suffering that comes from attachment to the delusions of our personal relative material reality. By caring for the entirety of creation, we experience unbelievable bliss. Freezing our minds on self to avoid this path causes the suffering of constant dissatisfaction. So many people feeling this way leads to the heart failure of our modern materialistic world. We make this heart better by admiring the values of those who care for creation.

✻ *Next comes the Kshatriya*, the person of noble heart who is seen as a natural leader, because he/she will take responsibility and risks for the sake of the community. Certainly, we admire people with such qualities in our society. Whether presidents and other leaders are real heroes, courageously devoted to truth and virtue whatever the consequences is not so clear. If they were, their ability to see ahead and lead others out of danger to a better future would stand out above all other considerations. The true hero inspires confidence, because of his or her integrity. Today it takes spin, assessing and manipulating the opinion of focus groups and money to lead a materialistic society. Yet, without courage, principled integrity and nobility in our individual natures, how can we overcome life's challenges and be a truly valuable example to others?

The contemporary 'quick fix', 'celebrity' culture, described earlier is material society's attempt to fill the gap left by the lack of true heroes, who cannot exist because our society does not understand and hence value the principles genuine heroes live by. Instead, we set up, preen and reward excessively those that are unready, and then fuel our envy and jealousy by knocking them down again. Whether we are looking to film and sports stars, politicians or just the 'beautiful people' who hang around them, the consequent disappointment creates the cynical view – there is no such thing as genuine heroism. Everyone is 'in it for themselves' in this materialist world. Such cynicism disappoints our hopes and dreams constantly – 'it has always been this way and always will be'.

For as long as we base achievement and success on empty and temporary criteria, it *will* always be like that and our lives will be essentially without hope. Comparing a person's actions against their essential astrological nature provides a genuine and reliable touchstone to assess how they are confronting their challenges. It enables everyone to be a hero and recognised as such.

Intuitively, we recognise that genuine achievement is always the success of mastering our own personal limitations. While it is an exquisite joy to watch a highly talented artist or sports person and great to be on the winning side; most of us have a soft spot for 'the little guy' – the 'giant killer' in sports competitions. We are inspired by those hidden artistic talents that emerge from the most unlikely of places – the pop idols who make it, even though they seem just like us.

Such feelings are based on a fundamental astrological and karmic truth. We are all born with limitations, talents and opportunities that come and go. Each of our lives in its own way is a constant challenge to recognise and make the very best use of what is possible for us. There cannot be a greater feeling of liberation and triumph than doing just this – experiencing our mastery – facing and transcending our karma. When we do, we recognise the Kshatriya potential that is within each of us.

Lacking such a genuine personal experience of nobility and being left with no more than living vicariously through mainly 'jumped up idols', we are disempowered, emptied of hope and dependent on low-level substitute sensuality. It is no accident that alcohol and being a sports spectator go hand in hand, and that major sponsors of sporting events are drink manufacturers, bookmakers, loan agencies and commercial media companies.

❋ *In the middle are the merchants (Vaishya).* These are the people who organise the supply of goods and resources. They keep the material fabric of society in order and in a balanced society support the religious and noble aspirants. The efficiency of this quality within each of us gives us the logistical support to do and go where we wish.

The proper and responsible marshalling and distribution of resources is a thing of beauty to express, behold and experience. While we can develop an art of learning from chaos, efficiency and high quality brings comfort and a liberating sense of certainty. Hence, our material providers and organisers are of immense value to our society. Quite literally, we could not live without them.

However, while all this should be accepted and celebrated, it does not mean that material wealth and the rules that regulate it are the 'be-all and end-all' that is. There are higher purposes to aspire towards. Why acquire and consume just for the sake of doing so? Are we really just the ants epitomised in Chapter 14? Are the limitations of modern material, mechanistic society the only things we would wish for in our own and our children's lives?

We have seen how our modern world loses its way when it sees the endless expansion of material possession and worldwide economical competition as the 'Holy Grail' - the be-all and end-all of everything. When business people's needs determine the political policy that sets the nature of our lives, rather than focusing on the best ways of providing material necessities that serve our chosen life-style, our priorities are dangerously out of order.

To rely on the fashion of contemporary business needs is to ignore the key higher levels of understanding that broaden perspective and make use of our full potential. Chapter 14 gave examples of waste and lost opportunities that come from mindless knee-jerk reactions to planetary cycles. It showed that using planetary cycles to understand and time clarifies what we can expect and helps us achieve our aims far more easily. Then, tasks seem less of an anxious struggle. We can rest in the satisfaction of a comfortable life, rather than wear ourselves out on the treadmill of illusory 'economic necessity'.

Quite simply, material decisions have to be made with respect for higher principles – our relation to the universal nature and selfless nobility. So many people finding such a notion fanciful, or even meaningless, reveals just how low our devotion to mechanical materialism has brought us. It explains why, for all our modern comforts, we continue to suffer and complain as much as we do.

✱ *Fourth are various servants (Shudra),* who gain great merit by the willing way they take on tasks. In traditional Indian society, to be served by those who take great pride in caring for others is an uplifting, almost spiritual experience. By accepting and behaving at our very best within the roles of server and served removes doubt and conflict. What happens is natural. The rancour, guilt and expectation that emanate from a confusion of roles is absent. The excellence of serving and being served is enjoyed and celebrated to the full.

That service can be a most purifying and liberating experience is unlikely to be acceptable in Western societies, where trade union and democratic struggles have fought long and hard for equality of opportunity and proper wages for work done. Service as a virtue in its own right is little understood in our world. Service at a price maybe – now that's another matter!

Yet, to see service, carefully supervised targets and rewards as inextricably linked is the root cause of considerable spiritual malaise in our modern materialistic societies. It is important to study service and reward on their own, and then we will see the dangers of making them interdependent and linking them formally.

We do not need to go to Indian culture to see why. Christ washed the feet of Mary Magdalene, told us 'it is better to give than to receive.'[92] Christian prayers urge us 'to give and not to count the cost.'[93] Experience confirms such wisdom. The more positive excellence we put into our day-to-day activities, the more satisfied we are with the outcomes. Quite simply, to get on with what needs to be done, to see good action leading to success and be pleased with other people's satisfaction is as much a cause for joy as any amount of money we may receive. Anyone who has employed a 'bargain-price cowboy builder' will know the agonies of the opposite being the case. Oh the agony of watching one's step, counting the cost and constant checking at every stage of the work in progress!

At the same time, to be generous in the way we reward others is just as good for the soul as being generous in the way we serve them. The pleasant surprise of being recognised, rewarded and praised more than expected can so focus the server's attention that it brings out talents people never realised they had.

One of the unfortunate and corrupting consequences of an egalitarian society based on materialistic self-interest, where no one is expected to do anything for nothing, is the castration of the magic fertility of generosity from human relationships. As employment law becomes more and more fine-tuned, many employers and employees find themselves having to take care to avoid generosity because it might create contractual precedents.

Isolated from the spontaneous generosity of others, we become more burdened with possessions and responsibilities in a world that not only sets a price on service but whose skilful advertisements and marketing encourage us to pay up large for 'protection'. Legal, loss of income and breakdown insurance are, a multi-billion pound market. Governments, local authorities, commercial enterprises as well as individuals are contracting out more and more of the responsibilities of their lives to expert enabling companies. The fastest expanding area of our economy is the service industry.

So the magic of spontaneous, freely given service and reward degenerates to a carefully calculated exploitative marketplace, whose skilful promotions trigger our desires and fears. This leaves us frightened to face the world and make our own decisions. We see compassion as exposing our vulnerability and even feel guilty when relying upon the kindness of others.

❋ *Then comes the group misleadingly referred to as the 'untouchables' (Harijans).* These people are seen as standing outside accepted society. In traditional Indian culture, the best known and certainly most exploited groups were those that took on society's least pleasant tasks –sweepers, washers of clothes, leatherworkers and animal slaughterers in a vegetarian society. Mahatma Gandhi and the independent Indian government he prepared the ground for, rejected entirely the simplistic prejudice behind such social categorisation of what can be invaluable work and honourable service.

However, the concept goes far deeper than this. Essentially the Harijan archetype represents those who are on the margins of conventional society for a number of reasons. They may do things that conventional people would not wish to do. They may even be beggars, prostitutes and criminals, but the group can also include those who reject the conventions of society for more regenerative reasons. They may be original artists, actors, musicians, and even idealistic social revolutionaries.

If we extrapolate this to our world where the values are so materialistic and invalid for reasons already given in this book, then many of our most admired artists and activists have in their day challenged social values and been considered social outcasts. Who of today's 'social outcasts' will be celebrated as visionaries in the future? The Harijan element may counter contemporary corruption. If it combines foresight with heroic Kshatriyan flair, it may contain the very seeds of our social redemption.

Paradoxically, the outcast element can go to the other extreme. Much that is corrupt and dishonest is institutionalised as 'natural and inevitable' in our modern society. People with such values, whose actions destroy social cohesion and represent the worst side of the Harijan archetype, can be richly rewarded and looked up to as leaders. Many marketing and political spin campaigns and their leaking manoeuvres are from that black world of untouchability. Yet masters of such methods can win elections, lead nations or direct international corporations. Throughout the world such people prop up and keep each other in power. Shrugging our shoulders and accepting such behaviour as inevitable and expedient (especially if we feel there is financial benefit for us) taints our world and confuses our children. How can we tell them what is right and wrong? How can we be surprised at the way their actions mirror back to us their view of our 'morality'?

Yet there is immense value in the regenerative melting pot at the untouchable margins of society. While it is important for any society and its individuals to be clear about what is unclean and should be outside normal behaviour, no one can be sure they are not, should they ever think they are!

Of course, each of us has all five of these qualities. We will make our modern society and ourselves classless and whole when we recognise and honour their positive expression within others and ourselves. It is vital that society should celebrate such core values. Our media and social actions need to explain and focus the implications of such standards of behaviour, and not just celebrate material success.

Individual happiness as the core of a happy society
While it is vital to select, teach, share and seek to integrate the key principles from world religions and moral philosophies, another didactic period of narrow, jaded and short-lived Puritanism is not the way. Uniquely, we do have the knowledge and technology today to work towards the dream of the Enlightenment that each individual person has a right to the pursuit of happiness. To do so, we have to acknowledge the Enlightenment's central failure of not defining clearly a concept of happiness and the nature of the individual.

To define happiness, it is necessary to have a system that clearly recognises and respects the individual predicament and his/her need for a relationship with ultimate truth or reality that many people call God. To suggest that mechanical reality based on relative observation will define ultimate truth in a relative universe of infinite mechanical possibilities could not be more illogical and unscientific! Mechanicalism as an absolute truth on its own can be no more than the cause of constant ongoing broken promises and disappointment – the root of unhappiness.

Quite simply to live to have things inevitably means the constant experience of not having things as well.

Happiness is better seen as an experience of inclusive coming together and wholeness, seeing ourselves as a recognised part of a compassionate universal community. This is why the early stages of political revolution are so ecstatic and celebratory. Earthly revolutions soon fade, as the will of the community is frustrated and abused by those who gain power on its behalf. We have to find a way of maintaining the experience of liberation and so enable the happiness of each individual all the time.

Fortunately, our time gives us a very special opportunity to do this. Before now, it has not been thought necessary to define the nature of ordinary individuals. Most were numerous and expendable. They were expected to dedicate themselves to nations, tribes and groups, who represented the supreme will of dominant leaders, or other special individuals.

Nowadays, most people accept the futility of judging people by means of misinformed and generalised notions of mass belief. It is just as unreliable and unfair to replace such criteria with contemporary blanket assumptions – the 'science' of regulations and laws, suggested by generalisations devised from piecemeal mechanical statistics.

To enjoy our right to happiness, we need a right to genuine personal understanding. Each of us brings personal strengths and weaknesses to every situation and is at a particular stage of potential and growth. Our astrological chart, its development through progression, and opportunities through transits, is the vital tool that identifies and describes everything about us. It describes, in a systematic way, the exact detail of each person's relative deviation from each other person. It allows for the fashion of the times in which each generation has and will live. What/who is the individual seeking happiness and how do I seek it is a personal quest that each of us has a right to embark upon and celebrate?

By connecting this constantly flowing and developing structure of unique astrological relationships between every individual and situation to essential compassionate heart values drawn from all world cultures, we can bring healing understanding to our world society. The sensitive insight such understanding provides will educate us about how we treat our planet. So, we will relate to it in a truly sustainable way – not panic from one disastrous course of action to far worse alternatives.

We start to progress by opening our minds: trying out, and then talking and writing about these ideas. Vitally, we need to establish channels that focus discussion and develop institutional structures to direct our cultures in accordance with such principles. The next chapter considers the implications of doing this in two key areas – cultural institutions and education.

Chapter 19
Establishing Essential Values in the 21st Century

May we all become living antidotes to war, torture and sickness, and to all physical and mental problems. Through the education of the good heart may all beings practise kindness, forgiveness, tolerance, humility and joy.

Lama Thubten Zopa Rinpoche

Day-to-day living in the modern world is a contradictory struggle between accepting the 'reality' of 'permanent limitations', while at the same time constantly refusing to accept anything is permanent by insisting we put right what 'is wrong'.

This profoundly illogical way of looking at life traps us in a vulnerable double bind. Any suggested reforms that might seem to change our familiar experience of education, relationships, work and pleasure are rejected as unrealistic, or even dangerous. 'You just can't be serious! It is not practical, or possible.' At the same time, we continue to express dissatisfaction and demand that 'something be done'. So, politicians and administrators conduct surveys to discover the desires closest to our hearts. Then, with skilfully ambiguous words, they suggest we can have what we want without uncomfortable change. Instead of delivering what we expected, those in power use it for their own interests and purposes. We become frustrated, cynical and feel impotent. 'They are all the same – in it for themselves. It has always been like that. You cannot change things.'

Reality is rather different. Whether we like it or not, things can and do change. However, this *real change* is rarely the result of conscious decisions on our part, or anyone else's. Sometimes things just happen, be they natural disasters or dramatic political events. We just have to adapt and get used to the new situation. Even when we do make effective policy decisions, very rarely are we able to control the specific outcomes. This does not mean we are powerless and unable to act as individuals to make things better. What can change with real effect is what we choose to focus our attention upon and hence our assumptions about it. Under Hitler, the German people accepted intolerance as natural. Since the Second World War, the same nation has rejected and marginalised fascism. Over recent decades assumptions about the role of racial relations in Western societies has been transformed. Courageous pioneers, opinion leaders and educational pressure groups have brought this about. It has led to people being ready for policy initiatives in the law, employment, housing and the like. Because the popular view against prejudice was strong enough, black footballers, newscasters, managers, lawyers and all races in just about every other area of society became accepted. As different races in all areas of society became commonplace, each began to judge and appreciate the other for their talents and individual personalities. Each saw the other as equally valuable to society. At first, resistance was immense. Within twenty years most prejudice has been marginalised.

So, when we look back over the many areas of society, culture and individual life that this book has shown could be benefited by the use of astrology, we should not dismiss such claims as impractical. In my lifetime, assumptions about racial purity, colonialism, the status of women, sexual relationships of all kinds, and what is tolerated on the media have changed beyond all recognition. When we use astrology in our lives, who knows what new benefits and understandings we may discover?

However, as with changes in women's rights and racial law and practices, the effects will be gradual, patchy and some outcomes may be difficult to predict, or even to accept. The liberation of women from the home leaves profound questions about the upbringing of children and the relationship between children and adults. From the 1980s, a greater openness towards talking about sexuality revealed there had been an unexpected amount of abuse of children by carers. It was an unpleasantness that needed to be addressed.

Understanding our astrology will open many doors and give personal power to those presently disempowered. Some in power may find their stature diminished and their motives exposed. The wise will welcome deeper knowledge; only the weak and manipulative will fear it.

At the same time, we should not expect more than is reasonable of astrology. Although it may give advanced and very helpful insights, it is an instrument of analysis; not an answer or solution. It helps us to ask, answer and understand the right questions, only if we permit.

Parts 3 and 4 of this book have already outlined a range of ways that the potential value of astrology could be explored. How society develops as a result will be decided by the outcome of research, experimental projects and pilot studies.

The outcome will be a vast melting pot of new understandings that will require channels of communication to exchange ideas and distribute knowledge. If we are to do this properly, it is vital that our systems of communication and education are cleansed of prejudice and counterproductive regulations and practices. This chapter will consider how both could be reorganised to include the highest principles of astrology. Then, once in the open, it can help heal communities both within and between countries and cultures.

Healing the media

How might the heart values of selfless understanding and our astrological individuality, outlined in Chapter 18, be institutionalised into our key core of cultural exchange – the modern news, entertainment media and the Internet? Can we find ways of using these myriad links between people to deepen foundation values in our society?

Firstly, for reasons explained in great detail throughout this book, the media and the opinion leaders that dominate its columns and airspace will need to think again about the arbitrary way they cheapen and dismiss astrology. Secondly, the benefits of the unbridled influence that media and promotional agencies have over the everyday lives of individual citizens need to be questioned and investigated. We may have rules about how this or that product, or service, is promoted, but who is questioning how the promotion industry itself is working and whether this is in the public interest?

When in 1932 Aldous Huxley wrote *Brave New World*, in 1948 George Orwell wrote *Nineteen Eighty-four*, and in 1957 Vance Packard wrote *The Hidden Persuaders,* they were seen by contemporary readers as 'timely warnings' and as such became set texts at colleges and universities. As I write this in 2007, it seems that the students that studied them assumed they had been given *Teach Yourself...* books on what they were expected to devote their adult lives to bringing about – not cautionary tales of how society could degenerate and destroy itself! For now (or soon to be), at the 'essential' and 'unavoidable' common place centre of our contemporary world we morally justify various practices: manipulating innocent minds to want what they do not need or had even considered necessary; spinning lies to be believed as 'truth'; seducing individual desire for corporate gain; and genetically engineering for the convenience and profit of those in power.

There are two central reasons for this happening. Firstly, the dominance of an amoral, mechanistic, growth-obsessed economy and insatiable taste for generalised business decision-making based on ever more statistical research. Secondly, the reading, viewing and consuming public are seen as a recipient customer base to be placated rather than an authority of tastes and opinions to be consulted. Advertising and media insiders regulate the industry. The public increasingly becomes this industry's creation and so is powerless to control it.

The truth and value of scientific development and economic expansion ad infinitum is taken for granted. If promotion helps that process and pays for what consumers can be persuaded to want, then it is in the public interest. Regulators do not question the value of any material development, as long as 'qualified experts in the field' have accepted it as valid. The decoration of the truth to seduce in a playful way or to suit what are assumed to be comfortable social norms seems 'pretty harmless'. Provided that a broadcast or an advertisement is not too frightening or coarse, it can play on fear and sexual desire – just a 'bit of fun'!

How can our broadcast media and the press be regulated, so they do more than merely serve the status quo and increasingly reduce the options available to a pliant consumer base? How can they question, go deep, challenge and exchange assumptions about core morality? Crucially, how can the media ask questions that radically question their own assumptions? Unless the very institution of cultural exchange and judgement is up for scrutiny, how can we live in a healthy society?

Because media values dominated by instant gratification and profitability are administered by appointed industry-insiders, not the public, the familiar is much more likely to be accepted. The unfamiliar will struggle to find a way in. The result is unbalanced and paradoxically inconsistent programming.

Brutality and sexual explicitness are now commonplace in our media. Some such presentations can be cathartic and purifying, others sensationalise unkindness for the sake of doing so. Rarely do regulators attempt to distinguish according to intrinsic purpose or effect. What physically is seen is usually the touchstone. The likely psychological effect on viewers' behaviour is more difficult to decide, and so ignored. Regulation tends to prefer boxes and categories.

We could use psychological expertise to classify programmes according to their likely influence. Then programmers could be charged a fee, which could be used to finance a number of new independent public service broadcast channels that deal with issues brought out by those very entertainment programmes. Particular moral or social issues could be addressed. Explicit sexuality, violence, drug abuse and crime fiction would have to pay a fee to finance non-commercial programmes that deal with the issues in an educational and purifying way. Advertisers of alcohol and food products would finance programmes about health and diet.

With the development of new technology, there are so many new 'hidden' ways to profit from broadcasting. Information about them needs to be brought to the forefront of viewer attention. Details of the fees paid and profits made by the advertisers, or placers of products, could accompany the advertisement. How much money do the phone companies make from programmes based on voting and competitions? Maybe a ticker showing profits from people phoning in to compete, make comments, or vote. Maybe the actual cost added to the price of the product for the advertisement should appear on the screen.

A monitoring channel should be established as the central core of regulation. It should be available free on all digital networks and on the Internet. Here the public would feed opinion regarding the rules of regulation. The public would elect the regulators and their advisors directly. Care would be taken to ensure these would represent many beliefs and all walks of life. Minorities would be protected. No one should be regulated against without a very careful airing of his or her views. The regulators and members of the public appearing together to answer criticisms and suggestions would develop regulations. Genuine public regulation of our television and radio would make our society alive and potent to what is being communicated.

Such a vision is radically different to the way that present regulation is organised. When the UK government combined the various elements of media and communication regulation into one central body called Ofcom on 29th December 2003, it appointed a board of business administrators and lawyers, industry insiders and its own past advisers to oversee it. While Ofcom responds to public complaints and instigates consultations, it creates consultative documents and makes its decisions behind closed doors. Public control of the decision-makers is limited to the distant prospect of influencing government appointments to the board. In this way the experience and associations of its board and the people it chooses to appoint determine the agenda and assumptions. Since most people appointed are the very insiders discussed above, the assumptions and interests of the media industry and the business community that finances it form a status quo that cannot be challenged. The notions that media dependence on advertising revenue may not be in the public interest, commercial benefits and costs should be more transparent, and the commercial sector should support public interest broadcasting, are unlikely to be taken seriously.

Central to Ofcom regulation of television and radio is its Broadcasting Code. Its Section 2 states that serious, non-fictional presentation on the media of an area of activities that could include astrology could be as harmful and offensive as presenting extreme physical and sexual abuse. It makes it very clear that no 'life-changing advice' with regard to 'health, finance, employment or relationships' should be given and such activities should not be presented when large numbers of children are likely to be watching.

It may be harmful to broadcast some elements of this broad category described as 'exorcism, the occult, the paranormal, divination and related practices'. However, to blanket them all together reveals dangerous and counter productive ignorance. Although astrology is not specifically mentioned, the breadth of the wording could well block very necessary discussion of what this book shows to be important ideas for our society and especially our children. Indeed, restricting in the media serious study and social experimentation of this area of knowledge is likely to encourage harm and offence, not diminish it.[94]

'Films, dramas and fiction generally are not bound by this rule.' This means that the most ludicrous misrepresentations of magic and the occult are frequently the only ones the general public see. This explains why the social workers who dealt with the Rochdale family case mentioned in Chapter 16 misunderstood so fatally what had happened in the family they were caring for. It also explains why the facile criticisms that are answered in Chapter 2 continue to appear in the media.

Such arbitrary dismissal and omission of astrology from our media leaves it on the margin of our society. From what this book has shown, it is clear than such absence denies us understanding of each other and the world we live in. It traps us in a culture of misunderstanding instead. Yet, there are many informative and entertaining ways that astrology could and should be built into the programming. A cosmic weather forecast, pointing out the cycle of the Moon, special planetary features and how these might affect some people more than others could be just as valuable as the familiar metrological one. Astrological analysis of general news, political and social events and personalities could put what happens in perspective. Using astrological terms in intelligent media discussion could be really enlightening. The language could encourage exciting new character possibilities in film and drama. Today astrology is so misunderstood that any mention of it on the media 'has to be' accompanied with contemptuous dismissal. In the 1997 General Election programme astrologer Russell Grant was seated alone at a separate and lower place than the table of political commentators – just a bit of fun!

Of course, astrology can be used superficially to deceive and exploit. So can many psychological techniques, if not skilfully and ethically applied. Programmes that are allowed often have their dangers, in the way that the public are advised about child and animal rearing. Many reality shows do little more than make an entertainment out of abusing vulnerable people. It would be interesting to know the role professional psychologists play in the strategies behind such programmes. Unqualified celebrities frequently give advice in interview shows, with no regulation to restrain them. Faced with all this, it would be much more appropriate for Ofcom to protect the public by devising a form of words that would set standards for *all* advisory activities. Rather than just picking on one area of subject headings and give carte blanche to the rest, they could develop a code for all.

Perhaps they could extend such a code to include the extremely misleading 'advice' contained in paid advertisements as well. Certainly the status of commercial advertising on the media is not considered as carefully as it should be. The harm caused to our children's education and everyone's self-image, health and expectations by manipulative advertising cannot be exaggerated. The 'easy money' that comes from advertising is not a bonus that provides what we enjoy for nothing. The BBC licence fee is not an infringement of our liberty. To think like this is seriously to miss the harm advertising does. The psychologically guided commercial bombardment of the modern world deadens our minds and spirituality. Everywhere are advertisements and logos. Increasingly, we spend so much time trying not to look that it is difficult to believe there is sense and honesty to be found anywhere. In case we do not notice them, the sporting pitch-side advertisements now use modern technology to flash and change constantly. We are treating ourselves and raising our children to have minds full of junk images!

Making the regulators and advisers subject to democratic selection, and constantly questioned and challenged on the media they regulate, would certainly provide an ongoing facility to discover whether they understand the difference between serving the media/business community and protecting the public.

The central aim of such suggestions is not to prevent or restrict broadcasting, but to enhance the information and sense of power the public has about what they are viewing. In a society that did not judge and smear, where the community from the time they were pupils in school and university constantly examined values; there would be less need for censorship than at present. Censorship implies innocence and vulnerability – the viewer being a victim and unable to judge for his/herself.

With modern economies throughout the world focused upon material exploitation of the masses, establishing people-power institutions to regulate such exploitation via the media may seem to be no more than an empty idealistic dream. If you feel this, read again the first section of this chapter and then study change through history – even just that of the last two hundred years.

As this book was being written, exposés of abuses in phone-line competitions on major television channels have put considerable pressure upon the regulators – even criminal investigation has been considered. These are the beginnings of an eradication of public trust in programme-makers and media administrators that will be difficult to restore.

Advances in computer technology have led to a rapid expansion of public posting on the Internet – especially from younger generations. As hardware and software capacity increase, the public will have ever more power to create for itself what it wishes to watch. Commercial television's control of the means of communication and information exchange may weaken, as dynamic, film-streaming websites become commonplace. The World Wide Web has the potential to provide infinite choice and hence unassailable public influence over what we can view.

Paradoxically, this will be done not by restricting but by the public themselves having the capacity to offer alternatives. The programme makers will no longer be able to lead, but will have to follow. Paradoxically, it is the very permissive anarchy of the Internet that gives the public freedom to choose, rather than being dominated and manipulated by special interest groups. More and more people will offer their own television channel. Could the days of the spinning moguls be limited?

Genuine public involvement in the media would mean that issues of morality and vested interest and the consequences of our actions would be in our hands; not those who patronise us from the perspective of their own special interests. The principles that guide what we value and do should not be decided for us by experts "from on high". They should be questions we examine in an ongoing way throughout our lives. Then principles, such as those in Chapter 18, rather than expediency and profit will guide what we decide. The agencies of communication in our society should be no more than that. They should enable and permit a much wider range of programmes and information. The true cost and nature of what we watch should be shown, not obscured. Then the public would have genuine opinions to express and the power to determine what happens in their lives. When we focus on principles, we are more likely to use this power to create a better, healthier and richer future for our families and ourselves.

By visualising a society with a system of communication based on principles that we are proud to teach our children, we can start to see the changes we need to make in our schools ands colleges. There is a way to organise education to inculcate the highest healthy core multicultural values in 21st century societies. It involves identifying a core we all share, as attempted in Chapter 18, then leaving every culture and religion free to practise as it wishes.

As we establish a principle-based core to written, oral and visual media communication in mainstream society, we need to celebrate and teach such values at the core of our school curriculum. This should take precedence above the teaching of any academic, sporting or other skills.

Social values and education

The relationship between a society and its educational system is a classic 'chicken and egg' one – which came first? We have to identify the kind of society we want and do not want, before we can initiate our children into it. Chapter 18 suggested values that might lead to warmth and respect between people? The more time we spend discussing, exploring and trying out such principles at work and play, the more behaviour based on fear, insecurity and greed will wither away. The need to spend and sacrifice everything in an impossible quest for security will be seen as unnecessary.

If community care and personal integrity were prioritised above measured academic success, our schools and universities could educate to create a compassionate heart in our culture. By passing this on to our children, key principles would become a purifying force in the 21st century. With our priorities so re-ordered, we would be able to enjoy the best of scientific discoveries in a world that is equipped to deal with conflict and recognise the complementary value of most religions.

Such a suggestion is not as far-fetched as it seems. Not that long ago the institutions, out of which our present British education system grew, did see service to the national and international communities as its key *raison d'être*. Even if the 19th century view of service was arrogantly insular in focus; by putting service first, it did have its priorities in the right order. Did British education lose, or never even find its way, after our country lost its imperial role? Perhaps we can make up for the mistakes of the past by restoring a correct emphasis in our contemporary educational system. To create such an example would be a truly great post-colonial contribution to world society!

Life becomes so much easier when money, possessions and economic progress are the servants of something higher. We need a system that monitors social institutions to respect individuals more deeply than their material value. We need schools that initiate our children into a society that values the quality, not quantity, of life.

In what follows we will consider the benefits of putting the core values identified in Chapter 18 at the central core of our national curriculum, *before* reading, writing, and mathematics. Why teach how to succeed, if we do not know the reason or value of doing so? All religions should work on this core together, yet still practise their own ways in the home and faith schools.

Such a key change of priority in our schools will enhance social values and prepare pupils for their adult role of being proactive participants in the regulation of media and cultural exchange. It will give all of us something to believe in and work on together, from wherever we stand in society.

In Britain as I write there is much talk about common community values, the need for a concept of 'Britishness'. Such a search will be empty and self-defeating if it does not have the courage to address the central malaise – our lack of respect for all people, humanity and the planet. As it is, we prize competition that sets person against person. We are persuaded that the only way to live and succeed is to manipulate the truth and distort regulation to serve our own self-interest. So, how can we expect our children to behave differently? Crucially, how can we be surprised when their antisocial behaviour is inconveniently of the same intrinsic type as our own?

From fragmentary values to a principled common core

Many issues surrounding behaviour in our schools are ignored, deliberately avoided or at best addressed in a piecemeal way, because there are no methods built into the school cultures to reconcile contradictory value systems and cultural prejudices. Much depends on the ethical maturity and energy of individual teachers. Even if they represent kindness and general tolerance, such 'clean-living middle-class values' may not help, when the 'law of a brutal jungle' is all the child knows. There may be factors, such as bullying, social and racial prejudice that are far more important to address before anything else in schools.

Yet, the need to advance in league tables forces teachers to keep to the curriculum and teach skills. So, education is seen as a competitive struggle for survival, based on resentment and suspicion. Surveillance strategies to maintain order, test regularly, prevent cheating and even crime; make education and the society that lies beyond seem like a never-ending treadmill. Even when school's examination results are good, what is the value and social benefit for pupils of such an initiation?

On the other hand, when we co-operate and work through problems and ignorance together, build a sense of community and responsibility, answer the needs of others and feel the reassurance of our own needs being answered, we experience and encourage joy in life; learning becomes a wide and open experience. When a community, and especially a school, understand and celebrate the contribution of all members, then tasks are undertaken without resistance. Standards rise as conflicts within ourselves and between people diminish. Encouraging pupils to adopt such attitudes can only enhance our communities, whatever conditions of wealth and hardship they face.

The notion that economic needs and commercial finance should dominate our educational system did not take hold in British education until the late 20th century. Before it is *too* late, we should reverse this so recent and ill-considered trend.   Certainly, we must develop our knowledge and skills to the highest standards. Yet, even more important than formal skills and academic study is how we think and talk about each other – how we can bring happiness to as many people as possible.

As well as teaching the basic values outlined Chapter 18 at the top priority core of each stage of the national curriculum, according to each age group's understanding, schools should apply these principles in the day-to-day organisation. Before anything else, our schools should be a shining example of positive cultural cohesion and relationships, continually developing ways and facilities to resolve conflict and misunderstanding. By creating such a community culture, we initiate our children into an adult community, where the angst, accusation, fear and disenchantment of modern life are lessened, not increased. Through experience as they grow up together, they discover that being at peace with each other is far more satisfying than having lots and lots of things but being isolated.

Feeling we are moving towards such a positive culture will give far more happiness and create far less conflict in society than the over-scrutinised, academic 'sweat shops' that many of our schools have become. It is even possible that a co-operative school environment will still achieve higher academic standards. Constant testing tends to produce counterproductive anxiety, as well as disgruntled anti-social failure – both lead to misunderstanding and the absence of a good heart.

It is worth repeating that it would be very much in the tradition of its education, and an ironic antidote to its past imperial hubris, if Britain could institutionalise such a multicultural interactional value system in its schools, and pioneer a process that cleanses the selfish degeneracy of the contemporary mechanistic materialism that its empire also pioneered.

Identifying and respecting pupils

The essential problem of our schools and the society its pupils grow into is that neither sees pupils as individuals with individual needs. From kindness of heart, the majority of our teachers may recognise such needs, but they rarely have the tools, time and money to define and honour an individual's intrinsic nature. Instead, teachers are reduced to categorising aptitude solely according to success or failure at academic tests and making comments based on psychological or sociological theory half-learnt at colleges of education.

Unbelievable as it might seem, the tool we need is available. It is the intrinsic, in-depth understanding of each unique individual that comes from a thorough reading of their astrological chart and its development. Just as we have seen its benefits in mental and physical health, politics, business and the law, even more so can astrology guide the educational process and liberate its pupils. It may be essential for every member of society to develop basic skills, but the best way to achieve this will vary far more than any subject-based teaching method can allow for. How often do teachers hear students ask 'What has that got to do with me'?

With a full, detailed horoscope at hand, what 'that' has do with the pupil this minute, today, tomorrow and for a quite a time in the future is abundantly clear. Imagine each teacher knowing the depth of detail, outlined in the Appendix, for every pupil or group in the class. In addition, imagine both teacher and pupil having an idea of the development of that pupil's chart and the strengths and weaknesses being experienced today and likely in the future.

When preparing the structure of the curriculum and individual lessons, having an idea of the element and triplicity emphasis of the pupils and the generational and sub-generational focus of the class's medium and outer planetary positions could be invaluable in devising teaching approaches and timing strategies. Why did this year's group respond so badly to a series of lessons that went really well last year? Maybe they were born with a different Saturn (they need a firmer, or less firm, approach), or Jupiter (the way they respond to opportunity is different) sign. In history, it may help to choose a topic that has a particular planetary configuration, which resonates with the pupils in that year group. Another group, because of their generational planets, may respond to a different approach.

When misunderstandings occur, when there are difficulties in discipline and relationships, referring to transits can often help timing. Even waiting a day, or an hour, for the Moon to move on a little can make issues less confrontational. So we avoid problems now and leave them to work out more easily in the future. At other times, an understanding of the flow of planetary cycles can encourage us to address difficulties and make a break through right away.

Underlying such a truly individualistic approach is a radically important change of emphasis away from criteria by which we accept and celebrate achievement, or reject and condemn failure. 'You are good/bad at mathematics, spelling, reading, geography, drawing, this or that sport etc.' Every pupil is measured against a hierarchy of educational achievements. 'You must try harder.' 'You did far worse (or better) than expected.' Such arbitrary and often ill-informed judgements take little account of what is happening in the pupil's life. There may be very good astrological reasons why the pupil could do better, did better in the past, but is not doing so now. On the other hand, the chart may suggest much sterner pressure should be put upon the pupil immediately. In reporting, it is important to hit the mark at the right time, not bleat on with the same old stuff and be ignored.

Inappropriate bad reporting saps pupil confidence. In contrast, an astrological analysis will show why a pupil tends to be good or bad at a skill and when and how this might change/be made to change. Effort at the wrong time, driven on by counterproductive intimidation, can lead to feelings of guilt and inadequacy. In contrast, knowing where and why we are strong and weak confirms and reassures us about what we intuitively know about ourselves inside. It gives us a right to be ourselves. It teaches us to draw upon our strengths. It helps us let go of anxiety caused by other people's expectations, or lack of expectation, about us.

Perhaps the most exciting thing about using astrology as part of the educational process is that it both meets the demands of the now-out-of-favour 1960s educational reform movement and answers its limitations. Astrology recognises individuality and is clear that education should draw out a pupil's essential capacity rather than impose inappropriate extrinsically contrived benchmarks. At the same time, with astrological support, the teacher is not left wondering how to inspire the pupil and whether there *is* anything to be drawn out at all. When you know someone's horoscope, you know clearly what is there and possible. So, it is much easier to discover and implement ways to develop potential.

Enabling positive, proactive school and local communities

To master and benefit fully from our modern scientific materialist world, we need societies of proactive, organically developing individuals – not a populace of demanding clients submissive to the instructions of experts. When our schools do no more than initiate pupils into vast networks of 'expertise' at which only a minority can be expected to excel, it is small wonder that people grow up to feel powerless. So the 'nanny state' becomes our indulgent parent. Ordinary citizens are left vulnerable, even self-indulgent and obese, demanding and ultimately unable to judge and influence what is done in their name. A 'spoilt child' atmosphere of name, blame and sue develops that can be easily manipulated by our expert 'masters' visions of greed and fear.

With one person or group in charge and pronouncing a particular policy and set of standards deemed desirable for achievement, we experience life as a battle to overcome frustration, misunderstanding and impotency – the opposite of community. Paradoxically, the more we honour individuals and ask them to contribute from their experience, the more proactive a family community our society becomes. Being recognised for what each of us is empowers and enables us to make a positive contribution to our world. Underlying everything is the need to know the consequences of our individual actions. Rarely should we pass on our responsibility for what we have done to others to 'sort out' on our behalf. A good sports team does not succeed because of a few stars, but because every team member plays full out to support each other's strengths. In the same way, a healthy community celebrates and supports the rich diversity of its members and works together to identify and overcome its issues and achieve its needs. Its strength is the sum total of the volunteered maximum effort of all – not the bullied regimentation of the many by the few.

Yet, the idea of a school working this way and being a shared central resource and focal point of the whole community ran into difficulties and has been out of fashion for some years. It was felt that allocating schools to communities could lead to depressed standards in some areas and enhance privilege in others – class status quo would be perpetuated. Experiments to create schools of mixed class, race and ability were attempted. Some educational authorities bussed children to areas outside their community to achieve this. Although well intentioned, the effect was the worst of all worlds. Communities became marked as failing and undesirable or the opposite. Children were disorientated. Parents who could afford it either used the private system, or moved house to areas with 'better' schools, where this did not happen. The tendency in recent years to free up parent choice beyond their immediate community has intensified the lack of social cohesion. All these factors have isolated community friendship and made extra-curricular activities dependent upon 'parent taxi' cars! Communities broaden out like spiders' legs as people make friends and have common interests further afield. In many streets, families may live adjacent to, not with, each other.

Of course, it is for each of us to choose the community we wish to live in and belong to. We may prefer to be private or socially active. We may wish for a privileged and special education for our children. Perhaps they may have talents, or disadvantages, that require special teaching. We may prefer to identify with an extended rather than a local community. None of this suggests we should organise a whole system on the basis of individuals competing for the best chance of academic success. To see education solely in this way radically undermines society by downplaying and marginalising care and responsibility to one's community, be it local or wider afield. As a result, a centrally controlled 'culture' of selfishness is created and used by everyone.

Following on from this is the breakdown of family and social responsibility and subsequent individual alienation. Where opportunity to progress in larger society is most limited, sink areas emerge that the authorities seek to control by Antisocial Behaviour Orders. Even though extra money is poured into schools in such areas to restore opportunity, the resources go to academic, not social, initiatives. However good an academic opportunity we give to all, we resolve nothing if we ignore social needs. To do this we have to get to know and respect the unfamiliar, even what may at first appear unpleasant. It is amazing what the most unlikely people will contribute to their community. We should not mock attempts to 'hug a hoodie'.[95]

We miss a wonderful chance to address this problem by consigning social and community activities to the periphery of the school and instead focus on assessing, rewarding and promoting individuals by academic results alone. When we do this, we turn away from an incredible opportunity for social healing. It comes from having a representative of just about every family in the community together in school for a major part of each day.

Many volunteers, community organisations and social workers do much to help and heal communities already, but most feel they are constantly working against powerful contradictory forces. Putting the great work of social cohesion at the heart of the curriculum, encouraging parents and children to work together in their area could improve their environment and answer its many needs.

Seeing schools as community centres could enable them to offer much more than academic excellence. Furthermore, pupils would go to school not only to study subjects, but also to engage in activities that may excite them far more. They may develop practical and people skills, address community problems. They could enhance the school's physical and social facilities. The first step in living well is to care for our environment, be it by building, painting, gardening, visiting the elderly, encouraging younger children, helping those with difficulties.

The school could become a centre of recreation for young people, a true alternative to commercial provision. By creating or contributing towards the creation of their own facilities, pupils would come to understand and respect what they have. Rarely do we destroy our own possessions. Imagine the benefits of school being at the core of a self-supporting community at every stage in life, giving opportunities for children to support each other and adults across the age levels. As well as bringing real benefit to others, it would be an invaluable alternative to the life experience of most adolescents today – a radical change from hanging around in aimless peer groups. No longer would their day be focused on struggling for personal freedom in classrooms that paranoiacally force-feed far more academic work than they need to succeed.

At the same time, school should be organised to ensure that an even higher standard of academic learning is available to everyone. This can be achieved once we realise that academic learning will only be rewarding and successful if there is genuine pupil commitment. As students advance through the present school system, increasing amounts of time are spent *pressuring* them to learn and perform, not teaching in a pure sense. If enforcement arguments and punishments over exactly how much work is to be done when did not degenerate the teaching environment; pupil commitment could be much higher – closer to 100 per cent. Then most of the content could be taught in far less time. Academic study should be open to all pupils, whatever their assumed ability, provided they will attend, behave and carry out projects on time. Where pupils do not wish to make such a commitment, the school community should offer many other options. A community needs to honour all kinds of greatness in individual expression – not just the skills that lead to competitive success. There should be social, cultural and service activities in our community schools. Whether what happens is beneficial, difficult, a need to be answered or the cause of a problem, there should be someone there to understand, help, celebrate, or commiserate.

Essentially, remember what can so easily be forgotten in a world where we think everything has to be paid for. The more we feel we are receiving from others, the easier it is to give respect to others in return. We feel respected when we are known and recognised for what we are, not when we have 'jumped through hoops' to be as others want us to be. Only when we feel understood will we accept the opinions of others as the reflective judgement of genuine friendship. We need interactive schools that serve interactive communities that recognise the benefits of diversity and celebrate the rich culture this creates.

Nor is it a problem if some of these communities consist exclusively, or almost exclusively, of one cultural sub-group. Good communities come together because they wish to do so. Distinctly different cultures do not threaten each other. They enrich the whole country. This is one of the great lessons of the USA and can become the celebration of genuine Britishness in the United Kingdom and elsewhere, provided we celebrate the good in other peoples' customs. The 2002 celebrations of Queen Elizabeth II's Golden Jubilee, mentioned in Chapter 7, climaxed with an amazing multicultural procession in London's The Mall. From the time of the rock concert a few days earlier to the firework display at the end, great happiness, peace and tolerance were experienced. This did not come by integrating a token person from each sub-culture or seeking to create multicultural groups. It was a triumphant celebration because in Britain at that time all cultures were allowed the freedom to celebrate what made them different. Long may this be so and may such values of tolerance and appreciation move to centre stage in much improved education in a whole range of very different community schools.

Envisioning a school society that heals social malaise

So it is eminently sensible to put understanding of life and community before studying those academic subjects that give us the skills to succeed. We are far more likely to work hard at functional skills, and do well in far less time, if we are highly motivated and feel no resistance to doing so. What is the benefit in creating a highly successful competitive society, if it is unprincipled and squanders its success? Hence, knowing each other and ourselves should come before anything else in any national and individual school curriculum.

To make maximum use of each individual, we need to understand each person's nature and needs and which events and times could bring greater success and happiness to pupils, their schools and the communities they serve. This book has shown that to suggest astrology should play a central role in this is not 'flat-earth' madness. The tools we use to assess individuals at present are fragmentary and contradictory. Experts argue. Fashions of diagnosis and treatment change in tune with the cycles of the outer planetary transits. We have seen that the notion of education for all is not two centuries old – the contemporary ethos far less than one century. The methods we use to judge behaviour are hardly established and often at odds with each other. The decision to focus our schools on training for business competition in the consumption-obsessed world market-place is even more recent and a matter of dispute as I write. Many may feel they do not remember agreeing to this in the first place.

Imagine a community that recognises and cares so deeply for each individual from the time they are born, through their maturing years, and initiates them into caring for their own caring community. If astrology could provide a language of analysis, which helps bring us together, would that really be such a bad and 'unscientific' thing? Would it not bring us together and enhance other scientific disciplines?

Nor is such a suggestion economically unrealistic. In Chapter 14, we saw the primitive limitations and consequences of an unbridled, expanding world consumer economy. We also saw that future fashions could lead to business efficiency and economic success with less work and waste. The more we are educated to understand what has, is and will happen, the less we will have to do and the easier it will be to do it. Accepting individual respect and the importance of community and using the insights of astrology is not a soft, dreamy, unrealistic attempt to escape the 'real world'. Quite the opposite, it is to open our eyes with true science to the deeper, essential nature of existence and liberate ourselves from ignorance that makes us slaves to fear.

Astrology, with its profound human understanding and its many potential benefits that are outlined in this book, has been around for thousands of years. In the 21st century have we developed sufficient skill and understanding for a majority of people to see its value and use its proactive language to enhance community relationships? As well as being an objective tool to monitor each pupil's progress and to understand various age and social groups, it will enable the school and its larger community to monitor themselves and sub-groups. It will also put in perspective those who offer themselves up for leadership. It can help us look back on past decisions and find good times to develop, or change, them.

Of even deeper educational value than astrology's functional benefits is the intrinsic wisdom of its key concepts. By being aware of the underlying flow of life, we are less likely to be surprised and threatened, more likely to rest and feel comfortable with what happens. By understanding the astrological archetypes that describe what lies behind human motivation, we are likely to be more understanding and forgiving, when times are difficult. In short, we have a language that makes sense. With it we can understand each other and what is happening to us. Astrology can help to educate a confident and articulate younger generation that will have the tolerance and insight to regenerate society, however hard or surprising the times ahead may be. We will stop fighting over 'limited resources' and pace ourselves to enjoy the space and wealth of what we have and can renew.

Of course, even such an aware country and world of such communities would always be no more than work in progress. This world is a place of learning. We cannot hope to create utopia – beware of those whose ideas and policies suggest that anyone or anything can. Rather, we need to seek the wisdom to recognise an enlightened order, where the best-hearted people rise naturally to the highest point of public esteem. This life for all of us is a time of learning to grow by cutting through delusion, so we can open our eyes and see ever clearer.

We can, however, create schools, colleges and communities that are structured to help this growing clarity, not confuse, corrupt and so make it impotent. We need a society, where spiritual and ethical idealism in all its varieties is tolerated and discussed; where individuals are recognised and valued for what they are; where being on a path towards better understanding and better living is far more important than the name of that path; where principles are celebrated above expediency. When we realise this, we will have the wisdom and merit to select true leaders and systems that ensure we will live in a healing society.

At the heart of that society as a servant, not master, of mundane and esoteric wisdom will be astrology because, as we have seen, astrology works.

Chapter 20

Astrology & Compassion - the Convenient Truth

We make a living by what we get, but
we make a life by what we give.
Winston S Churchill

In 2007, the popular YouTube website staged one of the preliminary debates between the Democratic Party contenders for the 2008 American Presidential race nomination. Comedy Central's *The Daily Show* showed clips of young voters reacting as they watched the debate on a large screen. Their insights were incisive and their reactions both disturbing and illuminating.

As always, the candidates' statements were incredibly carefully prepared and bland. They aimed to offer maximum hope of positive change while giving little specific commitment and minimum offence to likely supporters. This was not the first debate. So, most responses to questions were well rehearsed and familiar. As the candidates made the prosaic statements, the young people reacted by repeating the statement and then taking a quaff of alcohol.

"'Devoted to the American way" I'll drink to that!'

"'Help for those that really need it" drink'

If continued long enough, the result would have been an audience in mindless mirth and stupor, but look deeper. Then we see that the young people's behaviour is both intelligent and vitally relevant. By their actions they are consciously and deliberately illustrating that they recognise and see through political spin *and* by their drunkenness they show exactly what it does to people who listen to it. We are being treated as stupid and so turned into drunks.

As I write this in the British summer of 2007, the problem of teenage drunkenness and, especially, associated gang gun violence dominates the news. Natural public expressions of personal despair from the relatives of victims combine with determination to 'get tough' and organise informer networks by the authorities.

All this has not suddenly happened. It is a sign of social malaise. The suffering of the bereaved family is an expression of the constant suffering of their community over lesser issues every day. The call to report other people to the authorities is a sign of desperate ignorance of that community for years. It is a sign that local politicians have been handling and manipulating, not understanding and representing, the people who voted for them. The media and political machines we studied in Chapter 17 have created a self-indulgent and drunken society. If we can lie, invade and kill innocent families in countries overseas, then is it any less natural for 'our gang' to shoot at 'your gang' on the other side of town?

Such points are not made to justify and certainly not to excuse any of these terrible actions. Rather to cut through the blind hysterical reactions and encourage humble self-questioning, in place of unhelpful and empty self-righteous condemnation. If we are so powerful and so wise and so wealthy and capable doing so many clever things, why is it still so difficult for the world and its societies to live harmoniously with each other? If mechanical science and its psychological and sociological associates claim complete authority of knowledge, why can they do no more than wash their hands of such problems? Is profiting from scientific discovery, providing more and more tools to play our games of destruction and detection with, the sole purpose of science – the only 'sensible' way by which to live?

The limitations of the mechanical paradigm

As we have seen, the social malaise illustrated by the examples above and studied in depth by this book indicate we are reaching the limits of where the mechanical paradigm can take us as a society.

Materially, we have been on a wild and amazing ride of ever-expanding possibility. In one hundred years, nuclear physics and astronomy have advanced from seeing the atom as the smallest unit of matter to activating chain reactions that split one element into many others and could destroy the planet. They claim to be able to explain all the basic stages of the creation of the universe from a 14-billion-year-old 'big bang' and its immense heat that formed the core elements of hydrogen and helium. In the past ten years, we have developed global face-to-face communication, with its truly international economic marketplace and general information systems.

Yet amidst all these wonders, we can see that mechanical science is close to reaching the very limits of what it can discover from its three-dimensional perspectives. It can calculate the precise value of Pi to billions of places, but never to its final place. It can build telescopes to see distant nebulae and black holes and claim to look toward the creation of the universe. It can trace creation back to the 'big bang', but not explain or even conceive of what came before that. It can freeze matter from a state of gas to liquid, to solid, to Bowse Einstein Condensate, yet never reach more than incredibly close to absolute zero degrees.

Nor will it do so, because what we observe is determined by the instrument we use to observe it. If our only paradigm is to step outside to measure mechanical relationships in three dimensions then we will be lost observers in an uncaring universe. We will bear and raise our children not to care, with illogical ties of drunkenness and empty loyalty as mindless relaxation when the working day is done.

A convenient paradigm for the 21st century and beyond

We have seen that it is vital to put ourselves back into the frame of consideration; not as mere impersonal fragments of developing genetic code but as participating co-creators in a living, conscious, balanced and eminently fair universe.

The outer planetary cycles explained in Chapter 5 show such developments are timely today. Just as the relative movements of the Earth, Sun and Moon mean we see the last two as being together, opposed and back together again every month, so in the larger scheme of things every five hundred years Pluto and Neptune conjunct and, while they are still close together, are transited by Uranus to be joined by Jupiter and Saturn at a key time. Every two hundred and fifty years, Uranus opposes Pluto, while Neptune is harmoniously 120 degrees from Pluto. The conjunction of Neptune and Pluto in 1398/99 was followed by dramatic upheavals of consciousness through the Uranus transit in the century that followed. The consequent change of paradigm was in the end to place humanity in a godlike position as observer and re-inventor of the universe. The impetus for this accelerated at the end of the 15th century.

The conjunction of Neptune and Pluto in the early 1890s symbolised a similar paradigm shift. We are hardly now beginning to assimilate the implications of the dramatic discoveries and events of the century that followed. We have seen that much popular perception of science and some scientists is still stuck in the 18th century Newtonian mechanical view. Chapters 11 and 12 showed how much further we have to go in our conceptual development.

Developments of the past twenty years are similar to those between 1490 and the early 16th century. In those earlier years, advanced thinkers were just assimilating the impact of printing, starting to realise that the Earth was round and moved around the Sun. Man only beginning to see himself as an objective observer of the universe. The famous dictum of Descartes was two centuries away. Similarly today, we near the end of twenty years of dramatic discoveries and are just becoming aware of the implications of computer technology. Small wonder we simplify and muddle up modern science with the solid 'certainty' of 18th century thinking.

This time we can avoid an inquisition if we realise how much more complete and convenient reintegrating the art and science of human behaviour with conventional mechanics could be. As we have seen, the use of astrology is the key. Past societies and even contemporary ones have secretly used and usually misused the knowledge, because only a ruling elite was allowed to have it. This is rather like keeping knowledge of the workings of electricity from the main population. Not only would such a policy divide and create a dependent society, but it would corrupt the knowledge itself by confining its use to the limited minds of those in power.

The aim of this book is to encourage consideration of a more appropriate 21st century paradigm with new priorities. Its core is to see the conscious wholeness of the universe and to understand each creature's role within it. By this study we will realise that the essential message and meaning of our universe is excellence through co-operation, not efficiency forced by the threat of competition.

While a range of spiritual methods offer the traditional wisdom to awaken and illuminate the deeper meanings behind human art and science, this book has focused upon astrology's valuable role in this. It seeks to make astrology generally available and to ensure that the consequences of its use are understood and adjudicated by all.

Because astrology offers enlightened insights into the co-operative organisation of people, it accords with Darwin's notion of advancement. It helps us to recognise the finest skills in every creature and show how each skill can support another. As a result, enterprises become more inclusive and successful.

The most efficient and long-lasting economic organisations are those where participants share a unity of belief, compassionate dedication and a common conviction and purpose. Great joy comes when one's abilities and talents are recognised and rewarded.

To take only what we really need, and give as much as we have the power to give, is by far the most efficient way of organising an economy. To avoid exploitation and to do this effectively, we need a crystal-clear understanding of other peoples' nature and needs – their astrology. Then we can answer those needs with an enlightened compassion. In short, astrological understanding and compassion are the essential qualities for a species that seeks to survive as the fittest.

The weapons and power over nature we possess in the 21st century make the circumstances more total and the stakes much higher. We understand and can do so much that, with the necessary open minds and motivation, we may be able to work together far better than humanity ever has before. We may avoid catastrophe and develop into the most advanced species in recorded history.

Realising all this, the central aim of this book has been to transform today's dominant emotions of greed and fear into their antidotes – compassion and astrological insight. As we have said more than once, when you know the essence of other people, there are few of them you would fear or wish to harm. Ignorance is the true enemy, not other people. When we co-operate, we do not lose anything we really want. The emphasis of what is important changes: life becomes easier, more productive and how we really want it to be.

In the Dutch town of Makkinga, all the physical barriers that separated road users from each other were taken away and an obligation to care for everyone placed upon each user. Amazingly the idea worked. Cars slowed to walking speed and they, pedestrians, and bicycles found a way around each other. They needed no roads, pavements or cycle tracks. Space was used as it became available. Of course, such a scheme may be best suited to the centre of a small town, where there is little through traffic, yet it makes a relevant point about the easiest way for life to interact. The more we focus upon caring for each other and the essential realities of situations, the more we will find solutions that make us feel safe with what others do. The many rules strip us of the most important thing: the ability to be considerate. 'We're losing our capacity for socially responsible behaviour,' says Dutch traffic guru Hans

Monderman, one of the project's co-founders. 'The greater the number of prescriptions, the more people's sense of personal responsibility dwindles.[96]'

We can apply the clear insight of this example to help heal the times in which we are living. We can look at our capacity to give and the support we can expect from others. What do have and can do? What do we need? In the microcosm of our day-to-day lives and relationships, we decide and provide for each person's situation. We help them complete their lives satisfactorily. In the macrocosm of the world, we seek ways to make the peoples of all countries happy, by marshalling world resources to meet their requirements.

How much better might our lives and our world be if we focused on accepting every person or group for what they are? How would our lives improve if we defined rigorously what each person or group needs to sustain their values and we shared the available world resources to achieve such aims? Would we be getting closer to enjoying the benefits of a truly efficient world community?

Such idealistic dreams cannot be planned centrally, or achieved overnight. Yet by accepting such visions as common sense and prioritising decisions that lead to mutual understanding, we move in the direction of such idealism. We start to make life better for everyone. We create hope out of despair. We start to regenerate our lives. We wake up each day to the possibility of a better tomorrow.

To move in such a direction, we need to stop fearing and dismissing what we do not know. Instead, we should develop sympathetic insight that makes even the most distant and unusual become familiar. By welcoming what is different, we become open and surprised by how similar in essence every stranger's needs are to our own. Knowing this, we feel crystal-clear clarity and compassion. By making decisions on the basis of this compassion, we dissolve enmity and build support. We need and waste less and less, but have more and more that makes us feel better. We care for each other and the environment of our planet. We open our eyes to see that we can have everything we *really* want. We move beyond the 'inconvenience' that Al Gore described so incisively.

Through using astrology in this compassionate way, we ever-increasingly see and enjoy its convenient truth.

Appendix

Astrology's Key Concepts & How They Work Together

Introduction

Unlike the familiar generalised media Sun Sign columns, proper astrology charts are based on an exact time, date and place of birth and so are specific to each person or moment of time.

This appendix explains the key concepts of astrology and how astrologers fit them together. It is truly exciting to see how precise astronomical measurements of the actual movements of the heavens can be translated into ordinary language that describes our behaviour and experiences.

Packed into this appendix is the key information that you would learn in a six-week introductory astrology course. It is designed to be easy to refer to and use. With it, you can start to interpret your own and other people's birth charts.

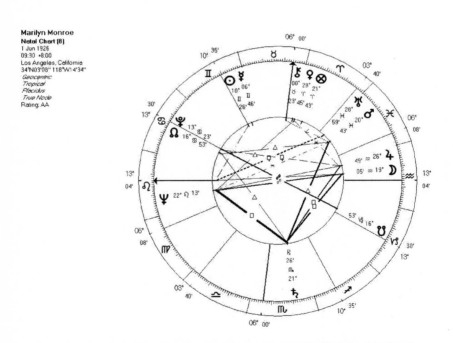

Figure 30 - The Birth Horoscope of Marilyn Monroe

The astrology chart

To measure the positions and relationships of the planets, we project the point on Earth we are studying outward to infinity in every direction. This three-dimensional ball we call the celestial sphere. This is divided into twelve segments known as the signs of the zodiac named after the constellations nearest to them. We use these twelve signs to measure the positions of the Sun, Moon and planets from our earthly (geocentric) perspective. We also note which signs are on the horizons and the higher and lower meridian, as the Earth spins on its axis.

These three-dimensional movements are simplified to a flat chart. Figure 30 is a chart drawn for the precise birth of the film star Marilyn Monroe.

* The outer band shows the twelve signs of the *zodiac.*
* The *planets* whose symbols are inside the zodiac band move at varying speeds around the zodiac in an anti-clockwise direction. The Moon changes sign every two and a half days. Pluto can take more than twenty years to change sign because its orbit is so much bigger.
* The long diagonal lines between the inner and outer circles indicate the beginnings of the *houses*. These are calculated by measuring the spinning and tilt of the Earth on its axis.
* The lines that connect the planets across the centre of the chart are called the *aspects*.

The sections that follow explain the meanings and associations of these planets, zodiac signs, houses and aspects. They also explain how these meanings can be combined to describe you and your life.

Reflect on the words and symbols and your understanding will grow. At the end are listed reference books and computer resources to help you calculate charts. Make up the charts of friends and relatives, as well as your own. Compare notes. Can you see astrology working in your life and those of others?

The planets in the zodiac signs
To simplify all this and make it usable for you right away, the meanings
of the zodiac signs and planets have been reduced to the single keywords
below.

Planet		Keyword	Sign		Keyword
☉	Sun	express	♈ Aries		urgently
☽	Moon	react	♉ Taurus		realistically
☿	Mercury	think	♊ Gemini		intelligently
♀	Venus	love	♋ Cancer		carefully
♂	Mars	act	♌ Leo		proudly
♃	Jupiter	expand	♍ Virgo		precisely
♄	Saturn	control	♎ Libra		adaptively
♅	Uranus	invent	♏ Scorpio		intensely
♆	Neptune	inspire	♐ Sagittarius		far-reaching
♇	Pluto	transform	♑ Capricorn		usefully
☊	Node	opportune	♒ Aquarius		knowingly
			♓ Pisces		sympathetically

Look at Marilyn Monroe's chart and combine the keywords. Her Sun is
in Gemini. So she expresses herself intelligently. Her Moon is in
Aquarius, so she reacts knowingly. Mercury is in Gemini so she thinks
intelligently. Venus in Aries loves urgently. Mars in Pisces acts
sympathetically. Jupiter in Aquarius expands knowingly. Saturn in
Scorpio controls intensely. Uranus in Pisces invents sympathetically.
Neptune in Leo inspires proudly. Pluto in Cancer transforms carefully.
When you put all these words together you will have the beginnings of a
description of Marilyn. By juxtaposing the contradictions and realising
that each meaning can express the positive and negative side of the
archetype, you begin to build a picture of a bright, effervescent,
romantically impulsive, independently minded and anxious person.

Through the web or by purchasing your own computer software
you can apply the same method to your own astrology birth chart.

The signs and the planets have far richer meanings than can be
expressed in one word. In the Planets and Zodiac sections that follow, a
rich spectrum of possible[97] associations is listed for each archetype. By
synthesising these meanings we begin to understand the breadth and
depth of the archetypes' potential to explain the nature of people, things
and what happens to them.

The planets

The planets are parts of a person's nature: the Sun - how you create; the Moon - how you react; Mercury - communicate; Venus - love; Mars - assert, etc. Reflect on the images below.

☉ The Sun * Helios * Hyperion * Apollo * kings and natural leaders * number 1 * Sunday * yellow and gold * the tonic do * giver of prana (life and heat) * flowering * the heart * gold * amber and topaz * myrrh, musk and frankincense * sunflower and birch * the energy of self-radiance and self-expression.

☽ The Moon * Artemis * Diana the Huntress * Selene * Luna * the mother * the psychic * numbers 2 and 7 * Monday * whitish * the tonic re * links the Sun with every living thing * gestation * breast and alimentary system * silver * crystal, mother of pearl, moonstone * camphor and frankincense * melons, broom tops and willow * the energy of reflection, how you react.

☿ Mercury * Hermes * the Messenger of the Gods * science and healing * commerce * thieves and vagabonds * number 5 * Wednesday * orange * the tonic fah * sight * childhood * respiration and brain * platinum * agate * clove * coriander and hazel * the energy of intelligence, how you communicate.

♀ Venus * Aphrodite * Goddess of Love * number 6 * Friday * green * the tonic la * touch * youth * throat and kidneys * copper * emerald, coral and quartz * strawberry * raspberry and rose * the energy of pleasure, how you love.

♂ Mars * Ares * God of War * number 9 * Tuesday * red * the tonic mi * taste * adulthood * muscles and genito-urinary system * iron * garnet, ruby and jasper * pine * sarsaparilla, cedar and holly * the energy of force, how you act.

♃ Jupiter * King of the Gods * Lord of Light * the emperor * the judge * the teacher * number 3 * Thursday * purple * the tonic sol * smell * middle age * liver and pituitary * tin * sapphire, amethyst and turquoise * jasmine * nutmeg, sage, oak and poplar * the energy of expansion, generosity, how you expand.

♄ Saturn * Kronus * God of the World and Time * the politician * the businessman * number 8 * Saturday * black * the tonic re * hearing * old age * gall bladder, skin and bones * lead * jet, onyx and black diamond * musk, poppy seeds and cinnamon * thistle, camomile, yew, ash, alder, cypress * the energy of limitation, structure, how you control.

♅ Uranus * God of the Sky * Father of the Titans * the reformer * the revolutionary * mustard brown * the tonic do * inner sight, clairvoyance * pineal gland * circulation * copper * turquoise and malachite * the energy of awakening, sudden change, how you invent.

♆ Neptune * Poseidon, holding a trident * God of the Sea * the poet * the deceiver * dull grey to black * the tonic re * inner touch, psychometry * nervous systems * silver * rock crystal and opal * the energy of mysticism, how you inspire.

♇ Pluto * Hades * God of the Underworld * the subconscious * atomic power * brown and maroon * the tonic mi * gonads, cell production and reproduction * iron * diamond, bloodstone topaz and agate * the energy of death and rebirth, how you transform.

The zodiac

How the planets manifest their energy is modified by the quality of their zodiac sign. Reflect on the associations listed on the next two pages.

♈ Aries * the Ram * cardinal * fire * positive * Mars * I am * the principle of ideation * God of Control * red * head and face * headaches and anger * Kali Phos cell salt * key of D flat * iron * bloodstone * fruit of all plants * pine and cypress * geranium, honeysuckle and nettles *all things of impulsive action, challenge, new beginnings.

♉ Taurus * the Bull * fixed * earth * negative * Venus * I have * the principle of ingestion * God of Obedience * indigo * throat and neck * illnesses of colds and obesity * Nat Sulph cell salt * key of E flat * copper * sapphire * roots of all plants * ash tree * apple and beans * all things that bring fullness - the richness and beauty of the earth.

♊ Gemini * the Twins * mutable * air * positive * Mercury * I think * the principle of communication * God of Wisdom * yellow * nerves, shoulders, arms and lungs * asthma and nervous disorders * Kali Mur cell salt * key of F * mercury * emerald * flowers of all plants * nut-bearing trees * lavender and carrot * all things that bring quick thinking and communication.

♋ Cancer * the Crab * cardinal * water * negative * Moon * I feel * the principle of assimilation * God of Harmony * ice blue * chest and stomach * indigestion, ulcers and chronic diseases * Calc Fluor cell salt * key of A flat * silver * pearl * leaves of all plants * rubber and all trees rich in sap * flax and privet * all things that bring anxious care and nurturing of life.

♌ Leo * the Lion * fixed * fire * positive * Sun *I will * the principle of co-ordination * God of Gratitude * golden * heart and sensory nerves * fevers and heart attacks * Mag Phos cell salt * key of D * gold * ruby * seeds of all plants * citrus and palm trees * sunflower, marigold and walnut * all things that suggest glory and life-giving energy.

♍ Virgo * the Virgin * mutable * earth * negative * Mercury *I analyse * the principle of discrimination * God of Justice * brown * intestines, joints, nervous system * bowel troubles and spasms * Kali Sulph cell salt * key of C * mercury * sardonyx * roots of all plants * hazel and nut-bearing trees * corn * morning glory, caraway and myrtle * all things that suggest correction and perfect manifestation.

Libra * the Scales * cardinal * air * positive * Venus * I balance * the principle of equilibrium * God of Reality * rose * kidneys * debility * Nat Phos cell salt * key of D * copper * sapphire * flowers of all plants * ash trees * lilac, garden mint and asparagus * all things that suggest harmony, acting with correct consideration.

Scorpio * the Scorpion/Eagle * fixed * water * negative * Mars and Pluto * I want * the principle of regeneration * God of Vision * dark red * sexual and excretory organs * piles, ruptures, venereal disease * Calc Sulph cell salt * key of E * iron * opal * leaves of all plants * bushy trees * carnation, rhododendron, broom and tobacco * all things that suggest desire, passion and transformation.

Sagittarius * the Archer * mutable * fire * positive * Jupiter * I see * the principle of projection * God of Victory * purple * liver, hips and thighs * blood disorders, tumours * Silica cell salt * key of F * tin * turquoise * ash and oak trees * dandelions and moss * all things that suggest vision, activity and generosity.

Capricorn * the Goat * cardinal * earth * negative * Saturn * I use * the principle of regulation * God of Power * black * knees and bones * rheumatism * Calc Phos cell salt * key of G * lead * jet and onyx * roots of all plants * pine and willow * hyacinth and onion * all things that limit, structure and control.

Aquarius * the Water Carrier * fixed * air * positive * Saturn and Uranus * I know * the principle of association * God of Love * turquoise * ankles and circulation * the illness of varicose veins * Nat Mur (common salt) cell salt * key of A * platinum and uranium * black pearl * flowers of all plants * most fruit trees * orchid, daffodil and hemp * all things that stimulate change and objectivity.

Pisces * the Fishes * mutable * water * negative * Jupiter and Neptune * I believe and often suffer * the principle of empathy * God of Mastery * soft sea greens * feet * illnesses from impure blood, especially gout * Ferr Phos (iron) cell salt * key of G flat * tin * amethyst * leaves of all plants * trees near water * water lily, tulip and fig * all things sensitive, mysterious and the fullness of experience.

Expanding planet in sign meanings

Now use the rich store of meanings and associations in the Planets and Zodiac sections to give more colour to the single keyword statements at the beginning.

It is important to remind ourselves again that all astrological qualities can be negative as well as positive. Too many ideas can cause unreliability. Impulsive infatuation, over-independence and an intense need to control what we want can make it very difficult for people to help us. Does this explain Marilyn Monroe's problems?

On the following three pages are some deeper, ready-made interpretations of the planets in zodiac signs.

Use these to interpret Marilyn's and your own chart. You could start to work on your friends' charts too, but remember your experience is limited. Just compare notes and learn.

Planets in ARIES indicate you will

☉	Sun	express yourself assertively
☽	Moon	react impatiently
☿	Mercury	communicate suddenly
♀	Venus	love impulsively
♂	Mars	act aggressively
♃	Jupiter	expand bravely
♄	Saturn	control with difficulty
♅	Uranus	invent restlessly
♆	Neptune	inspire over-idealistically
♇	Pluto	transform powerfully
☊	Node	take quick advantage

Planets in TAURUS indicate you will

☉	Sun	express yourself practically
☽	Moon	react charmingly
☿	Mercury	communicate persistently
♀	Venus	love beautifully
♂	Mars	act truculently
♃	Jupiter	expand physically
♄	Saturn	control methodically
♅	Uranus	invent inappropriately
♆	Neptune	inspire indulgently
♇	Pluto	transform materialistically
☊	Node	look for wealth

Planets in GEMINI indicate you will

☉	Sun	express yourself diversely
☽	Moon	react accommodatingly
☿	Mercury	communicate brightly
♀	Venus	love flirtatiously
♂	Mars	act restlessly
♃	Jupiter	expand without boundaries
♄	Saturn	control diligently
♅	Uranus	invent unreliably
♆	Neptune	inspire impressionably
♇	Pluto	transform unusually
☊	Node	understand immediately

Planets in CANCER indicate you will

☉	Sun	express yourself nurturingly
☽	Moon	react intuitively
☿	Mercury	communicate with discrimination
♀	Venus	love maternally
♂	Mars	act moodily
♃	Jupiter	expand caringly
♄	Saturn	control uncertainly
♅	Uranus	invent social norms
♆	Neptune	inspire affectionately
♇	Pluto	transform society
☊	Node	be a source of protection

Planets in LEO indicate you will

☉	Sun	express yourself radiantly
☽	Moon	react egocentrically
☿	Mercury	communicate proudly
♀	Venus	love with pleasure
♂	Mars	act dominantly
♃	Jupiter	expand imperially
♄	Saturn	control reliably
♅	Uranus	invent chancily
♆	Neptune	inspire without responsibility
♇	Pluto	transform forcefully
☊	Node	be full of yourself

Planets in VIRGO indicate you will

☉	Sun	express yourself precisely
☽	Moon	react fastidiously
☿	Mercury	communicate exactly
♀	Venus	love dutifully
♂	Mars	act with anxious diplomacy
♃	Jupiter	expand discursively

♄	Saturn	control correctly
♅	Uranus	invent with individual style
♆	Neptune	inspire fanatically
♇	Pluto	transform scientifically
☊	Node	celebrate perfection

Planets in LIBRA indicate you will

☉	Sun	express yourself harmoniously
☽	Moon	react peacefully
☿	Mercury	communicate properly
♀	Venus	love accommodatingly
♂	Mars	act with over-compensation
♃	Jupiter	expand with justice
♄	Saturn	control at all costs
♅	Uranus	invent conservatively
♆	Neptune	inspire romantically
♇	Pluto	transform nervously
☊	Node	benefit through friendships

Planets in SCORPIO indicate you will

☉	Sun	express yourself intensely
☽	Moon	react with desire
☿	Mercury	communicate shrewdly
♀	Venus	love passionately
♂	Mars	act ruthlessly
♃	Jupiter	expand attractively
♄	Saturn	control reluctantly
♅	Uranus	invent dangerously
♆	Neptune	inspire deeply
♇	Pluto	transform totally
☊	Node	expect satisfaction

Planets in SAGITTARIUS indicate you will

☉	Sun	express yourself idealistically
☽	Moon	react generously
☿	Mercury	communicate optimistically
♀	Venus	love open-heartedly
♂	Mars	act courageously
♃	Jupiter	expand with vision
♄	Saturn	control by alienation
♅	Uranus	invent far-sightedly
♆	Neptune	inspire energetically
♇	Pluto	transform far-reachingly
☊	Node	feel all is possible

Planets in CAPRICORN indicate you will

☉	Sun	express yourself usefully
☽	Moon	react realistically
☿	Mercury	communicate with order
♀	Venus	love cautiously
♂	Mars	act forcefully
♃	Jupiter	expand responsibly
♄	Saturn	control strongly
♅	Uranus	invent resolutely
♆	Neptune	inspire thoroughly
♇	Pluto	transform dictatorially
☊	Node	manage masterfully

Planets in AQUARIUS indicate you will

☉	Sun	express yourself independently
☽	Moon	react tolerantly
☿	Mercury	communicate knowledgeably
♀	Venus	love universally
♂	Mars	act enthusiastically
♃	Jupiter	expand with hope
♄	Saturn	expect self-control
♅	Uranus	invent progressively
♆	Neptune	inspire idealistically
♇	Pluto	transform co-operatively
☊	Node	master originality

Planets in PISCES indicate you will

☉	Sun	express with understanding
☽	Moon	react with empathy
☿	Mercury	communicate emotionally
♀	Venus	love totally
♂	Mars	act dreamily
♃	Jupiter	expand with devotion
♄	Saturn	control modestly
♅	Uranus	invent mysteriously
♆	Neptune	inspire fascinatingly
♇	Pluto	transform privately
☊	Node	understand completely

The houses

The time and place of your birth is important, because it tells us where the Earth was on its turning when you were born. From this we calculate the zodiac sign rising in the East and so can divide the circle of the chart into twelve sections (houses). Which house the planet and zodiac sign are in reveals what area of your life the planetary meaning is focused upon. The twelve areas are listed below.

1	Personality, physical appearance
2	Possessions, feelings
3	Short journeys, non-parental family, communications
4	Home, mother, social values
5	Creation, love affairs, fun, speculation
6	Work, health
7	Marriage, relationships, how things come to you
8	Shared possessions and feelings, sexuality
9	Long journeys physical, metaphysical
10	Public image, career, ambition
11	Service, organisations, social life
12	Secrets, institutions, inner life, privacy, self-reliance

You can now extend the method and be more specific. For example, Marilyn's Neptune in Leo in the 1st house explains her fascinating goddess-like personality. Saturn in the 4th house indicates her difficult early home life and search for older men as father figures. Her Jupiter and Moon in 7th house explain why the whole world seemed to feel they had the right of a relationship with her. Apply this method to your own and your friends' charts.

The aspects
Events in life do not happen in isolation. What occurs in one area has a
bearing on others. If you buy a house (4th house), your possessions will
increase (2nd house is 60 degrees to 4th), but you may need support from
others (8th house 180-degrees to 2nd), but this will enable you to live in
the house (8th 120 degrees to 4th). If you fall in love (5th house), it will
develop your relationships (7th house 60 degrees to 5th) and challenge
your sexual attitudes (8th house 90-degrees to 5th), and so on. The
planets make such angular relationships to each other. Some aspects
indicate easy flows of energy, others more difficult flows. Both
possibilities together create the opportunities of our lives. Below are the
symbols, degrees, names and meanings of the main aspects.

☌	0	Conjunction	easy or difficult, depends how planets fit
⚺	30	Semi-sextile	mildly friendly
□	45	Semi-square	somewhat stressful
✶	60	Sextile	friendly
□	90	Square	very stressful
△	120	Trine	very harmonious
□	135	Sesqui-square	awkward
⚻	150	Quincunx	strain
☍	180	Opposition	confronting

Now you have all the elements to interpret more fully. Below, a start is
made on Marilyn's chart.

Interpreting Marilyn Monroe's chart
With Sun and Mercury in Gemini in 10th house, being harmonious to
Jupiter and Moon in the 7th house in fellow air sign Aquarius, Marilyn
loved freedom and to open herself out to all kinds of people and ideas.
With Venus in Aries in the 9th house, however, she was easily infatuated
with ill-considered enthusiasms that did not last, and with Mars and
Uranus in Pisces in the 8th house found it natural to expose herself
sexually. While this got her out of a deprived home situation (Mars trine
to Saturn in the 4th house), with that Saturn in a T-square with Neptune
and Moon/Jupiter, it exposed her to abuse and constant exploitation.
With Neptune so public in the 1st house and so afflicted to her home
foundation and relationships, it is not surprising that her death is
shrouded in scandal and mystery and that it was through drugs that her
life came to an early end.

You will notice how these interpretations enrich the keywords by drawing on their associations. This is the art of astrology.

How to look to the future

There are many methods of developing the chart to show how you have grown and will continue to grow through your life, and the situations you will have to face.

To do this, we take complete astrological charts drawn for past and future dates and compare them to the birth chart of a person or event. This provides a wealth of concepts to compare and consider - as varied and rich as life itself. Below are some areas you may wish to study in the books and computer programs suggested at the end of this Appendix.

Transits

Here we compare the positions of the planets on any particular day with positions in the chart of the time of birth. Transits can also be used to explain the timing of events and cycles and flows of history.

Progressions and directions

There are various methods to discern the unfolding of a person's nature through life. Secondary progressions look at the charts in the days immediately after the day of birth, as if they were years of a person's life. If you are born with the Sun in Aries, sometime in the first 30 years of your life it will progress into Taurus. At this time, the individual develops a more materialistic and rounded demeanour. Tertiary progressions take a day for a month of life. Solar arc directions advance every planet a day for a year of life, as if it were the Sun.

Birth charts, transits and progressions as dynamic patterns

Modern computer software (such as Solar Fire that is mentioned below) can animate and reveal the patterns behind all this complexity, even for beginners. By comparing experiences and events in a person's life with patterns graphically displayed on a computer screen you actually see astrology working.

How to find out more

Astrology is both a science and an art. The calculations and the key meanings that relate to each concept are scientifically precise, but the depth of interpretation and conclusions you come to from juxtaposing the images together is an art.

The more charts you interpret, and then compare to the people, institutions and events they represent, the more proficient you will become. Developing your experience like this is the best way to learn. The more you do this, the easier it will be for you to understand and assess the claims and assertions in the main chapters of this book.

A good professional astrologer will have considered tens of thousands of charts and developed methods too varied to be explained here. A good astrologer will also have much more experience of the myriad ways the cycles combine at each unique moment of time.

To help you improve your understanding by tapping into this knowledge, below is just a small selection of beginners' resources. Visit the web sites below for further contacts and information

Classes, teach yourself and software possibilities
If you wish to learn thoroughly, taking classes with a recognised astrological school is by far the best way – see information below.

Initially, however, computer technology makes it possible to teach yourself and start experiencing the basics of astrology.

Solar Fire V6 deluxe computer software performs the calculations and helps with the interpretation. It created the charts in this book. Astrolabe Inc, whose site also offers a free natal chart generation service, publishes it worldwide. Visit:
http://www.alabe.com.
Below are additional contacts:
http://www.astro.com offers information and a chart service
http://www.astrosoftware.com/ for Kepler software
http://www.matrixastrology.com/ for Winstar software
http://www.timecycles.com for Io Macintosh software

Consultations, organisations and other information
Lists of schools are to be found in the web sites below. If you do not wish to study, but find out more about yourself, consulting a professional astrologer can be a most beneficial and liberating moment in your life, when full expertise and experience can be focused on your present situation and future.

Also, the sites opposite give links to consultants and classes.

http://www.astrologicalassociation.com
http:// www.uraniatrust.org
http://www.isarastrology.com
http://www.astrologer.com/metalog/
http://www.professionalastrologers.org/

Books to enhance basic skills
The serious astrologer will still learn how to construct a horoscope manually and build up interpretation skills from the books of established experts. Below are some key books, and the sources of calculation data. At the end of many chapters are further lists to take you further. Find these and other books at your local bookshop.

Ronald C Davison *Astrology*
Margaret Hone *The Modern Textbook of Astrology* [Revised Edition]
Derek and Julia Parker *Parker's Astrology – New Edition*
Sue Tompkins *The Contemporary Astrologer's Handbook*

Vital reference books for manual calculations
The American Ephemeris for the 20th Century
The American Ephemeris for the 21st Century
The American Tables of Houses
The International Atlas and American Atlases
(All from ACS Publications - various dates)

THE MORE YOU GET BUSY WITH ASTROLOGY, THE EASIER IT WILL BE TO SEE WHETHER THE KNOWLEDGE WORKS AND IS USEFUL.

Thank you. If you feel ready now is the time to return to chapter 4 of the main book.

Notes

Chapter 1
[1] This is the conclusion of Games Theory - the John Nash and RAND Corporation nuclear war strategy.

Chapter 2
[2] The geneticist, Richard Dawkins, for a long time the professor for the public understanding of science at Oxford University, is a most notable example.

[3] Geoffrey Dean, *Recent Advances in Natal Astrology*.

[4] Famously offering £1,000 to anyone who could prove this to his satisfaction.

[5] Michel Gauquelin *The Truth About Astrology*.

[6] Refer to Ertel's book and perhaps the *Correlation* arguments

[7] Richard Tarnas *The Archetypal Cosmos* last section of Part II of *Cosmos and Psyche* by. This is the first of a number of occasions we will be referring to this author's significant scholarship.

[8] Barnham was a 19th century showman, whose phrase 'there is one born every minute' is often used to debunk astrologers by suggesting that most people are easy to convince. Several high-profile television programmes have sought to demonstrate that ordinary people cannot tell the difference between a con artists pretending and a genuine astrologer. Similar results would be likely, if a therapist, psychologist or many other experts replaced the astrologer we consult every day.

[9] The Telegraph Group of Newspapers mounted very similar media campaigns against astrology in 2003 (referring to Geoffrey Dean and Ivan Kelly Journal of Consciousness Studies 10 No. 6-7, 2003, pp175-198l) and in 2006 *Personality and Individual Differences* Available at Science Direct Volume 40, Issue 7, Pages 1323-1504 (May 2006). In both cases, astrologers undertook none of the research and, in any event, it did not invalidate astrology as the newspapers claimed.

Chapter 3
[10] The number varies as more powerful instruments add more information and hence theories advance.

[11] See this chapter's Further Reading for Dr Percy Seymour's books

[12] Refer to the web link below
http://news.independent.co.uk/world/science_technology/article2171687.exe

[13] Dr Percy Seymour Appendix 1 of *The Birth of Christ – Exploding the Myth*

[14] Richard M Pasichnyk *The Vital Vastness -- Volume One: Our Living Earth*

[15] On 28th December that year, *The India Daily* printed the full text of the paper by N.Venkatanathan, N.Rajeswara Rao, K.K.Sharma and P.Periakali, which can be read at: www.indiadaily.com/editorial/12-28c-04.asp

[16] Astrological Mandalas see chapter's Further Reading.

Chapter 5

[17] This is a basic beginners table of rulerships and strengths and weaknesses. Where there are gaps the ruling planet can be considered to be exalted and the detriment planet in fall. However, there are more advanced systems that include the more recently discovered outer planets, the planetary nodes and even Chiron.

[18] Chiron is a planetoid with an oblique, uneven orbit around the Sun. It was discovered in the 1970s and many astrologers derive its interpretation from the Greek story of Chiron – the centaur who learned how to heal by coming to terms with his own wounds – hence the "wounded healer".

[19] A grand cross is a complex combination of tension aspects made of angular separations of 90 or 180-degrees – two oppositions and four squares, between four or more planets.

[20] This is the moment when the Sun returned to its natal position, not clock time anniversary

[21] Astrologers find the degree that is exactly equally distant between two planets that they call the 'midpoint' is an especially strong focus point.

[22] George Bush Snr. 1145 EDT 12th June 1924, Milton, Massachusetts, USA

[23] Bill Clinton, 0851 CST, 19th August 1946, Hope, Arkansas, USA.

[24] Refer to her book for information about Joan Quigley's advice to Ronald Reagan during seven years of his time in office.

Chapter 7

[25] Joan Quigley's book *What Does Joan Say?* mentioned in the chapter's bibliography gives a full account of this.

[26] William Lilly, *Christian Astrology* [Modern edition edited by David R Roell].

[27] B V Raman *How to Judge a Horoscope Volume 1 & 2, Muhurtha – Electional Astrology.*

[28] When the transiting Saturn returns to the exact point if was at birth is known as the Saturn return. It indicates a stage in life when Saturn has triggered difficulties and encouraged order in every area of the native's chart.

[29] The Part of Fortune is determined by adding the Moon's position to the ascendant position and subtracting the Sun position, or exchanging the Moon and the Sun in the calculation for night births. It is felt to indicate that fast moving part of the chart, where unusual good fortune can be found , whatever other circumstances may be.

[30] Working with the Planets *The Astrological Journal,* Vol. 44, Number 3, May/June 2002

[31] Working with the Planets, *The Astrological Journal,* Vol. 44, Number 4, July/August 2002.

[32] Daniel Yergin *The Prize,*

[33] Red Line Agreement, time not given, 31[s,t] July 1928, in Ostende Belgium.

[34] Iran Oil Nationalised, 0000, 1st May 1951, Tehran, Iran, (nationalised by decree that took effect at this moment).

[35] Ayatollah Khomeini Returns to Iran time not known, 1st February 1979, The army handed over power to him on 11th February.

[36] All degrees from here on are rounded up or down to the nearest degree and provided to give a rough idea. Readers are encouraged to construct the charts and study them in more detail.

[37] Working with the Planets, *The Astrological Journal*, Vol. 48, Number 3, May/June 2002.

[38] Working with the Planets, *The Astrological Journal*, Vol. 49, Number 4, July/August 2003

[39] 12th House Rules OK *The Astrological Journal*, Vol. 39, Number 4, July/August 1997.

[40] Tony Blair, 0610 BST, 6th May 1953, Edinburgh, Scotland.

[41] Birth certificate as reported in Caroline Gerard's *House of Commons 1992 to 1997*

[42] A method of raising capital for building and other public infrastructure projects through the financial markets, which involves repayment over an extended period of time in the future.

[43] Working with the Planets, *The Astrological Journal*, Vol. 48, Number1, January/February 2006.

[44] Data was given to Annabel Herriott in person.

Chapter 8

[45] *City of God*, Book V.

[46] *Paradise Lost*, Book IV – lines 997 to 1005.

[47] Chogyam Trumpa Rinpoche's *Cutting through Spiritual Materialism* defines and explores this theme brilliantly.

Chapter 9

[48] For a scholarly, in-depth account of the roots of contemporary culture, the reader is referred to *The Passion of the Western Mind* by Richard Tarnas.

[48] Page 345 Richard Tarnas *The Passion of the Western Mind*

[50] Trans. Ven. Thubten Tsultrim, *The Heart Sutra*.

Chapter 10

[51] In his *Autobiography* (1924), Vol 1, p. 246, Twain attributed this statement to Benjamin Disraeli

[52] Original article *Guardian Unlimited* © Copyright Guardian Newspapers 2006 published: 7th August 2003

[53] A gene named VMAT2 controls the flow of monoamines within the brain.

[54] Quoted from the Evolutionary Psychology section of Wikipedia the free on-line encyclopaedia.

[55] Extract from his presentation, entitled 'The Evolutionary Psychology of Religion' to the annual meeting of the Freedom from Religion Foundation, Madison, Wisconsin, 29th October 2004, on receipt of The Emperor's New Clothes Award.

Chapter 11

[56] Born in 1886, Olaf Stapleton was a younger contemporary of H G Wells and a major influence on Arthur C Clarke, author of 2001.

[57] Professor Marcus du Sautoy *The Music of the Primes.*

[58] *Brazil* – Terry Gilliam's 1985 film.

[59] Robin Heath - *A Key to Stonehenge.*

[60] Charles Piazzi Smyth *Our Inheritance in the Great Pyramid .*

[61] See Bibliographies at the end of this and Chapter 3.

[62] Richard Tarnas *Cosmos and Psyche.*

Chapter 12

[63] Refer to Chapter 5 for data and chart

[64] For his first term Noon EST, 20th January 2001, Washington DC.

[65] Dependent arising is a phrase well known in Buddhist philosophy. Because nothing can happen without a cause, everything that exists can only do so in a relative sense and hence is dependent upon other factors. Nothing therefore can arise or exist on its own but neither can anything not exist - all is dependent arising.

[66] In her *Handbook of Medical Astrology.*

[67] Laing and Esterton *Sanity, Madness and the Family.*

[68] *Catcher in the Rye by* J D Salinger is the story of a young person's angst and hence dismissal of the corrupt, self- indulgence of his contemporary society. It became a "call to arms" for many people in Chapman's generation. However, Chapman's self-destructive isolation prevented him from being part of any movement for social change. Isolated he took far too much upon himself with horrific results. Ironically, he assassinated the very man that many in his generation looked to for answers to the very social corruption!

[69] Making the same search at the time of writing a few weeks later, throws up numerous, mainly unhelpful findings.

[70] The ascendant takes only 40 minutes to transit the entire sign of Aries.

[71] *Minority Report* is a film starring John Travolta, in which a psychic is used to foretell crimes so that the perpetrators can be arrested before the crimes are committed!

[72] Visit the link below for full information.
http://news.independent.co.uk/world/science_technology/article2171687.exe

[73] This is not beginners' work. A knowledge of the complexities of the full natal chart and medical astrology methodology is essential.

[74] Paracelsus was a 16th century doctor and astrologer, who is often referred to as the 'father of toxicology'.

[75] Dr Pat Harris *Astrological Research in the Field of Psychology*

[76] Dr Pat Harris *The Application of Astrology to Health Psychology: astrological and psychological factors and fertility treatment outcome* (2005), British Library (access available from 2009).

Chapter 14

[77] Asserted in the documentary film *The Smartest Guys in the Room.*

[78] It is usually assumed that such a 'someone' will take the form of a scientific discovery.

[79] The relegation of Pluto to a 'dwarf planet', implemented by a rump of delegates at the end of the 2006 IAU conference, does not affect the observations made by astrologers since the discovery of Pluto in 1930. Pluto is not claimed to be the cause of developments determined by its cycle; rather it is a reference point around which patterns are observed. The actual sequential 'cause(s)' may be many other factors, whose combined effect is synchronistic with the cycle of Pluto.

[80] If we look at the previous two cycles, two years after Pluto entered Capricorn in 1269, Marco Polo commenced his 24-year journey to the Far East and China. On 31st October 1517 almost exactly a year after the next ingress, Martin Luther nailed his Ninety-Five Theses to the door of the Wittenberg Church and laid the ground for Christian division and the English Reformation, which was implemented by Acts of Parliament in 1531/12, as Pluto was leaving the sign.

[81] Between 1830 to 1835 the next crucial time of revolutionary social change, Uranus returned to oppose the 1798/92 position Pluto had occupied.

Chapter 15

[82] Anti Social Behaviour Orders – a British legal device to restrict the movements of citizens whose actions are held to be disturbing the community.

[83] On these three occasions, other very special astro-cycle circumstances applied alongside the Mars station.

[84] There were considerable price changes in other markets as well

[85] http://en.wikipedia.org/wiki/Bhopal_Disaster#Background_and_causes

Chapter 17

[86] The Title of Al Gore's film that described the effect of carbon emissions upon global warming and climate change.

Chapter 18

[87] Readers from outside the United Kingdom should not be confused. Although referred to as 'public schools', the Public School system in Britain is in fact fee-paying and private. For the best schools, future pupils names have to be put down well in advance of admission and family background is an important factor in gaining entrance.

[88] For further detailed information refer to http://en.wikipedia.org/wiki/Sephirah

[89] 1 Corinthians 13.

[90] For more information visit www.16guidelines.org. The 16 Guidelines are being developed and promoted by the Foundation for Developing Compassion and Wisdom, a UK-based educational charity. See www.essential-education.org.

[91] Lama Zopa Rinpoche.

[92] St. Paul – 1 Peter 1:9.

[93] From a prayer by Saint Ignatius of Loyola.

Chapter 19

[94] Readers living outside the United Kingdom may recognise similar prejudiced restrictions in their own country's media and legislature.

[95] David Cameron, the leader of the British Conservative Party has been frequently mocked for making this statement, which was a honest and positive attempt to encourage people to understand and help heal what he refers to as 'Britain's broken society'.

[96] Reported in SPIEGLEONLINE 16th November 2006
http://www.spiegel.de/international/spiegel/0,1518,448747,00.html

Appendix

[97] There are a number of systems that associate planets and zodiac signs with particular stones, colour, planets and so on. These lists are not complete in every category. Some alternative associations may be more suitable for some other astrological systems. These ideas are just to get you started. You are encouraged to check up and research further.

INDEX